TEACHING AND LEARNING IN INTERNATIONAL SCHOOLS

LESSONS FROM PRIMARY PRACTICE

Endorsements

It is very rare to find an educational text that leads the reader from principles into practice. Teaching and Learning in International Schools does exactly that, and in a style that brings you along on a journey rather than intimidating with jargon and theory. Each chapter contains relevant and rich content that takes us through a wide range of ideas around teaching practice, pedagogy and teacher skill development. As an educator it is easy to forget how many tools we use every day, and how many strategies we take for granted. Teaching and Learning in International Schools helps us to examine and reflect upon all of these practices. The 'teacher voice' is strong and brings the theory into real-life, makes it more authentic and gives confidence to the reader that we can do it too! The photos, reflection questions and example planners really help with the story-telling. Congratulations to the writing and editing teams because this is a text that is much needed in national and international education, putting principles into practice and building confidence for the teaching community.

Malcolm Nicolson
Former Head of IB MYP and DP Development,
Director Erimus Education

This book is a welcome contribution to the resources available not only to those who wish to pursue a career in international education but to any beginning teacher or those simply wanting to refresh their thinking about how to apply contemporary practices to the classroom. It is heartening to read such a collection written by practicing educators. The suggestions in the book provide some very useful examples of theory in action and the authors are careful to ground their recommendations not only in their lived experience but in the relevant literature. I am sure there will be much in this collection that will resonate with international educators. The thoughtful questions posed throughout the text have the potential to guide some important conversations and prompt positive, professional growth.

Kath Murdoch
Seastar Education Consulting

Our titles are also available in a range of electronic formats. To order, or for details of our bulk discounts, please go to our website www.criticalpublishing.com or contact our distributor, NBN International, 10 Thornbury Road, Plymouth PL6 7PP, telephone 01752 202301 or email orders@nbninternational.com.

TEACHING AND LEARNING IN INTERNATIONAL SCHOOLS

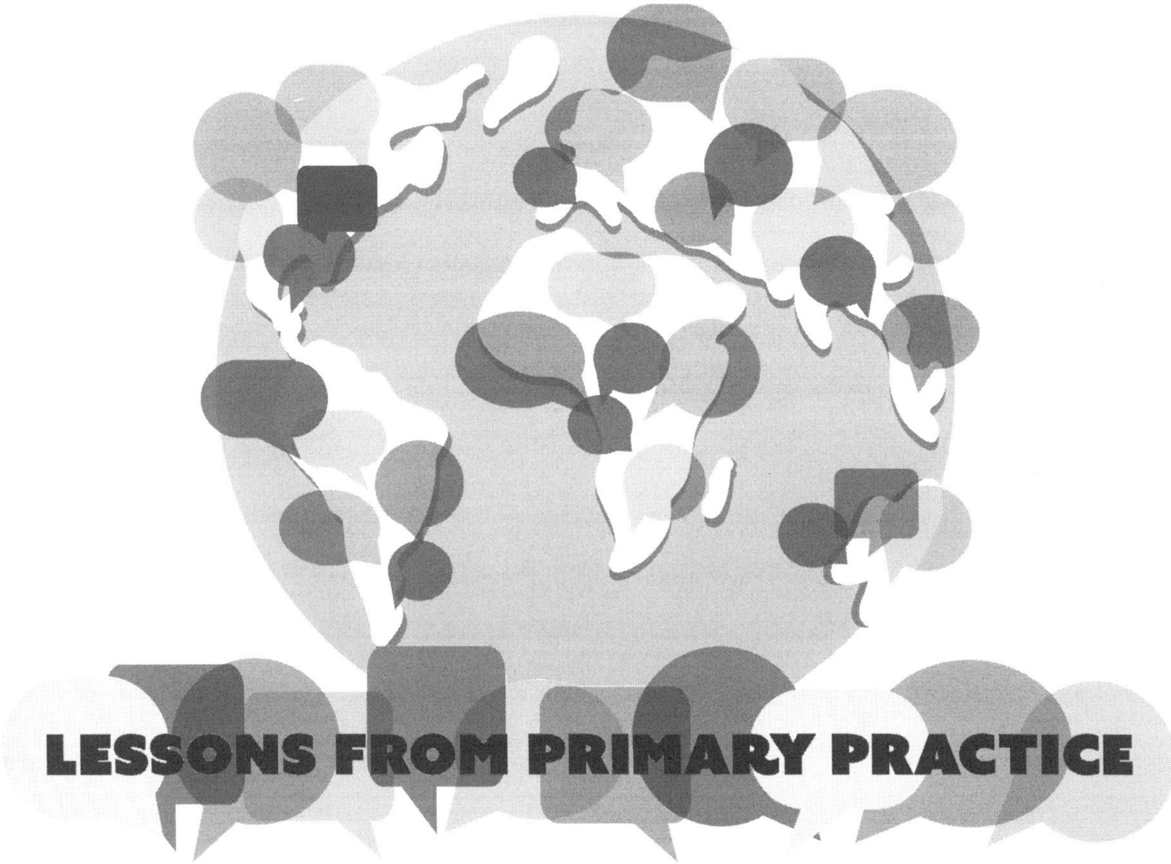

LESSONS FROM PRIMARY PRACTICE

Editors: Anssi Roiha and Eryn Wiseman

First published in 2021 by Critical Publishing Ltd

All rights reserved. No part of this publication may be reproduced, stored in a retrieval system, or transmitted in any form or by any means, electronic, mechanical, photocopying, recording or otherwise, without prior permission in writing from the publisher.

The authors have made every effort to ensure the accuracy of information contained in this publication, but assume no responsibility for any errors, inaccuracies, inconsistencies and omissions. Likewise, every effort has been made to contact copyright holders. If any copyright material has been reproduced unwittingly and without permission the Publisher will gladly receive information enabling them to rectify any error or omission in subsequent editions.

Copyright © 2021 Helen Absalom, Maria Ballester, Nicole Boerma, Sridevi Brahmadathan, Anne Brandwagt, Brandi Brittain, María Campos Ippólito, Kris Coorde, Jennifer Diepman, Wychman Dijkstra, Oana Dobarcianu, Panagiota Fameli Buwalda, Idalet de Haan, Marcelle van Leenen, Marianne Lauritzen, Brian Lynam, Kelsey Middleton, Elvira Oskam, Melanie Post Uiterweer, Raakhee Ramaiya, Anssi Roiha, Katharina Scherpel, Megan Tregoning, Rynette de Villiers, Carren Ward, Dakota Wilkinson, Eryn Wiseman, Ana Yao and Josephine Zelleke.

British Library Cataloguing in Publication Data
A CIP record for this book is available from the British Library

ISBN: 978-1-913453-49-7

This book is also available in the following ebook formats:
MOBI ISBN: 978-1-913453-50-3
EPUB ISBN: 978-1-913453-51-0
Adobe ebook ISBN: 978-1-913453-52-7

The rights of Helen Absalom, Maria Ballester, Nicole Boerma, Sridevi Brahmadathan, Anne Brandwagt, Brandi Brittain, María Campos Ippólito, Kris Coorde, Jennifer Diepman, Wychman Dijkstra, Oana Dobarcianu, Panagiota Fameli Buwalda, Idalet de Haan, Marcelle van Leenen, Marianne Lauritzen, Brian Lynam, Kelsey Middleton, Elvira Oskam, Melanie Post Uiterweer, Raakhee Ramaiya, Anssi Roiha, Katharina Scherpel, Megan Tregoning, Rynette de Villiers, Carren Ward, Dakota Wilkinson, Eryn Wiseman, Ana Yao and Josephine Zelleke to be identified as the Authors of this work have been asserted by them in accordance with the Copyright, Design and Patents Act 1988.

Cover and text design by Out of House Limited
Project management by Newgen Publishing UK
Printed and bound in Great Britain by 4edge, Essex

Critical Publishing
3 Connaught Road
St Albans
AL3 5RX

www.criticalpublishing.com
Paper from responsible sources

Contents

Meet the editors — vii

Meet the authors — ix

Introduction — 1
Anssi Roiha and Eryn Wiseman

PART 1 CORNERSTONES OF EFFECTIVE TEACHING — 5

1. **Student agency** — 7
   Brandi Brittain and Josephine Zelleke

2. **Differentiation** — 19
   Anssi Roiha, Nicole Boerma and Maria Ballester

3. **Classroom management** — 36
   Oana Dobarcianu and Dakota Wilkinson

4. **Collaboration** — 51
   María Campos Ippólito

PART 2 PROGRESSIVE PEDAGOGICAL APPROACHES — 67

5. **Play-based teaching and learning** — 69
   Elvira Oskam, Jennifer Diepman and Marianne Lauritzen

6. **Concept-based teaching and learning** — 86
   Eryn Wiseman, Kelsey Middleton and Sridevi Brahmadathan

7. **Enquiry-based teaching and learning** — 104
   Anne Brandwagt and Brian Lynam

8. **Transdisciplinary teaching and learning** — 119
   Katharina Scherpel and Raakhee Ramaiya

PART 3 DEVELOPING SKILLS FOR THE FUTURE — 131

9. **Teaching computational thinking and digital pedagogy** — 133
   Wychman Dijkstra, Kris Coorde, Ana Yao and Panagiota Fameli Buwalda

| 10. | **Rethinking literacy**
Marcelle van Leenen | 151 |
| 11. | **Towards new mathematical thinking**
Idalet de Haan | 163 |
| 12. | **Fostering multilingualism**
Melanie Post Uiterweer, Anssi Roiha and Helen Absalom | 185 |
| 13. | **Intercultural competence**
Carren Ward, Megan Tregoning and Rynette de Villiers | 201 |

Index   220

Meet the editors

Anssi Roiha

I am an experienced educator and have gained insights into several educational contexts. I have worked as a teacher and student support specialist at the International School Utrecht in the Netherlands and as a special education teacher in Finland. I hold PhD and MEd degrees and I am specialised in foreign language pedagogy, differentiation and intercultural education. Currently, I work as a university lecturer in foreign language pedagogy at the University of Turku in Finland where I conduct research and train pre-service teachers. With this book, we want to provide teachers with concrete and practical examples that can be used in international schools across the world. The book is also useful for pre-service teachers as well as for parents whose children go to an international school.

Eryn Wiseman

I am an experienced teacher and education consultant, having worked in international schools in various roles to support teachers and administrators with the development of ethos in, approach to and execution of enquiry and concept-based teaching and learning. Drawing on over 20 years of teaching experience, I am well placed to facilitate the development of those new to the profession (as well as those who have been teaching for a little longer). I know how confusing the first steps into an international school can be, and that many of the resources available are theoretical. With this book, we hope to provide practical examples for all.

Meet the authors

Helen Absalom

I am in my 30th year of teaching having taught all age ranges from kindergarten to high school within a variety of national and international curriculums and International Baccalaureate schools in the UK, Spain, Turkey, Poland, India and the Netherlands. I originally come from Wales and am currently teaching English as an Additional Language (EAL) at the International School Utrecht. I have headed English language departments and trained teachers in additional language acquisition, home-language maintenance and multilingualism and presented at a variety of conferences in Europe and Asia. I have designed curriculums for a number of schools and written and delivered training programmes for the British Council and UNICEF, as well as the Turkish and Chinese ministries of Education. I am an experienced trainer for English as a Second Language (ESL) in the mainstream and an examiner for Cambridge ESOL. I am also a trained CIS school visitor and I hold a master's degree in TESOL.

Maria Ballester

I was born and raised in Barcelona, Spain. I hold a bachelor's degree in primary teaching with a specialisation in foreign languages and a master's degree in personalised education. I have taught in different schools as a class teacher and I am currently working as a kindergarten teacher at the International School Utrecht in the Netherlands. My philosophy as an educator is that each child is unique and special; the teacher's role is to help the students to discover themselves and develop their potential. In order to do that, the environment that is created in the classroom needs to be harmonic and secure for the children.

Nicole Boerma

I have been teaching in Dutch primary schools since 2001. I have a bachelor's degree in primary education from the PABO (Pedagogische Academie voor het Basis Onderwijs). I also have an MA degree in educational sciences from the Rijksuniversiteit Utrecht. More recently, I obtained a master's degree in special educational needs from Fontys Hogeschool in Utrecht. I teach primary and secondary, Dutch language acquisition and Dutch language and literature. Additionally, I work as a student support co-ordinator at the International School Utrecht, where I have been teaching since 2012. As the students at the school are from very diverse backgrounds, the level of Dutch varies, thus creating a need for differentiation. Next to this, I draw on personal experience as a mother of a dyslexic son.

Sridevi Brahmadathan

I was born and brought up in India. After completing my bachelor's degree in mathematics, I worked for different companies. As part of the corporate social responsibility, I got a chance to help promote education in remote pockets of India. Following that, I obtained a bachelor's degree in primary education and worked for four years in a primary school in India. I moved to Europe in 2014 and have been working at the International School Utrecht within various grades since April 2016. I want to promote conceptual level thinking in my teaching and application of this understanding in problem-solving and mathematics.

Anne Brandwagt

I was born and raised in the Netherlands. I am an experienced teacher, specialised in the early years. I taught for five and a half years at the International School Utrecht and have also been teaching in Indonesia and Curacao. I am looking forward to a new chapter in my life and will start to teach Grade 4 students in Malaysia in 2021. I am passionate about education and love to learn about different cultures. I have worked in many different school systems; however, once I started teaching the International Baccalaureate, I became immediately inspired by the concept of enquiry-based teaching. Creating lessons in a playful manner and letting subjects come to life for children is something that I love doing.

Brandi Brittain

I am originally from Texas in the United States, but I have taught in Spain and Australia for many years working with students from kindergarten to Grade 6. I am currently a kindergarten teacher in the Early Years Programme at the International School Utrecht in the Netherlands. I hold a bachelor's degree in primary education and multiple certifications in English language learning. In my experience with students of many different backgrounds, one aspect that holds true to all students is that agency provides them with an opportunity to shape their own learning and provide authentic learning experiences.

María Campos Ippólito

I was born in Granada, Spain. During my studies, I moved to England for six months where I experienced all the benefits of multiculturalism. After finishing my studies as a bilingual primary education teacher, I moved to the Netherlands where I joined the International School Utrecht and immersed myself in IB workshops and in the school programme. After four years of living abroad, I decided to move back to Spain where I continue to work and develop myself. As a teacher, I want to find out my students' individual needs. I build a connection with them that creates an environment that encourages respect and motivation towards learning.

Kris Coorde

I am from the Flemish region in Belgium, and I have lived in the Netherlands for over a decade. I studied American studies at Utrecht University and worked for a history show on Dutch national television. Looking for a new challenge, I got my primary teaching degree while a teaching assistant at the International School Utrecht, where I have since taught in kindergarten, Grade 2 and Grade 4. I am currently a Grade 5 teacher with a passion for computer science, maker education and student agency.

Jennifer Diepman

I am a music teacher and director in the Netherlands and received my degree in music education in Cleveland, Ohio. I believe that play-based learning is important so that students of all ages may learn various subjects through play and discovery. Play-based learning has been implemented into my nearly 20 years of public school teaching experience and I hope that many others see the advantages of play-based learning in various educational settings as well.

Wychman Dijkstra

I grew up in a bilingual environment in Friesland in the Netherlands, speaking Dutch and Frisian at home. In 2010, I finalised my master's degree in international relations and organisation. I finished my teaching degree at the Marnix Academie in Utrecht in February 2019. Currently, I am working as a Grade 4 and computational thinking teacher at the International School Utrecht. I love to teach the children about nature, but also technology and computational thinking and philosophy, thus bringing the mind, the digital world and the real world outside the classroom together.

Oana Dobarcianu

I am an experienced teacher and I have been working for many years with children ages three to seven. I graduated from the University of Education and Psychology, Bucharest, Romania. After teaching many years in my home country of Romania, I moved to Dubai, where I completed my education with a master of strategic human resource with major in cultural differences. While studying for my master's degree, I taught British/international curriculum at the Kangaroo Kids Nursery Dubai. In 2012, I moved to Norway where I worked at an international school. In 2017, I started working at the International School Utrecht. I love to create resources that promote a positive class culture and an environment in which kids feel safe, calm and like they can be their best selves.

Panagiota Fameli Buwalda

I grew up in Athens, Greece, and I have been living in the Netherlands since 2013 with my Dutch husband and our two children. I hold a bachelor's degree in primary education and a degree in music and contemporary singing, and I am currently completing my master's degree in computers in education at the University of Athens. I have taught in primary schools in Greece and the Netherlands. In 2016, I started teaching at the International School Utrecht where I am experiencing the beauty of enquiry-based teaching and learning. Since 2019, I have been the early years student support specialist at the school, a role that allows me to give my students additional support and tools to further develop and shape their own learning.

Idalet de Haan

I was born in South Africa and I worked at the International School Utrecht in the Netherlands from 2015 to 2018. I obtained a bachelor's degree in foundation phase education from the Northwest University and an honours degree in learning support at the University of Pretoria. I have nine years of teaching experience and I have mostly taught at primary level, particularly in Grade 3. My passion for mathematics stems from my personal experiences in school where the concepts were not always taught for understanding. I have attended various Primary Years Programme workshops involving the teaching and learning of mathematics. I currently live in South Africa and give workshops to teachers and parents on active teaching strategies and enquiry-based learning.

Marianne Lauritzen

I come from Norway where I used to teach mathematics and science in secondary school, in Grades 8–10, before moving to the Netherlands in 2015. I am currently the ICT co-ordinator at International School Utrecht, where I also teach mathematics in secondary. During my time at the teachers' academy, I wrote my pedagogy final paper on the importance of gaming to enhance learning and the principles behind gamification is at the core of my teaching philosophy.

Marcelle van Leenen

I have 20 years of experience co-ordinating and teaching language and literacy programmes in international schools. I have led workshops on language and literacy and instigated various whole-school initiatives: connected learning, language and literacy across the curriculum, co-teaching and mother tongue maintenance. While working at the International School Utrecht, I was a digital literacy coach. Currently, I work as the head of primary at an IB World School in Latvia. I am an IB workshop leader and school visitor and have experience in international conference presentations, consultations and teacher training sessions.

Brian Lynam

I was born and raised in Dublin, Ireland. I am a passionate Primary Years Programme teacher and have taught extensively in international schools around the world. I take great pride in my students' learning and ability to become independent thinkers and always promote awareness, respect and equality in class. I have taken great steps to improve and develop my knowledge of the enquiry cycle and I enjoy sharing and discussing ideas with other educators.

Kelsey Middleton

I am originally from Durban, South Africa, where I completed my bachelor's degree in education, specialising in foundation phase. I have lived abroad for five years, teaching within the British curriculum in Munich for two years, and I am currently a Grade 2 teacher at the International School Utrecht. I am fascinated by concept-based education and actively employ it in my teaching.

Elvira Oskam

I come from the Netherlands and have a background in both secondary and primary education. I am an early years specialist at the International School Utrecht. I believe strongly in play-based learning and guide not only my colleagues at school, but also the parents within my kindergarten community.

Melanie Post Uiterweer

I was born in the Netherlands and spent a large part of my childhood in Germany where I acquired my International Baccalaureate diploma. I came back to the Netherlands to attend the PABO (Pedagogische Academie voor het Basis Onderwijs), and gained experience in teaching in different school systems. I was a classroom teacher in a public school in Aruba for seven years. Currently, I work as a language specialist at the International School Utrecht teaching Dutch language acquisition. I work with students from kindergarten to Grade 5. Working in an IB school has broadened my view and increased my interest in language learning.

Raakhee Ramaiya

I grew up in England and have a Hindu background. I have taught in a variety of schools from special needs, to mainstream, to language schools around the East and West Midlands in England. Having a BSc honours in psychology with English literature, I have a lot of curiosity and interest in thoughts, actions and human behaviour. My experience mainly consists of working with early years students. Working in an International Baccalaureate setting inspires me to teach in new and dynamic ways to help children shape their learning based on their interests and acquired knowledge.

Katharina Scherpel

I grew up in Düsseldorf, Germany, in a German/American family and attended the international school there. After receiving my IBDP diploma, I moved to Los Angeles and studied business and communication there. After receiving my bachelor's degree in primary school education, I started teaching at the International School Utrecht where I have worked as an English language acquisition teacher and a teacher in Grades 1–3. Currently, I work at an international school in Germany as a Grade 5 teacher. Teaching at international schools has given me many opportunities to develop professionally, for example, by participating in a variety of IB workshops and collaborating with my colleagues in different grade level teams.

Megan Tregoning

I was born and raised in South Africa. I completed my bachelor's degree in education, specialising in language, at the Nelson Mandela Metropolitan University. I moved to the Netherlands to further my knowledge on an international scale, where I have stayed for the last four years. I currently work as a Grade 3 classroom teacher at the International School Utrecht. I have worked with children aged five to 15 from various socio-economic and schooling situations. I believe I have as much to learn from my students as they learn from me.

Rynette de Villiers

I was the head of the International School Utrecht for six years before taking on the role as principal of the Amsterdam International Community School. As an IB educator for 16 years and a leader of international schools for many years, I have gathered practical experience in engaging with international communities, communicating and working with a very diverse cultural population. Attending among others CIS (Council of International Schools) deep learning symposiums on cultural competence has helped me to develop a well-rounded approach to intercultural competence within a school community.

Carren Ward

I was born and raised in Southern California, but I have been living in the Netherlands with my family for several years. I have taught at various primary schools for almost 20 years. I have earned a CLAD (Cross-cultural, Language and Academic Development) credential, attended several cultural competence workshops and am currently working at the International School Utrecht as a teacher mentor and a Grade 2 teacher. My interest in intercultural competence partly stems from my background as I have grown up surrounded by people from various cultures and have lived a prominent period of time abroad.

Dakota Wilkinson

I grew up in Australia, often travelling up and down the East Coast. I studied at the University of the Sunshine Coast where I graduated with a bachelor's degree in early childhood and primary education. During my studies, I was lucky enough to work collaboratively with many behaviour management specialists and this grew my passion to encourage positive behaviour in my classes. In my experience, great classroom management strategies can help the environment and students to become more independent, trusting, honest and safe. I am currently working as a Grade 4 teacher at the International School Utrecht.

Ana Yao

I am a Japanese-Brazilian and grew up in Brazil before moving to Europe to study graphic design at Central Saint Martins College of Art and Design in London. After moving to the Netherlands, I continued my work as an art director in the photography industry for a number of years, before branching off into the education sector led by my passion for working with children, education, creativity and technology in an international context. I see the importance of empowering students with computational and critical thinking in a fast-changing world where digital life becomes as important as real life.

Josephine Zelleke

I am French and Ethiopian and I grew up in Tanzania. From a young age, I learnt about the beauty of multiculturalism within international schools. I studied psychology at university prior to completing my PGCEi, and I then worked at international schools in Tanzania and in the Netherlands. I have a passion for teaching and for helping students grow into independent, strong individuals. I practise student agency within my class, and foster an independent environment in which the children learn how to resolve conflict on their own, and learn to trust in themselves and their thinking.

Introduction

Anssi Roiha and Eryn Wiseman

The number of international schools has mushroomed in the past few decades. In particular, the International Baccalaureate (IB) has dramatically expanded its reach in recent years. As a result, more and more teachers are working in international schools. However, there seems to be a lack of books about effective pedagogy in an international school context. This book aims to respond to this need by being future-facing and offering fresh insights into international education. Research on how teachers best teach and how students best learn is constantly being updated and views change. For instance, increased access to information and the recognition of how important creativity and divergent thinking is in learning are forcing schools to redefine their educational approaches and curricula. As a result of the educational field changing quite rapidly, many teachers seem to struggle with how to sensibly implement new trends in practice. In order to remain afloat in an ocean of information, much of it extremely theoretical, teachers need practical explanations and examples. This book endeavours to provide exactly that: a wealth of practical examples.

The authors of this book are teachers from the International School Utrecht in the Netherlands, who are passionate about what they do. They come from a variety of countries and educational contexts and, due to their backgrounds, are able to incorporate many theories, perspectives and elements from different curricula to their educational practices. This diversity permeates the book which combines theory and practice in a comprehensible way by providing a multitude of concrete examples on many current topics.

The primary audience for the book is practitioners working in international schools. The fact that this book is written by teachers for teachers makes it easy to relate to. The book will also be useful for pre-service teachers who are forming their teaching philosophies and collecting a toolkit for best educational practices. Additionally, parents whose children are attending an international school or who are considering placing their children in an international school are likely to be interested in this book.

The book contains 13 chapters divided into three parts. In Part 1, which comprises four chapters, the authors share their take on the cornerstones of classroom practice. Chapter 1, *Student agency*, is by Brandi Brittain and Josephine Zelleke. This chapter focuses on student agency both in theory and in practice. The authors examine the benefits of student agency and discuss the practices that can be employed to foster it in early years and primary education.

Chapter 2, *Differentiation*, is by Anssi Roiha, Nicole Boerma and Maria Ballester. In the first part, the authors explain the student support procedure at the International School Utrecht and how differentiation is embedded in it. The remaining part of the chapter outlines a wide range of differentiation practices in five dimensions of teaching, which are teaching arrangements, learning environment, teaching methods, support materials and assessment.

Chapter 3, *Classroom management*, is by Oana Dobarcianu and Dakota Wilkinson. This chapter introduces a wide range of practical examples on how to use positive classroom management strategies to ensure a peaceful learning environment for each learner. In a narrative form, the chapter takes the reader through different classrooms and showcases how classroom management is manifested with learners of different ages.

Chapter 4, *Collaboration*, is by María Campos Ippólito. The chapter defines collaboration and discusses its benefits. By using the International School Utrecht as an example, the chapter demonstrates how collaboration between the whole school community serves the learning of both the students and staff.

Part 2 presents a selection of innovative and emergent pedagogical approaches that differ from mainstream teaching and includes four chapters. Chapter 5, *Play-based teaching and learning*, is by Elvira Oskam, Jennifer Diepman and Marianne Lauritzen. The authors first define play-based learning and talk about the types and levels of play. The chapter also illustrates how play-based learning can be manifested in primary years and middle years as well as in various subjects.

Chapter 6, *Concept-based teaching and learning*, is by Eryn Wiseman, Kelsey Middleton and Sridevi Brahmadathan. The authors explain how concepts can be used to strengthen a school's curriculum. Moreover, the chapter illustrates how teachers can use concepts in their teaching as well as explores the main challenges of concept-based teaching and how to overcome them.

Chapter 7, *Enquiry-based teaching and learning*, is by Anne Brandwagt and Brian Lynam. This chapter describes why enquiry-based teaching and learning is important for the children of tomorrow. The authors outline various strategies to set up an enquiry-centred classroom and discuss how to utilise assessment in enquiry-based teaching.

Chapter 8, *Transdisciplinary teaching and learning*, is by Katharina Scherpel and Raakhee Ramaiya. The authors first define transdisciplinary learning and explain the philosophy behind it. This chapter describes concretely how to approach teaching through transdisciplinary themes and emphasises the importance of collaboration and planning.

Finally, Part 3, which contains five chapters, gazes towards our and our students' future and addresses the skills that will be emphasised then. Chapter 9, *Teaching computational thinking and digital pedagogy*, is by Wychman Dijkstra, Kris Coorde, Ana Yao and Panagiota Fameli Buwalda. The authors focus on the role of computer science in learning and talk about topics such as digital literacy, digital wellness and computational thinking. The chapter describes several actual lessons on how to implement the above topics in practice.

Chapter 10, *Rethinking literacy*, is by Marcelle van Leenen. This chapter presents practical examples of how learning about and through new media literacies can be incorporated into the enquiry classroom. The chapter delves into topics such as participatory culture and connected learning and discusses how teachers must also keep up with the shift towards an increasingly digital world.

Chapter 11, *Towards new mathematical thinking*, is by Idalet de Haan who explains how to teach mathematics with enquiry- and concept-based approaches. The chapter stresses the importance of building mathematical knowledge from concrete to abstract and using real-life examples to help students to build a solid understanding of mathematical concepts. The chapter also discusses how to differentiate and assess mathematics in a student-centred way.

Chapter 12, *Fostering multilingualism*, is by Melanie Post Uiterweer, Anssi Roiha and Helen Absalom. The authors first define multilingualism and present an overview of previous research on multilingual education. The chapter highlights how multilingualism and different languages can be brought to the forefront in second/foreign language education and in other subjects.

Chapter 13, *Intercultural competence*, is by Carren Ward, Megan Tregoning and Rynette de Villiers. The authors explain the concept of intercultural competence and its various phases. The chapter discusses the importance of intercultural competence in the twenty-first century and introduces practical ways to address it at a whole school level as well as in the classrooms.

As with all book projects, it has been a long road to get to this stage. We want to give our heartfelt thanks to the authors of the book who alongside their own teaching work took time to write these chapters. We would also like to express our gratitude to several people working at the International School Utrecht who provided many valuable examples for the chapters. We would especially like to thank Lindsey Dudgeon, Amy MacGregor and Natalie Benedetto for their insightful comments and suggestions. As a token of our gratitude for the school's strong commitment to this book project, and as proponents of lifelong learning, we have decided to donate all the royalties for the book to a fund for teachers' professional development at the International School Utrecht. We hope that this small gesture will, for its part, ensure that the teachers working there are given the opportunity to constantly develop and update their educational knowledge, skills and expertise.

Part 1

Cornerstones of effective teaching

1 Student agency

Brandi Brittain and Josephine Zelleke

Tell me and I forget.
Teach me and I remember.
Involve me and I learn.

B Franklin

INTRODUCTION

Student voice and choice is the teaching practice that encourages the idea that children can be their own teachers, by allowing them the independence to choose their passions and ways of learning. Historically, education has focused on a one-way framework in which teachers would teach, and students should listen. Recently, there has been an increased focus on the theory and practice of making education a partnership between the teacher and student, and also between the student and school. By encouraging students to become active participants in their own learning, the classroom environment has evolved from a place of learning to a place of deeper understanding. Allowing students the opportunity to independently learn within their own framework creates a classroom where questions are encouraged and learning is personalised.

This chapter focuses on student agency both in theory and in practice. It examines the benefits of student agency and how these practices have been implemented at the International School Utrecht (ISUtrecht). This chapter is divided into two parts: first, we address the benefits of student agency in teaching practices, and second, we showcase how ISUtrecht has implemented this framework in its own system.

FORM

What is student voice and choice?

Student agency is a practice that has become a growing movement in many education systems (St John and Briel, 2017) and its primary motivation is to include students at the centre of learning, by incorporating their identity, values, passions, culture and environment (Core Education, nd). Student agency refers to students taking autonomy and responsibility of their own learning, while student voice concerns using that responsibility and classroom opportunities to communicate their thoughts and ideas (Victoria State Government, 2020).

On a micro level, student agency can be a strong tool in the classrooms for teachers who take a more democratic approach (Morrison, 2008), such as allowing the students to choose their method of preferred testing. Morrison (2008) argues that student agency should also be applied on a macro level, which extends the idea of student choice being applied to the whole school, suggesting that the students are involved in constructing the entire curricula.

While student agency and student voice are intrinsically linked (Victoria State Government, 2020), student voice alone refers to *'students in dialogue, discussion and consultation on issues that concern them in relation to their education, but in particular, in relation to pedagogy and their experiences of schooling whether as a student cohort, individual class groups or within a forum construct like a student council'* (Fleming, 2015, p 223). In other words, student voice allows students to communicate their thoughts, whether that may be concern or curiosity, within an educational context. The practice of student voice helps foster learner independence within the class, which allows students to have a *'significant and meaningful input into decisions that will shape their learning experiences and those of their peers either in or outside of school settings'* (Jobs for the Future & the Council of Chief State School Officers, 2015, p 26).

Vaughn (2018) argues that student agency can be grouped into three dimensions: dispositional dimension, which focuses on the students' personal dispositions and how they can become willing and eager to take action; the motivational dimension, which focuses on student self-efficacy in which students reflect on their own emotions and beliefs to complete the task at hand and take effective action; and the positional dimension, in which the student takes into consideration their environment and uses that as a context to make decisions. By implementing student agency and student voice in one's classroom, the teacher *'recognises that learners have the ability to shape and make decisions regarding their education in ways that adults cannot anticipate'* (Robertson, 2017, p 41). An additional note of importance is that in many classroom environments, students come from different socio-cultural backgrounds, lending further argument as to why it is important for all students to have a say in what or how they learn.

Research findings on student agency

There are many benefits to implementing the practice of student agency in the classroom, which is why there is an increase in the number of teachers and researchers who understand the importance of listening to what students have to say (Robertson, 2017). Furthermore, numerous researchers argue that a lack of a student voice in the classroom can lead to feelings of alienation, powerlessness and disengagement among the students (Mansfield et al, 2018).

Arguably, the most important benefit is that the students are more engaged within the classroom (Healey et al, 2016). By offering students a platform for them to not only express their ideas but also have a choice, they are empowered to understand that they have a right to have input regarding their own education (Annan, 2016). Moreover, student agency allows students to stand up for their rights in terms of their learning, but they also become more resilient in both the academic aspect of learning and personal learning (Mansfield et al, 2018). This is because student agency involves finding solutions to real-life problems in a safe environment where the teacher helps them persevere through trial and error, whereby learning is seen as a continuous effort, which extends beyond the classroom (Annan, 2016).

Williams (2017) argues that by allowing students to choose their own books from the library, teachers can increase student interest in recreational reading. He believes that by allowing students the choice of where, what and when they read

> *they read more; they read longer; they read later into life; they learn more; their reading, writing, and mathematical skills improve; their spelling improves; their vocabulary expands; and their knowledge builds. All of these benefits just from reading for fun!*
>
> (Williams, 2017, p 13)

Furthermore, a study in 2007 found that student voice and choice affects both the achievement levels and student satisfaction levels (Hanover Research, 2014). By allowing students to become advocates in their learning, they become more passionate and find the work that they are doing both purposeful and personal (Annan, 2016; Harvey and Chickie-Wolfe, 2007).

Another point to consider is the social benefits of implementing student voice and choice in schools, one example being the strengthening of student well-being. Kohn (1993) states that by allowing students to have more control in their lives, they experience more self-determination, in addition to feeling more positive and active. Kohn (1993) further suggests that student agency allows students to develop their own beliefs and values, noting 'the only way children can acquire both the skills of decision making and the inclination to use them, is if we maximise their experiences with choice and negotiation' (para 15) as teaching democratically instils autonomy. In addition to students becoming more self-aware, implementing the student agency pedagogy promotes children to become more active and competent members in the community, by seeking more social and educational change (Mansfield et al, 2018).

By putting trust in students, they become more independent, self-aware and more intrinsically motivated as learning and education is not seen as goal-orientated but rather as a value (Morrison, 2008). Furthermore, it strengthens the relationship between student and teacher (Mansfield et al, 2018), as well as unburdens the teacher from having to make constant decisions and monitoring the students, which creates an active, collaborative learning environment for both parties (Kohn, 1993).

FUNCTION

The second part of this chapter examines student agency through the conceptual lens of function. We have looked at what agency is and now we look at how teachers plan for it in the classroom. This is broken into early years and primary grades to examine how it looks across the different ages.

How can student agency be structured in planning?

Formal planning

Much of the planning for student agency is integrated in planning for enquiry-based learning (see Chapter 7). Formal lesson planning occurs both as a team and individually. When learning experiences are planned as a team, they begin as suggestions but then evolve into something deeper. These are put in the planner to have a repertoire of planning ideas to choose from but also noting the students' enquiries into the concepts in the unit. This sets up the classteacher to be able to allow the students to choose the direction of their learning. Below are some examples from both the early years and the primary grade teams at ISUtrecht.

EARLY YEARS

The kindergarten team has a unit of enquiry on family and friends. They created a hook in the form of a role play that spotlighted the connections between a student and the people involved in the student's life, such as friends and family. When each class went back to their rooms to do a visible thinking activity, one class wanted to learn more about their families and another class wanted to know more about their friends. Although these teachers planned the unit together, they listened to their students' ideas, thoughts and wonderings. One class began with families, while the other started with friends. This allows the students to have a choice in the direction of their learning and makes it authentic because the teacher follows the connection of the class.

Furthermore, the early years team's formal plan for student agency is in the individual lesson plans. The teachers often reflect on lessons they have planned and ask themselves questions such as '*Where can the students have meaningful choice in this?*' The choices may vary from small things such as sitting where they would like to as big as allowing the students to choose what they learn about that day, and how they learn it.

During a unit on community helpers, a teacher wrote a lesson plan in which the learners would create questions to ask the concierge about his job. The idea was that they would leave the class to find and ask him these questions. This demonstrated their questioning, thinking and speaking skills, a total package lesson plan. But during the teacher's reflection prior to the lesson, she asked herself '*Where is the students' voice?*' So, she changed the lesson plan to say, '*Create questions for XXX for an interview*'. She did not know who they would come up with. What if the learners decided they wanted to ask their parents or someone famous? It would change the idea of walking around the school, but would it still practise their thinking, speaking and questioning skills? Yes. Would it give them ownership? Yes. Would they still be learning the knowledge behind interviewing? Yes. This is how '*XXX*' became a welcome and normal part of this teacher's lesson plans and also taught her how to be more flexible. If the students wanted their parents, it was okay, she would make copies and send them home to do the interview. If the students wanted someone famous, it was okay. The students could make a video and send it to them. It is important that these choices still maintain the knowledge and skills that are to be practised. Allowing students to choose key parts of the lessons also teaches teachers to think on their feet, which, in turn, teaches the learners to be thinkers and problem solvers.

PRIMARY

As the learners get older and move into primary from the early years, they are capable of higher levels of agency in the classroom. This development of independence and thought is taken into account during the formal lesson planning process. In Grade 4, the students are involved in constructing the central idea and the lines of enquiry. The learners think about the concepts that they want to learn about within the unit and under the transdisciplinary theme. The Grade 4 team also involves the students in creating learning intentions. This is so the students think about how they want to learn the concepts, what they are learning to do by using the approaches to learning (ATLs), and what they are learning to be through the learner profile. The ISUtrecht Grade 2 team involved their students in the creation of their most recent summative assessment. They posed the task to choose a classic story and tell it from the perspective of another character. The learners got to choose the story, the character and how they communicated that story; whether it was through written work, acting it out, a song, a puppet show or whatever other medium they chose to tell the story.

ISUtrecht primary grade teams also plan formal learning time which does not always involve their direct teaching. Many teams ensure that they build in plenty of time for reflection throughout the entire day. This allows students to work together and reflect upon different parts of their learning. Many primary classes create peer-to-peer feedback systems. These systems work together with the reflection times. In doing so, the students are able to take ownership over their personal learning processes and continue to grow as learners. Some classes involve students in the home learning process as well. In Grade 4, students are given a choice as to what authentic at home task they want to complete to reinforce their classroom learning. By choosing what the students want to continue to work on at home, they are taking ownership of their own learning as well as gaining a deeper understanding of their own strengths and weaknesses.

Informal planning

Informal teaching moments are the moments that are outside the formal lesson plans. These include transitions, morning stations, snack time, free play, outside play, lunch, quiet time, genius hour and library. Within these times, the students have the choice to decide on what they want to do, read, play, etc.

EARLY YEARS

In an ISUtrecht kindergarten classroom, formal teaching only makes up about 30 per cent of the day and the rest of the time is for informal learning. These moments are important in creating the feeling of ownership within the classroom. At the beginning of the academic year, the students create the classroom and class jobs. They help decide the classroom layout with regard to furniture and classroom environment. For example, the children can decide where some of the displays should go. During the day, free play is offered at least once and outside play usually twice. Students are allowed to choose which station they want to play in during free play. Within many of those stations, materials are provided from the student's personal interests to help provoke more learning while they play. For example, there is a student who loves dinosaurs. Even though it is difficult to incorporate dinosaurs into a unit of enquiry about community helpers, the teacher provides the child with something of his personal interests during his free play, including books about dinosaurs in the class library, and dinosaur toys in the small world play station. When possible, the teacher includes dinosaurs in stand-alone mathematics and language lessons. During outside play, students are provided with open-ended play materials that allow them to create and play using their imagination and creativity, while allowing an opportunity for them to create their own choices and to start developing their voices (see Chapter 5 for play-based teaching and learning).

The students are allowed to create their own provocations for the morning stations. In some early years' classrooms, students choose the stations they will engage in when they enter the class. They also create the questions that provoke the play at that station. For example, one five year-old in a kindergarten class chose to put paper and coloured pencils on the table. At the time, one of the related concepts of the unit was relationships. The provoking question she created for the table was *'What does a family look like?'* which also showed her understanding of the key concept of form. At snack and reading time, the students choose the book being read aloud and then their own book to read afterwards. They are allowed to sit anywhere in the class while they read.

PRIMARY

Much like in the early years, the primary teachers involve their students in many aspects of the planning of the class. Each classroom starts as somewhat of a blank slate. The students are given the voice to create their own essential agreements which is a key part of the Primary Years Programme (PYP). This being a part of the PYP already lends itself into fostering student agency in the classroom. Students in a Grade 4 class are also given the choice of how they like their learning environment to be arranged. This is something that all of ISUtrecht is working towards. Some classes choose the desk setup and where they hand in their work as well as where their reading corner or play areas are situated in the class. Though certain aspects of the timetable are set such as specialist hours and lunch, other classes then allow the students to choose the routines and parts of the schedule.

In the primary grades, ISUtrecht has a time slot called *genius hour* (see Chapter 2). During this time, which is dedicated for the learners to explore and enquire into their own interests, the teachers help guide the students towards their chosen end goal. In the years that ISUtrecht has conducted genius hour, it has been organised in various different ways. For example, ISUtrecht once held genius hour classes by grouping the children, regardless of grade level, into interests of the learners. Recently, ISUtrecht conducted genius hour by grade-level groupings arranged by interest. The premise of each practice remained the same: allow the children time to enquire into what they want to learn about. This is a key example of how voice and choice is fostered within the ISUtrecht community.

How can student agency be supported and modelled during a lesson?

Student agency is when learners have a voice and choice in their own learning, a guided and supported discovery of one's passions, thoughts, strengths and weaknesses. Although children should be encouraged to make personal decisions and have the freedom to speak their thoughts, student agency is having the framework and foundation for what choices to make, within the context of the classroom or lesson.

EARLY YEARS

In early years, a large part of the teaching process is modelling. Early years teachers model how to learn, how to act, how to think and how to speak. This also includes modelling how to have a voice and make a choice. Teachers model to the students how they can use their voices to speak their opinions, as well as demonstrating how to make personal choices within the classroom. Some children who come into early years have had little opportunity to make personal choices that impact them individually, due to a variety of reasons, and may often be told what to do, rather than offered the opportunity to have a say.

The teachers in early years start to foster agency by modelling how to express ideas and share thoughts. At ISUtrecht, one classroom has a small idea display which promotes the learners to share their ideas of how they can learn. The sticky notes from the learners are ideas on how they can practise their letter sounds, how they can celebrate the 100th day of school and how they can learn more about the weather.

An example of how student agency is fostered in early years was on Valentine's Day. An early years teacher covered a table with crafting material and posed a question to the learners: '*What can you do with these materials?*' The first student to join the table asked the dreaded question '*What are we supposed to do here?*' to which the teacher responded with '*What do you want to do here? The question asks what you can do with the materials*'. The young girl stopped for a moment to think and repeated her original question and the teacher repeated her question. With a moment of thought, the girl understood that she was being allowed to make a choice and immediately showed her creativity and engagement of the task.

PRIMARY

Modelling can be a teaching technique that gets overlooked especially if the teacher comes from a more traditional teacher-centred background. Though modelling is highly important in the early years, it is just as important in the primary grades. A Grade 4 teacher at ISUtrecht takes these ideas very seriously. The teacher says '*I try to model how I take ownership of my own learning by thinking out loud and showing that I am a learner too. I say why I have chosen a certain strategy for learning and I show them where I found it*'. The teacher also models to the students and colleagues at ISUtrecht her constant learning with a very active Twitter and blog.

As mentioned above in the section *Informal planning*, students are given the choice to arrange aspects of their physical environment. In the ISUtrecht mission statement, it says: '*Our learning environment is one in which every person can express themselves safely and freely*'. By creating a democratic environment in which students can feel safe and free to take risks because what they say is valued, the teachers at ISUtrecht support the students in shaping their social-emotional environment.

How do we differentiate student agency?

Student agency does not look the same for every learner in an ISUtrecht classroom. Students learn differently; therefore, they also need to be granted their agency differently.

EARLY YEARS

In some early years classes, there can be learners as young as four and others as old as six and a half. This creates a huge space to differentiate; as a teacher would differentiate to a child's language abilities, they do the same for the child's choices. In one lesson, a teacher may be able to provide the older students with an open question that allows them to enquire and make choices on how they show their learning, yet the younger students need a bit more guidance. So, while the teacher lets the six year-olds choose how they show their learning, he or she may then turn and allow the four year-olds to choose another aspect of their learning and guide them on how to show their learning.

An example of how agency can look different from student to student in a class was in a lesson in an early years classroom about community helpers. Six year-olds were able to choose how they wanted to show their learning and given open-ended materials such as playdough, building blocks and drawing materials. The four year-olds were asked to join the drawing station where they were provided with supports, like photographs of community helpers, which helped them to learn how to show their learning. They were able to choose what they drew and which materials they used from pencils, crayons or markers. Choice was still an aspect of the learning, but it was a different choice than with the older students.

PRIMARY

At the start of the year, many primary classes enquire into what learning is. Along this process, they learn how people learn and, in turn, how they best learn. As the year progresses, the children and teachers use this knowledge to guide their learning journey. Teachers differentiate the choices based on the child's individual abilities and interests. For example, a new student who has limited language acquisition skills will be given simpler texts to read; however, the choice of multiple levelled texts is still available to the student (see Chapter 2 for differentiation).

CONNECTION

The third part of this chapter delves into student agency through the conceptual lens of connection. We have looked at what student agency is and how it works in the planning stages, and now we examine how this connects to the students' learning in real-life situations. We show what a day in a kindergarten class and a Grade 3 class looks like and how student agency is used through the day (see Table 1.1).

CONCLUSION

This chapter has shown how ISUtrecht looks at student agency through the conceptual lenses of form, function and connection. It is now important to decide what to take from it. Below are essential questions on how to get started with implementing student agency in the classroom and what school-wide factors affect the process.

How to get started with student agency?

First of all, teachers have to learn to let go. For many teachers, the idea of losing control of the class is that nightmare that wakes them up in the middle of the night. Therefore, it is natural to want to hold a tight grip on every aspect of the day. However, in order to let the students' voices and choices be heard in the classroom, the teacher has to let go a bit. When a teacher wants to start incorporating student agency, it is good to look at the timetable. What moments in the day could the learners choose something? Where in the lesson or daily routine can their voices be incorporated?

Another way to start the implementation is to make student agency a title head in the lesson plans, next to the outcomes, materials and differentiation. In the beginning, it is easier to write a lesson and reflect on it. While reflecting, ask: '*Where can the students choose something?*' Start with something small. Maybe the students choose where they sit, who they work with or what writing material they use. These small choices start to foster an environment where choice and thought become normal and comfortable. Then move into bigger, more thought-provoking choices: '*Where can the students choose something in their learning?*' Ask the students: '*How do you think we can learn about this? How can you show what you know about this topic?*'

Lastly, just give it a try. Start letting things go, planning in the agency and then do it. Watch what happens when the learners choose how they show their knowledge instead of the teacher telling them how. Watch as students realise that their voices are valued. At times, things may not work, but that is okay. It is a moment to reflect and think of how to guide that area of agency better to get the desired outcome.

What helps agency schoolwide?

There are certain factors that make creating agency in the class easier. Some of those come from schoolwide policies and philosophies. Being a teacher who is allowed agency in their teaching better allows him or her to implement agency for the students. To further explain, it is important to examine the team meetings at ISUtrecht. The subject of a

Table 1.1 A day in an early years and primary class at ISUtrecht

Kindergarten	Grade 3
• Children set the tables with the stations they want for the following day and create the provoking question to accompany the station. • Children choose how they want to tell the teacher good morning: high five, hand shake, hug or dance. • Attendance is a student-led activity in which they answer a question that a student created and a child then lets the teacher know who is not present by looking at who has not answered the question. • Children choose which station to play in with their parents in the morning. • Children do all tidying up on their own taking responsibility for their classroom. • Children's questions guide the enquiry into the unit. • Children choose in which language we say good morning. • Children are allowed to choose who they have discussions with during whole group. • Children often choose how they show their learning. • During reading time, children choose their own books and where in the class they want to read. • A child leads the opening of the stations for free play. • In play, children choose their own station and can move freely between them. • Children choose where they sit for lunch and snack. • Children lead the dismissal routine and complete a class checklist to make sure that they have everything they need to go home. • Children choose how to say goodbye at the end of the day.	• Children choose the location for displays. • Children choose the layout of the classroom. • During discussions, children are allowed to sit anywhere they wish. For example, on the tables, on the carpet or on a chair. • Children sometimes help decide what to do during a 30-minute time slot. • Children decide what music they listen to when reading or working quietly. • Children decide when they want to go to the bathroom. They simply remove the bathroom pass, and place it on their desk so that the teacher knows where they are. • Children decide what classroom jobs they think are important at the beginning of the year. • Children choose what topic they do for genius hour. • Children choose their own library books. • Children choose their motivational poster. • Children coined the term '*Golden Study*' whereby they can work on whatever they want once they have finished. The only rule is that it must be related to classwork. For example, they can use the computers to research a fact that they heard in class, or they can practise their comprehension questions in interview form.

recent meeting was documenting differentiation in our support and attendance system. There was a bit of confusion as teachers were being asked to document how they differentiate in their lesson, except each team documents their differentiation differently. Instead of telling us that all teachers would have to change and conform to one standard way, our PYP co-ordinator recognised the value in the way each of us documented it and said we would have to find a different way that allowed the teachers to still have a voice in how we document. Having a management team that allows the teachers to have agency trickles down to having teachers who allow students to have agency.

Another factor in a school that helps promote agency is the curriculum and pedagogy. At ISUtrecht, the International Baccalaureate PYP curriculum with the pedagogy of enquiry-based learning is used. These two things alone help to create agency in the classroom. Aspects of the PYP and enquiry-based learning such as the essential agreements and using student wonderings to lead teaching make agency a key part of the classroom without the teacher even having to do much. The way our school is shaped from our mission statement to our daily agreements helps the teachers at ISUtrecht promote and maintain student agency in the classroom.

Learning is a partnership, and in order to foster a feeling of belonging and personalised learning, teachers need to relinquish some control, and allow students to become active members of their own learning – because when a student is included in the learning process, they become unstoppable.

Reflective questions

1. Who do you believe should drive student learning and why?
2. How do you provide students with opportunities to work in groups and practise agency?
3. Can your students identify their own strengths and weakness as learners?
4. How would students identify, describe and explain their own agency in your classroom?
5. How do you create a supportive environment that fosters students' ability to take risks and fail?

REFERENCES

Annan, J (2016) *Student Agency in Interactive Learning Environments*. [online] Available at: https://static1.squarespace.com/static/5dd1b5c9da15f732723fe4c6/t/5e576bec4e2df00530a061e1/1582787567116/2+Student-Agency-in-Interactive-Contexts-V2-9-06-2017-.pdf (accessed 12 September 2020).

Core Education (nd) *Learner Agency: Final Research Report*. [online] Available at: www.core-ed.org/assets/Uploads/Learner-Agency-CORE-Research.pdf (accessed 12 September 2020).

Fleming, D (2015) Student Voice: An Emerging Discourse in Irish Education Policy. *International Electronic Journal of Elementary Education*, 8(2): 223–42.

Hanover Research (2014) *Impact of Student Choice and Personalized Learning*. [online] Available at: www.gssaweb.org/wp-content/uploads/2015/04/Impact-of-Student-Choice-and-Personalized-Learning-1.pdf (accessed 12 September 2020).

Harvey, V S and Chickie-Wolfe, L A (2007) *Fostering Independent Learning: Practical Strategies to Promote Student Success*. New York: Guildford Press.

Healey, M, Flint, A and Harrington, K (2016) Students as Partners: Reflections on a Conceptual Model. *Teaching & Learning Inquiry*, 4(2): 1–13.

Jobs for the Future & the Council of Chief State School Officers (2015) *Educator Competencies for Personalized, Learner-centered Teaching*. Boston: Jobs for the Future.

Kohn, A (1993) Choices for Children: Why and How to Let Students Decide. *Phi Delta Kappan*, 75(1): 8–16, 18–20.

Mansfield, K C, Welton, A and Halx, M (2018) Listening to Student Voice: Toward a More Holistic Approach to School Leadership. *Journal of Ethical Educational Leadership*, Special issue 1: 10–27.

Morrison, K (2008) Democratic Classrooms: Promises and Challenges of Student Voice and Choice, Part One. *Educational Horizons*, 87(1): 50–60.

Robertson, J (2017) Rethinking Learner and Teacher Roles: Incorporating Student Voice and Agency into Teaching Practice. *Journal of Initial Teacher Inquiry*, 3: 41–4.

St John, K and Briel, L (2017) *Student Voice: A Growing Movement within Education That Benefits Students and Teachers*. [online] Available at: www.worksupport.com/documents/StudentVoiceAgrowingmovementwithineducationthatbenefitsstudentsandteachers.pdf (accessed 12 September 2020).

Vaughn, M (2018) Making Sense of Student Agency in the Early Grades. *Phi Delta Kappan*, 99(7): 62–6.

Victoria State Government (2020) *Dimension: Empowering Students and Building School Pride*. [online] Available at: www.education.vic.gov.au/school/teachers/management/improvement/Pages/dimension3empowering.aspx#link11 (accessed 12 September 2020).

Williams, P (2017) Student Agency for Powerful Learning. *American Library Association*, 45(4): 9–15.

2 Differentiation

Anssi Roiha, Nicole Boerma and Maria Ballester

*If a child can't learn the way we teach,
maybe we should teach the way they learn.*

Ignacio Estrada

INTRODUCTION

Students' individual differences are getting increasing attention in education and the long-standing one-size-fits-all approach is generally seen as outdated. However, the diversity of classrooms all around the world is making it difficult for teachers to take each learner's individuality into account. Differentiation is often presented as one solution to the problem as it is considered to be a necessity for different learners to achieve the same goals. Yet, many teachers lack the resources, knowledge or expertise to differentiate their teaching in a systematic and profound manner. As a result, the most effective differentiation practices which tackle the heterogeneity of the students are often not implemented in classrooms.

This chapter focuses on differentiation in teaching. In essence, differentiation is a teaching approach that takes each student's uniqueness, interests and needs into account. Differentiation is a proactive, student-oriented and systematic pedagogical approach that permeates all teaching. With differentiation, teachers can offer successful learning experiences and enhance each student's learning process in the best possible way. In differentiated classrooms, teachers allow and normalise different work methods for different students. Thus, not everyone needs to do exactly the same activities at the same time nor in the same way.

In this chapter, we draw on examples from the International School Utrecht (ISUtrecht) which is a relevant context for differentiation as the classes there are relatively heterogeneous due to the students' diverse language skills and learning profiles. Teachers at ISUtrecht employ numerous differentiation practices to provide the best teaching for each student. Initially, we briefly conceptualise differentiation and introduce its theoretical underpinnings as well as provide a concise literature review on the topic. However, the main emphasis of this chapter is on various differentiation practices and strategies. The practical part starts by outlining the student support procedure at the school. The remaining part is divided into five dimensions: *teaching arrangements*, *learning environment*, *teaching methods*, *support materials* and *assessment*. In this chapter, we capitalise on the varied experience and expertise of the authors and examine differentiation from many viewpoints by providing a myriad of practical examples in all the aforementioned dimensions.

WHAT IS DIFFERENTIATION?

Differentiation is often interchangeably used with individualisation and personalisation and there has been some ambiguity in the conceptualisation of the terms. Individualisation and differentiation often refer to the type of instruction in which all learners are expected to achieve the same goals by various support practices. Personalisation, in turn, refers to an approach in which individuality is even more extended ranging from the learning objectives to the pace of learning (Bray and McClaskey, 2012). In this chapter, we adhere to the term differentiation and see it as somewhat synonymous with personalisation. That is, we broadly define differentiation as a holistic teaching approach in which teachers proactively modify their teaching to maximise each student's learning potential (Tomlinson, 2014). For instance, according to Tomlinson (2014), differentiation should be based on students' readiness, interests and learning profiles and be primarily targeted at content, processes and products. Thousand et al (2007), in turn, define differentiation as being proactive and circular. According to them, teachers should become aware of their students' special needs and individual features as well as strengths and use those as the basis of differentiation. Ongoing assessment is also a pivotal feature in differentiation as teachers should constantly assess and evaluate their differentiation practices and modify them based on the feedback received. All differentiation should always stem from the students and their individual features, such as learning profile, self-esteem, interests, capabilities, needs, motivation, personality and history (Roiha and Polso, 2020).

Differentiation is not a theory of its own but rather includes many theoretical underpinnings. For instance, differentiation reflects the constructivist learning theory which emphasises learners' own activity and motivation in the learning process. Moreover, students' prior perceptions and beliefs are significant as they guide the learning and meaning-making processes (eg Rauste-von Wright et al, 2003). Students' own interests and pre-knowledge are assumed to be the starting point also in differentiation. In light of this, differentiation can be seen as one way to apply the principles of a constructivist learning theory in practice.

Another theoretical concept relevant to differentiation is Vygotsky's (1978) Zone of Proximal Development (ZPD) that relates to his sociocultural theory. Simply put, ZPD refers to the distance that is between the student's actual development level and the potential development level available through assistance from others. According to Vygotsky, each student's ZPD is unique and independent of age (Vygotsky, 1978). Teachers are expected to be aware of their students' ZPD in order to provide appropriate and suitable challenges for each learner. Thus, in an ideal situation, each student would always work on tasks and activities that correspond to their individual ZPD.

Differentiation has also underpinnings of Gardner's (2008) theory of multiple intelligences. In his theory, Gardner distinguished nine different forms of intelligence: *musical intelligence*, *bodily-kinesthetic intelligence*, *logical-mathematical intelligence*, *linguistic intelligence*, *spatial intelligence*, *interpersonal intelligence*, *intrapersonal intelligence*, *naturalistic intelligence* and *existential intelligence*. According to Gardner (2008), every person has traces of all the aforementioned intelligences, but their degree varies among individuals. In his view, schools should increasingly acknowledge all forms of intelligence as traditional uniform teaching favours mostly linguistically and logic mathematically oriented students. Gardner's theory has received a lot of criticisms, for instance, for the lack of empirical research and the use of the term intelligence. However, with respect to differentiation, the theory importantly highlights students' different learning profiles which should be taken into account at school. Differentiation can be seen as a pedagogical application of Gardner's theory as it similarly acknowledges the uniqueness of each student.

RESEARCH FINDINGS ON DIFFERENTIATION

While the research on differentiation and its benefits is still in its infancy, some studies nevertheless indicate that differentiation can improve students' learning outcomes and be a useful teaching approach regarding all learners. For instance, peer support and remedial teaching as well as individual and systematic feedback as means of differentiation have been found to reduce learning difficulties in mathematics (Baker et al, 2002; Fuchs et al, 2005). Also the use of flexible grouping and individual assignments have been shown to enhance the learning of both weak and gifted students (DeBarsyshe et al, 2009; Reis et al, 2011; Koeze, 2007; Shaunessy-Dedrick et al, 2015; Tieso, 2005). Students have also performed better in national tests when they have received differentiated teaching even though the tests have not corresponded to this level (Grigorenko et al, 2002). In addition, a few studies have indicated that differentiation can engage students in learning and form a more positive attitude towards school (Karadag and Yasar, 2010; McCrea Simpkins et al, 2009). Despite the promising research results, many teachers regard differentiation as challenging and arduous to implement. Issues such as the lack of time and resources, impractical physical classrooms, large class sizes, uniform teaching materials and the heterogeneity of the students are often brought forth as factors that prevent teachers from differentiating (eg Roiha, 2014; Tomlinson and Imbeau, 2010). The purpose of this chapter is to lower the threshold for differentiation by providing useful practices for teachers in several dimensions of teaching.

DIFFERENTIATION IN PRACTICE AT INTERNATIONAL SCHOOL UTRECHT

Student support

As we are all different learners, some students will always need different types of teaching and support to be able to successfully follow the curriculum. With that in mind, it is important that each school has a systematic and comprehensive support system in place. Even though the emphasis of this chapter is on differentiation in various dimensions of teaching, we first briefly outline the support policy at ISUtrecht to give an overview of how students' diversity is considered at the school. It is important to note that ISUtrecht is a mainstream school which is able to offer support to students with only mild learning disabilities or temporary learning difficulties. The International Baccalaureate (IB) curriculum itself offers many possibilities for meeting the students' needs. In addition, at ISUtrecht, we distinguish the three following levels of support in all of which differentiation has a central role.

1. *Tier 1 Regular in-class support*: Provided by a classteacher or class assistant (eg extra instruction and homework to solve minor issues).

2. *Tier 2 Specific support*: Working towards SMART-formulated aims, academic or behavioural, written down in a Support Plan (SP) by the classteacher together with one of the student support specialists. The support is provided by the classteachers as well as a student support specialist. The extra support sessions are given as often as possible in class during the regular lessons.

3. *Tier 3 Specific support*: Arranged when a student has been diagnosed with a disability or is having severe behavioural or social emotional issues. SMART-formulated aims, written down in an Individual Educational Plan (IEP), will be evaluated and adapted on a regular basis.

When the regular in-class support is considered insufficient, the subsequent support procedure starts by filling a form in which the classteacher describes the strengths, challenges and main concerns about the student, earlier interventions that have been carried out to support the student and their effectiveness. Parents add to this form as their commitment and approval is important during the whole support procedure. Additionally, the student support specialists need information on the student's language background to rule out any possible English language acquisition issues. Depending on the student being a native or non-native English speaker, the need for support will be discussed either in the student support team or in the English Language Acquisition (ELA) team. If a new student enrolling in the school does not have adequate English proficiency and is still learning the language, this can have a major influence on the school results and even the behaviour of the student. Therefore, we want to give the students who have a non-English academic background enough time to improve their English language skills, while simultaneously asking the parents to continue supporting the mother tongue development at home as research clearly indicates that the development of one's first language is very important to help one reach one's full academic potential (Clark, 2002) (see also Chapter 12).

At ISUtrecht, the students with inadequate English proficiency will receive ELA support twice a week, arranged by the ELA team. If a student needs extra language support on top of the regular ELA support, this is agreed between the ELA team and the student support team. Sometimes, it can be challenging to distinguish whether a student requires ELA or learning support. When a student is not considered an ELA student anymore – usually after two years of structural education in English – any continuing challenges in English might indicate a learning difficulty or even learning disability. These concerns will be discussed with the teacher and the support team and appropriate aims and interventions will be decided on and documented in an online support plan. Interventions can, for instance, be extra reading, spelling or mathematics instruction, exercises connected to unit work or online tools. The students are also expected to regularly practise at home. The interventions can be implemented by the classteacher or one of the support specialists. We primarily aim to arrange the support in class to promote inclusive education. However, when considered necessary, mostly for reasons of concentration, the support will be pulled out.

Continuous assessment is a central feature in the support system. After four and eight weeks of received support, an evaluation is made to see whether there has been progress in the student's performance. If necessary, the aims will be adjusted after four weeks depending on the level of progress. After eight weeks, a decision is made whether the support should be continued or discontinued. This procedure is repeated a maximum of three times. If, as a result, no or not enough progress is observed, further investigations will take place. In this case, parents will have to give their consent to external testing in order to obtain more information on how to support the student in a proper way. This final step is carefully considered and testing is recommended only if we are convinced that it is necessary and will benefit the student. When a learning disability is diagnosed, the students will receive continuous support as stated in their IEP. For instance, in order to demonstrate their learning properly, oral assessment is permitted to dyslexic students as an alternative to a written one.

In addition to learning difficulties, the support at ISUtrecht is also targeted at students who need extra challenges and demonstrate more advancement in certain areas. This support is mostly implemented by the classteacher as in-class support by providing the students with higher order questions and assignments relying on the levels of Bloom's Taxonomy of thinking skills (Bates and Munday, 2005). In order to challenge the more abled students, they will be asked to analyse, synthesise or evaluate what they have learnt.

In general, differentiation is embedded in the teaching philosophy at ISUtrecht. The teachers take the students' individuality into account, for instance, by covering the students' interests and needs, adapting teaching methods and the support materials, differentiating students' learning objectives, implementing many ways of assessment and creating a personal and close relationship with each student. In order to make sure that the teachers are creating an atmosphere in the class in which all of the students are able to freely express themselves and enhance their potential, it is important to pay attention to different aspects of teaching. In the remaining sections of this chapter, we introduce several differentiation practices that can be implemented in schools. We have divided the chapter into five key dimensions of teaching (see Figure 2.1).

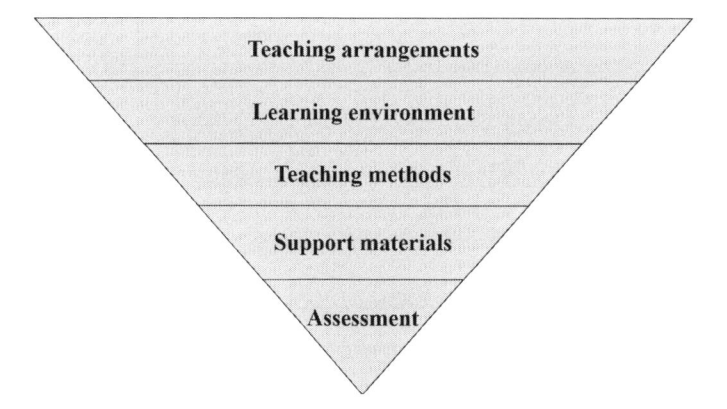

Figure 2.1 Five dimensions of differentiation
(Adapted from Roiha and Polso, 2020)

Dimension 1: teaching arrangements

The first dimension consists of various teaching arrangements which can be implemented at both a class and school level. One example is flexible grouping in which students are divided into various groups based on different criteria so that the teachers can provide more tailored teaching to each group. The grouping can be based on ability levels, interests, social relations or students' working styles. It is important to pay attention that students are not always grouped based on the same criterion as flexible grouping should not have a stigmatising effect nor should it negatively determine the student's perception of her/himself as a learner. Furthermore, it is essential that the composition of the groups is constantly altered and students' placement in a certain group continuously reassessed. One key element in successful differentiation that relates to flexible grouping is peer support. In essence, it means organising opportunities for the students to facilitate each other's learning.

At ISUtrecht, many teachers have systematically employed flexible grouping. In kindergarten, for example, the students do not have a specific chair and table to sit while working. That way the students move in a flexible and free way around the classroom and choose the spot they feel more comfortable in during a specific activity which allows various types of collaborations. In upper grades, flexible grouping coupled with peer support is employed to attend to the students' different levels, needs and profiles in specific activities and subjects such as reading, writing, mental mathematics or spelling. For instance, at the start of a mathematics unit, the teachers may conduct a pre-assessment to get to know their students' pre-knowledge of the topic. Based on this, the students are divided into different groups so that the teaching can be better tailored to their current needs. It is useful to implement this type of policy across the whole grade level to maximise its effect. That way each teacher can instruct a more homogenised group, for instance, a few hours per week in certain subjects or topics which makes the teaching more effective. As the vehicular language at ISUtrecht is English, which is not the mother tongue of most students in the school, the teachers also aim to place the ELA students in the same group with their mother tongue peers so that they can support each other's learning (see Chapter 12).

A teaching arrangement that functions as a good example of differentiation is known as genius hour. The idea is said to originate from the business world where many innovative companies allow their employees to spend a portion of their work time on their own projects as it is expected to increase productivity (Genius Hour, nd). In genius hour, the same idea is transferred to a school context. The arrangement is fairly simple to implement in practice. The basic idea is to give students the time and opportunity to work on topics of their interest. However, the topics should be such that they require problem solving and critical thinking. Even though genius hour is very much student-oriented, the teacher's role in choosing the topic and narrowing the scope is essential. Students are expected to work on the same topic for a relatively long period of time, for instance, the whole semester or even an entire academic year. One lesson per week can be reserved for this arrangement with all classes which also allows the use of flexible grouping within and across grade levels. It is important that students plan their project thoroughly before delving into the actual work.

Continuous and ongoing assessment is an important part of genius hour. After every genius hour lesson, students should reflect on their work and set goals for the next time, for instance, in their genius hour journals. It is also worth investing in the presentation of the final products. For example, parents can be asked to come to school for a genius hour project presentation day. Students also learn while listening to each other's presentations. In genius hour, students learn to plan, execute and assess their work. They also take more ownership of their own learning. Furthermore, this sort of teaching arrangement often sparks intrinsic motivation and promotes creative learning. The teacher's role is to work as a facilitator in the learning process. From a differentiation viewpoint, the arrangement differentiates already in itself. Some students remain on a more superficial level in their enquiries, while the most gifted students practise more abstract thinking. Teachers also learn a lot about their students; what interests them and what are their preferred working styles. This is valuable information for further differentiation. The arrangement fits well with an approach that emphasises holistic and cross-curricular learning. Genius hour is a useful arrangement for acknowledging especially the more abled students. Students' experience of genius hour is usually very positive. They are excited to get to choose their own topics and decide on how to proceed with the project. For instance, during genius hour at ISUtrecht, the students have investigated black holes and climate change, studied Braille and learnt coding.

Differentiation means providing appropriate challenges to all students including the more abled ones. This is carried out on a daily basis in the classroom by the teachers. In addition, it is sometimes beneficial to provide pull-out sessions to the students who are in need of extra challenges at school. Teachers can use several measures to identify and determine who these students are. It is important not to rely on a single but rather on several indicators when deciding which students would benefit the most from this kind of support. Often, teachers make valuable observations in class and are aware if a student is not challenged enough and if the activities are too easy. School grades and performance at school also give a preliminary indication which students would possibly benefit from extra challenges. In addition to these, teachers can use standardised ability tests to endorse their decision. It is also important to listen to the students themselves and consult the parents as they may offer valuable information for the teacher. It should be borne in mind that extra challenges should not be provided only to students with exceptional achievement but also to students who stand out in terms of their creative or critical thinking skills.

At ISUtrecht, we have recently launched a pilot arrangement to provide extra challenges to a number of students in small groups. We have formed two groups based on the students' age. The group of older students has consisted of fifth graders and the group of younger students of second and third graders. The students who have taken part in the arrangement have shown exceptional problem-solving skills and abstract reasoning as well as demonstrated a high intrinsic motivation for learning. The older students have engaged with their personal enquiry projects an hour per week. The projects have been thoroughly planned beforehand and the students have formed enquiry questions to guide their learning. For instance, one student has enquired into quantum mechanics and another into mythical creatures. The students have practised student agency in planning and deciding on their projects and learning (see also Chapter 1). The focus with the younger students has been more on collaborate learning skills. The students have first solved a few mathematical escape rooms after which they have created their own escape room for their peers to solve. The arrangement is still in its infancy but the initial experiences have been highly positive from both the students' and teachers' perspectives.

Dimension 2: learning environment

The second dimension concerns learning environment which receives a lot of attention at ISUtrecht. For instance, the school's mission statement declares the following:

> *We give special attention to the physical and social environment we learn and work in. We value and care for the natural world and model responsible behaviour. Our learning environment is one in which **every person** can express themselves safely and freely.*
>
> (International School Utrecht, nd)

The above quotation exemplifies how students' individuality is acknowledged also regarding the physical and social environments in which they are learning. In this chapter, we focus on learning environment from the viewpoint of differentiation. At first, we discuss the atmosphere in the class and how it can help teachers to personalise their teaching practices followed by a few examples on how the physical learning environment can promote differentiation.

Imagine that you have a group of 25 students in your class. You are aware of most of their interests and needs, but as they are all different, you only have the resources to fully focus on a small group of students at a time. This is where the classroom environment helps you to address every student's needs and interests at the same time. The physical environment you create with the grouping of the desks, the resources displayed and the provocations provided will be your extra arms, hands, eyes, mouth and ears. That way the environment can be used as the third teacher much like Reggio Emilia pedagogy suggests (Edwards, 1993). Properly arranging the learning environment enables the teacher to walk, observe, interact and guide the students while they are learning in an independent, dynamic and inspirational way. The teachers at ISUtrecht do this on a daily basis in their classrooms. They endeavour to attend to each student's interests and needs with the help of the learning environment. The teachers think about the atmosphere they want to create and the provocations to provide to the students in order to stimulate them, not only by words but also by what they can see and perceive around them.

The ISUtrecht staff believes that each student is unique and special. Therefore, the teacher's role is to guide the students, observe them and help them uncover their full potential. However, the idea is that the students are responsible for their own learning process as much as possible. From this perspective, the classroom environment aims to provide the best facilities for the students to learn, whether this is on the floor, at their desks or on a chair or sofa. For instance, in the early years, the classrooms are organised by enrichment corners. Armstrong (2006) proposes organising the class in different areas that refer to each of Gardner's (2008) multiple intelligences. He calls them '*work centres*'. Following this view, the classroom can have a spatial intelligence corner (eg for drawing or with 3D construction materials), a bodily-kinesthetic corner (eg crafting materials), a logical-mathematical corner (eg board games and various mathematics manipulatives), a linguistic corner (eg books, magazines or reading and writing resources), a naturalistic corner (eg exhibition table with some natural elements such as plants, stones, sticks, objects made of wood), a musical corner (eg musical instruments or a CD player), an interpersonal corner (eg role plays, discussions) and an intrapersonal corner (eg a tent or an isolated place to allow the students to be alone). Students often have the option to choose the corner they like to work in. Sometimes, the teacher will guide students to a corner of which they would benefit, even if this is not their initial choice. The possibilities are multiple in order to provide the students a space where their needs and interests as well as their personal abilities and intelligences are taken into account.

In all the primary years classrooms, the tables are organised in groups or a semicircle as opposed to the more traditional way of lining the desks in rows facing the board. These seating arrangements enable the use of peer support and collaborative learning which are emphasised at ISUtrecht. Contrarily, facing all the tables towards the teacher would highlight the importance of the teacher's voice, but at ISUtrecht, the discussions and reflections between the students are valued more. In addition, most teachers' desks are placed in the corner of the classroom and primarily used to store their laptop and stationery material. This diminishes the traditional view of the teacher being the most powerful character with the biggest desk in front of the class. Instead, this arrangement creates an atmosphere in the class that facilitates a closer relationship between the students and the teacher and among the students themselves. Within the groups, the students can be placed according to various criteria. For instance, the students with the same mother tongue or the same learning style can sit in the same group to support each other's learning. The students who have trouble concentrating can be placed facing the board with their backs against the window.

At ISUtrecht, the desks are just one place for studying. All the classrooms also have a big soft carpet to encourage the students to work, think, reflect and discuss topics on the floor. This offers another perspective and for most students, a more comfortable and informal place to work. The carpets are also often used for whole class discussions during which students normally sit in a circle so that everyone can see each other's faces. This further creates an atmosphere that reinforces the connections between the members of the group. With the help of these discussions, the teachers get to know their students' interests and needs which is highly beneficial for their teaching and differentiation. Many classes have the routine of every day gathering on the carpet to share their experiences, anecdotes or news. Furthermore, during free time, and particularly with the younger learners, the teachers often play with their students or observe them to learn about their interests in a very informal way.

In general, it is important to let the students move in a flexible way in the classroom and allow them the chance to support their peers and help each other. However, it is also equally important to acknowledge that the students are not always in the mood to work with others and would prefer to have some quiet and relaxing time. Therefore, it is important that the classrooms have venues for different types of learning situations. These can be an individual desk at the corner of the classroom or even in the corridor or a private hut made up of pillows and room dividers in one corner. An option is to encourage flexible seating so that students can choose their own space that fits their current needs which is the policy in many classes at ISUtrecht.

Dimension 3: teaching methods

The third dimension covers teaching methods and how differentiation is embedded in them. In general, the Primary Years Programme (PYP) strongly promotes constructivist, conceptual and enquiry-based learning. This enables learners to ask and explore their own questions and construct new knowledge from their own curiosities and interests. In that way, the students have an active role in their learning and the teacher's role is more of a guide or facilitator in the process. This type of approach to teaching, which differs a lot from the traditional approach in which the teacher transfers the knowledge to the students, allows the students to learn in various ways that are more connected to their own personal learning styles. In general, the teaching approach at ISUtrecht is a natural and favourable way to differentiate as the learning is very individualised and student-oriented. Moreover, this approach helps the students to understand and enhance their potential as they have the freedom and flexibility to develop themselves in a personalised way feeding their proper desire to learn. When students do most of the question asking and answer seeking, their individuality is shown to us. As teachers, we then need to design learning engagements that promote discussions, collaboration, creativity and critical thinking suited to their needs. The PYP is designed to foster the development of the whole child both in the classroom and in the world outside. This means that with our teaching methods, we provide a holistic development and do not focus only on the intellectual dimension but also on the emotional, social and physical aspects as well. We all see the students as unique individuals and aim to build a relationship with every child. We focus first on the students' emotional and social well-being and when that is considered to be in order, we move on to the academic side.

In all the primary years at ISUtrecht, the teaching and learning process follows a similar structure. During the year, we work on five or six main transdisciplinary topics that are considered necessary depending on the students' ages, general needs and interests. Teachers then think about a central idea for each topic and plan a hook, which is a provocation to engage the students to think and wonder what they already know and what they still want to learn about a topic. Teachers take notes from those discussions and start planning from the students' inputs. The activities in the lessons are a combination of guided and free enquiry (see also Chapter 7). For instance, the classes have joint discussions on the carpet or the students work individually or in small groups with the guidance and support from the teacher(s) in the classroom. ISUtrecht believes in the potential of every student in the class which is important to show to them and reinforce their confidence and self-esteem by giving them time to explore and learn independently which echoes the philosophy behind differentiation. An atmosphere in which one is not afraid to try, make mistakes and try again without being judged promotes meaningful and constructive learning.

Finally, part of our teaching methods are the reflections on what the students have learnt. We engage them to be critical and autonomous thinkers. Therefore, ISUtrecht teachers provide reflection routines to connect individual thoughts, enquiries and discoveries with the rest of the group. In this way, it is not only the teachers who share their knowledge but the students also teach each other and co-construct meaning. The reflections reveal a lot about the students' understanding and makes their thinking visible. Some teachers, for example, use a jar for '*I wish my teacher knew…*' notes for this purpose. Another effective way of reflecting the students' learning is a gallery walk in which the students rotate in class to observe what others have done in class. In line with differentiation, we take the students' individuality into account in the process and guide them to reflect on their learning in the ways and depth that is suitable for each learner.

Dimension 4: support materials

The fourth dimension deals with various support materials which can be used to support students' learning. In upper grades, information and communication technology (ICT) is used for this purpose on a daily basis in the classrooms, through a combination of tablets, computers and smart boards. Students use these devices to develop their research skills by searching for information on the internet. Tablets are also used as a tool to photograph, record, document and reflect on the learning. Some classroom teachers use various online portfolios and platforms with their students. These are natural ways of differentiating teaching. ICT also allows flipped learning to be implemented with the students who need extra support at school. For instance, the students can be instructed to watch short videos and familiarise themselves with a topic at home before it is covered at school. That way they have a surface-level understanding of the topics in advance which helps them to better acquire what is being discussed at school. The role of technological devices in learning is more thoroughly discussed in Chapter 9.

With younger learners, the use of ICT is more reduced and the focus is more on other types of support materials such as natural objects to explore and connect with the real world, wooden toys based on Montessori approach (Montessori, 1964/2014), language and mathematics games created by the teachers, puppets, playdough, paint, role-play props and story books. Younger learners also have an arrangement called '*golden time*' which takes place once a week. During this period, students can choose an important toy from home that they want to bring to school and share with their friends. This is also an excellent way for the teachers to get to know their students' interests and likes.

In general, it is important that the classrooms have a lot of manipulatives, games and other resources that the students can freely use to support their learning. It is helpful if these have their own labelled places in the classroom so that all the students can access them easily. Classes should have a culture in which students can flexibly use the appropriate resources needed when engaging with various learning activities. Particularly with younger learners, teachers need to guide students to reflect on their learning and which materials would help and support their learning. When this is done systematically, in time students will learn to go and get the appropriate support materials for each activity by themselves. Teachers can actively create a classroom culture in which the use of various support materials is normalised. For instance, the fact that some students may need a chair cushion to sit on to concentrate better or others a magnifying glass to read fluently should not be a taboo in the classroom.

Learning materials and their use also involve differentiation. In general, teachers often tend to create several types of worksheets for the same activity to take different learners into account. This is, of course, helpful for many students but also very time-consuming for the teachers. Although the teachers at ISUtrecht rely on teaching materials much less than in traditional teaching, they still occasionally use, for instance, worksheets. As a way to move past the preparation of several different worksheets, the teachers often provide the students with open-ended questions that can be answered according to the students' individual abilities. All students can also be given the same kind of worksheets but they can complete them in differentiated ways. For example, some students can only focus on the easier exercises, while others are also able to complete the more challenging ones. Another positive aspect of providing the whole class with the same worksheets is that the students are not that easily stigmatised.

Dimension 5: assessment

The final dimension focuses on assessment which can be broadly divided into *pre-assessment*, *formal assessment* and *summative assessment*. Even though they have very different purposes, they all provide the teacher with valuable information on what and how to differentiate. In general, differentiation is effective only when it is based on actual information about the students' learning profiles. In order to obtain this information, an ongoing assessment in all its forms is needed. This way meaningful and purposeful differentiation can be implemented, for instance, with regard to content, amount of work, pace of learning or learning process. It is important to bear in mind that as each student is unique and has different ways of learning, we also need different methods for assessing them. The traditional approach with formal exams or tests does not acknowledge the individuality of all students as it requires them to do the same task, in the same way and in the same time frame. This type of uniform assessment does not respect students' uniqueness and differences in learning and in demonstrating their understanding. If we ask all the students to work in the same way, we also limit their creativity.

At ISUtrecht, we assess the students in three different periods: at the start (pre-assessment), during (formative assessment) and after the learning process (summative assessment). We conduct a pre-assessment which has a twofold purpose as it reveals what both the teachers and the students themselves already know about a topic and what they still need to focus on. The methods of pre-assessment vary from whole group discussions to written assessments such as questionnaires or checklists. Formative assessment, in turn, takes place during the unit and can be carried out employing different methods such as observation, anecdotal notes, performance assessment, open-ended tasks, checklists or documentation. Finally, at the end of the unit, the students have a summative assessment which can also be conducted in various forms. Different methods of assessment are, for instance, written essays, role plays, drama, interviews, experiments, tests, quizzes, posters, oral presentations and conversations. It is important to note that teachers do not need to rely on the same assessment methods with all students but they can be differentiated based on their individual needs. Some students can, for instance, write an essay, while others can demonstrate their learning orally. Regardless of the assessment methods, all students should be aware of *what* is being assessed as well as *how* and *why* it is assessed.

The teachers at ISUtrecht use various strategies to assess their learners in a personalised way. These are mainly agreed on in collaborative meetings between all involved parties such as teachers, specialists and assistants. During these meetings, both the learning outcomes and the corresponding assessment criteria are decided on. With younger learners, the primary learning objectives are set by the teachers. The objectives are adapted to each student's abilities and teacher support is given when needed. With older learners, in turn, learning intentions are partly decided together with the students. Based on these learning intentions, success criteria are jointly agreed on as a class with the teacher guiding the process. The criteria are used as the basis of assessment and the students can use them to reflect on their own learning. In that way, the students have more ownership and agency in the assessment process. In addition to the assessment criteria, the ways of demonstrating understanding can be decided together with certain students or the whole class.

Often students receive a numerical certificate after each semester in which their learning is assessed in a somewhat limited way. At ISUtrecht instead, the students receive written reports of their learning two times in an academic year. The teachers also meet with the parents the minimum of two times during the school year to discuss the students' learning and progress. These practices allow the teachers to assess the students in a more personalised way and the parents also get a better understanding of their children's learning and performance. The teachers can also focus on the strengths of each student while addressing the targets of development in a constructive manner. It is worth remarking that even though a school would not have a policy of organising these types of oral progress meetings, teachers can always arrange them for individual students if needed.

Currently, at ISUtrecht, summative assessment plays the main role in the learning process, mostly taking place in the last week of the unit. In the future, we want to focus more on formative assessment and provide students with more agency in deciding their own learning goals and methods of assessment also with younger learners. Additionally, the intention is to increase the role of peers and parents in the assessment process as well.

CONCLUSION

Differentiation is a way of considering teaching with students' individuality constantly in mind. It is a pervasive approach that permeates all teaching and extends to all dimensions covered in this chapter. Occasionally, even small changes and adjustments in teaching or classroom routines can have a substantial effect on students' learning. The purpose of this chapter has been to provide insights and ideas on how to approach differentiation in teaching. The most central practices are summarised in Table 2.1 opposite. It is important to keep in mind that not all practices are transferrable to all contexts as such. However, when differentiation is at the core of one's teaching philosophy, one approaches all teaching with the mindset of providing each learner with appropriate challenges. There is never an endpoint to differentiation but it is rather a constantly evolving process. Similarly, at ISUtrecht, we are regularly revisiting and developing our differentiation practices so that they best serve each individual learner. In the future, we want to increasingly allow the students to demonstrate their learning in various ways as we would like to give each student more agency on what to learn and how to assess this. We also want to involve the parents more in their children's learning. We are in a continuous process towards a curriculum that will be even more focused on the progress of individual students instead of a curriculum that uses grade-level expectations. The following quotation serves as a premise for this journey:

> *There are no year level expectations in a series of achievement standards. No one is at, on, above or below expectations. Every student is simply at a level of development defined by what learning is developmentally appropriate.*
>
> (Care and Griffen, 2009, p 56)

Reflective questions

1. Is the support system in your school systematic and comprehensive? How could you develop it?
2. Do all the dimensions mentioned in this chapter receive equal attention in differentiation in your teaching/in your school?
3. Can you come up with differentiation methods which would benefit all students in your class?
4. Do you always assess all students the same way? Can you think of alternative assessment methods for some students?
5. Do you take the students' opinions into account when designing differentiation practices?
6. Do you involve the parents in differentiation?

Table 2.1 Differentiation practices in a nutshell

1. Teaching arrangements
- Group students flexibly within and across classes (based on learning styles, abilities, interests, etc). Students can work on different topics or subjects.
- Make systematic use of peer support.
- Provide opportunities for more abled students to challenge themselves.
- Book one hour a week for fully differentiated work (eg genius hour).

2. Learning environment
- Choose the classroom seating arrangements individually. Not all students need to have their own designated place in the classroom.
- Arrange various learning spaces that allow different types of work in your classroom (ie reading, silent work, group work, hands-on work, etc).
- Display only the pertinent and most essential materials (too much stimuli can be counterproductive).
- Make use of the various learning spaces of the school.

3. Teaching methods
- Create a flexible work culture in the classroom. Not everyone needs to do the same things, the same time or the same way in the classroom.
- Implement enquiry-based learning in which the students set themselves individual goals and partly work on different topics.
- Focus on each student's positive sides.

4. Support materials
- Use ICT resources to support students' learning.
- Use online portfolios for differentiation.
- Equip the classroom with a lot of resources for different types of learning.
- Create a culture where students can freely make use of all the resources in the class.

5. Assessment
- Conduct a pre-assessment at the start of a unit. Based on that, set individual goals for the unit in collaboration with the students.
- Make sure the students know *what* is being assessed as well as *how* and *why* it is assessed.
- Use self- and peer assessment in a differentiated way.
- Use formal assessment individually to guide the students' learning.
- Methods of summative assessment can be, for instance:
  - ✓ Written exams
  - ✓ Presentations and projects
  - ✓ Plays
  - ✓ Recorded videos
  - ✓ Posters

REFERENCES

Armstrong, T (2006) *Inteligencias Múltiples en el Aula: Guía Práctica para Educadores.* Barcelona: Paidós.

Baker, S, Gersten, R and Lee, D-S (2002) A Synthesis of Empirical Research on Teaching Mathematics to Low-achieving Students. *The Elementary School Journal*, 103(1): 51–73.

Bates, J and Munday, S (2005) *Able, Gifted and Talented*. London: Continuum International Publishing.

Bray, B and McClaskey, K (2012) *Personalization vs Differentiation vs Individualization*. [online] Available at: http://kathleenmcclaskey.com/personalization-vs-differentiation-vs-individualization-chart/ (accessed 2 January 2020).

Care, E and Griffen, P (2009) Assessment is for Teaching. *Independence*, 34(2): 56–9.

Clark, B A (2002) First- and Second-language Acquisition in Early Childhood. In Rothenberg, D (ed) *Issues in Early Childhood Education: Curriculum, Teacher Education, & Dissemination of Information. Proceedings of the Lilian Katz Symposium November 5–7, 2000*. Champaign: ERIC Clearinghouse on Elementary and Early Childhood Education.

DeBaryshe, B D, Gorecki, D M and Mishima-Young, L N (2009) Differentiated Instruction to Support High-risk Preschool Learners. *NHSA Dialog*, 2(3): 227–44.

Edwards, C P (1993) *The Hundred Languages of Children: The Reggio Emilia Approach to Early Childhood Education*. Norwood: Ablex Publishing.

Fuchs, L S, Compton, D L, Fuchs, D, Paulsen, K, Bryant, J D and Hamlett, C L (2005) The Prevention, Identification, and Cognitive Determinants of Math Difficulty. *Journal of Educational Psychology*, 97(3): 493–513.

Gardner, H (2008) *Multiple Intelligences. New Horizons*. New York: Basic Books.

Genius Hour (nd) *What is Genius Hour?* [online] Available at: www.geniushour.com/what-is-genius-hour/ (accessed 12 September 2020).

Grigorenko, E L, Jarvin, L and Sternberg, R J (2002) School-based Tests of the Triarchic Theory of Intelligence: Three Settings, Three Samples, Three Syllabi. *Contemporary Educational Psychology*, 27(2): 167–208.

International School Utrecht (nd) *Mission Statement*. [online] Available at: www.isutrecht.nl/organisation/mission-statement/ (accessed 12 September 2020).

Karadag, R and Yasar, S (2010) Effects of Differentiated Instruction on Students' Attitudes towards Turkish Courses: An Action Research. *Procedia – Social and Behavioral Sciences*, 9: 1394–9.

Koeze, P A (2007) Differentiated Instruction: The Effect on Student Achievement in an Elementary School. Doctoral Dissertation. Paper 31. Eastern Michigan University.

McCrea Simpkins, P, Mastropieri, M A and Scruggs, T E (2009) Differentiated Curriculum Enhancements in Inclusive Fifth-grade Science Classes. *Remedial and Special Education*, 30(5): 300–8.

Montessori, M (1964/2014) *The Montessori Method*. New Brunswick: Transaction Publishers.

Rauste-von Wright, M, von Wright, J and Soini, T (2003) *Oppiminen ja Koulutus*. Helsinki: WSOY.

Reis, S M, McCoach, D B, Little, C A, Muller, L M and Kaniskan, R B (2011) The Effects of Differentiated Instruction and Enrichment Pedagogy on Reading Achievement in Five Elementary Schools. *American Educational Research Journal*, 48(2): 462–501.

Roiha, A (2014) Teachers' Views on Differentiation in Content and Language Integrated Learning (CLIL): Perceptions, Practices and Challenges. *Language and Education*, 28(1): 1–18.

Roiha, A and Polso, J (2020) *How to Succeed in Differentiation? The Finnish Approach*. Woodbridge: John Catt Educational Ltd.

Shaunessy-Dedrick, E, Evans, L, Ferron, J and Lindo, M (2015) Effects of Differentiated Reading on Elementary Students' Reading Comprehension and Attitudes Toward Reading. *Gifted Child Quarterly*, 59(2): 91–107.

Thousand, J S, Villa, R A and Nevin, A I (2007) *Differentiating Instruction: Collaborative Planning and Teaching for Universally Designed Learning*. Thousand Oaks, CA: Corwin Press.

Tieso, C (2005) The Effects of Grouping Practices and Curricular Adjustments on Achievement. *Journal for the Education of the Gifted*, 29(1): 60–89.

Tomlinson, C A (2014) *The Differentiated Classroom: Responding to the Needs of All Learners*. Alexandria, VA: ASCD.

Tomlinson, C A and Imbeau, M B (2010) *Leading and Managing a Differentiated Classroom*. Alexandria, VA: ASCD.

Vygotsky, L S (1978) *Mind in Society. The Development of Higher Psychological Processes*. Edited by Cole, M, John-Steiner, V, Scribner, S and Souberman, E. Cambridge: Harvard University Press.

3 Classroom management
Oana Dobarcianu and Dakota Wilkinson

INTRODUCTION

This chapter approaches positive classroom management skills and strategies through the early years and upper primary school. The world has changed dramatically over the years as the lifestyles of children are different and digital technology has positive as well as negative influence on their life experiences. We have realised that classroom management is not managing students, it is rather building a strong, solid relationship with each student and allowing each individual child to have agency (see also Chapter 1). Teachers are busy educators striving to adapt their teaching style to the digital and informational revolution, feeling the intense pressure to provide more academic experiences in their school. Therefore, we want this chapter to be an accessible and energising reading experience. Included are a wide range of practical examples on how to use positive classroom management strategies to influence and change students' behaviour in school from each stage of the cycle. We focus specifically on small and large group classroom management strategies and skills.

THEORETICAL BACKGROUND

There are various theories of managing a classroom, each with a different background reflecting the psychological and epistemological tradition at the time when they were developed. To understand learning then, we must understand the theories and the thoughts behind them. In this sense, we have Edward Ford's (1999) *'Responsible Thinking Process'* that has the prime goal to coach the educators how to teach their students to grow a sense of responsibility for their own actions and to show consideration for everyone around them. On the same line in the theory *'Teacher Effectiveness Training'*, Thomas Gordon (1974) raised an important question: *'What makes the difference between teaching that works and teaching that fails?'* The element that plays the main role is the quality of the teacher–student relationship. This model gives the teachers the right skills for meaningful communication and conflict solving so much needed in order to have high-quality relationships with their students and to decrease the conflicts and increase learning time.

B F Skinner (1954) sustained the idea that to change a behaviour, we need to modify the environment and he promoted scaffold instruction, small units, repletion and immediate feedback. John Dewey (1916/1966), in turn, advocates in his theory that the children are capable of learning and behaving agreeably with one another having the instructor as a facilitator. He promoted the idea that educational environment should include a natural approach that implicates direction and guidance. In his book *Teacher and Child* (1972), Ginott promoted the principles of asking questions and listening to students to create an open and safe environment to express ideas and show acceptance and respect. The educators will facilitate meaningful discussion that will include every class member and give value to their ideas and input.

When teaching at the International School Utrecht (ISUtrecht), we find our inspiration in some of these theories as well as in '*The Choice Theory*' formulated by William Glasser (1998). This theory states that everything we do is to behave and almost all our behaviour is chosen and urged to satisfy the five basic needs: *survival*, *love and belonging*, *power*, *freedom* and *fun*. According to the philosophy of this theory, the teachers are identified as managers who run effective classroom activities to satisfy students' needs by developing positive relationships with the students to enable them to master success. The focus falls on love and belonging as this will allow learning to increase while disruption is reduced. According to Sullo (2011), students are able to '*connect, feel a sense of competence and power, have some freedom and enjoy themselves in a secure environment*' (section: How choice theory impacts learning, para 6).

STUDENT AS FOCUS FOR CREATING THE LEARNING ENVIRONMENT

Dealing with young students can be challenging, particularly in kindergarten as it is their first school experience and the main goal of our teachers is to make the children fall in love with the concept of school and education. A love that needs to be fed on regular basis in order to make it grow as the school will be a child's main occupation for the next 12 years at least. In order to achieve it, we have designed and developed several positive strategies to help us manage the class dynamics during our formal and informal activities.

In classrooms, we want to create an environment where children feel respected and valued as this is the foundation for creating positive behaviour in our children. Instead of thinking that behaviour is something that needs to be managed, we believe that children need to be involved in reflecting on their own behaviour, by talking about self-management, for example. In the Primary Years Programme (PYP), this is part of the approaches to learning (ATL) skills. The ultimate goal is for students themselves to see why certain behaviour is desirable. We do this by modelling and giving praise to behaviour that is exemplary. So, instead of asking the noisy students to be quiet, we rather thank and praise the ones that are.

Some teachers also like to create an environment where students see that their actions can be linked to the learner profile (International Baccalaureate, nd) which is used often during classroom discourse as it is also part of our daily learning intention. A display idea is to have a learner profile detective board in the classrooms and have students actively look for demonstrations of the learner profile.

Part of feeling valued is being in a democratic place to learn. For example, the traditional '*hands-up approach*' reduces engagement and does not promote quality discourse. Instead, '*lucky dip*' strategy in which the teacher randomly picks a student's name is a great engagement enhancement, as students need to make the choice to listen actively because if they are chosen, they will need to share their ideas. We involve students and give choice in all aspects of the classroom and learning. The year starts by making essential agreements together, asking students' input in how we use the space in the classroom and what kind of classroom routines we will use.

POSITIVE USE OF ASSESSMENTS WHEN CREATING A LEARNING ENVIRONMENT

We find it important to assess students in an inclusive environment to support the classroom management. The assessments can be separated into three different sections, including *diagnostic, formative* and *summative* assessments. Opening lessons with different types of diagnostic assessment will discreetly eliminate any chance of embarrassment and anxiety, therefore allowing students to be open and truthful and confidently say if they do or do not have the understanding needed for the lesson (Cologon, 2014). 'Yes/No cards', 'throw in' and 'word splash' are all activities that students can participate in anonymously to demonstrate their understanding on a topic. This type of assessing is positively reinforcing students' ideas and relating them to what they are learning. It develops an environment where students feel safe and supported and have a willingness to share their experiences. This allows teachers to have an accurate reflection on what students have an understanding of and what needs to be worked on before moving on to another subject (Killen, 2016).

Formative assessment will be beneficial for both students and teachers to collaborate on ideas. Discussions, interviews and 'show and tell' are quick easy assessment strategies that focus on the understanding rather than the product (Killen, 2016). Here, teachers decipher whether or not these students are critically thinking and have the knowledge and understanding (Hattie and Timperley, 2007). All of the formative assessment strategies can be done either one on one, or in small or larger groups. It allows for the students who are not confident in their ideas or standing in front of people a chance to do it in front of one person first (Cologon, 2014). As well as building their confidence to speak to an audience, students can develop little videos to present to the class. This is for the students who have limited ability to present or students who are tech-savvy and feel they would present better if given the opportunity to do so via a movie. Bringing technology into the classroom will help students collate and explore their ideas in a simpler form while still achieving everything they need to be achieving (Cuttance, 2001). Using tablets also promotes presentations and the need to share their work to other peers to receive feedback and reflect on their processes (Killen, 2016; Cuttance, 2001).

Finally, summative assessment can be included, for instance, in the form of the science journal. Science journals are a way to record information from the learning. They provide a written copy of the learning that was encountered during the unit plan through the students' ideas (Killen, 2016). The science journal is a hard copy piece of evidence that teachers use to accurately mark and modify against specific criteria.

Diagnostic, formative and summative assessment strategies have been added to become inclusive of all learning styles and abilities (Cologon, 2014). There will be many more discussions in small and large groups to have an understanding of the discovering and exploration that happens during the unit. Misconceptions and unanswered questions can be addressed during these times as well as many available times for one-on-one conversational feedback between the teacher and the student (Cologon, 2014). Constant feedback to students will positively reinforce continual learning and discovering (Hattie and Timperley, 2007). Adding positive ways of conducting assessments or assessing students can deeply affect a classroom and what is happening during this usually stressful time for a child. By allowing students to become part of the planning and by bringing assessments into a lighter and more positive perspective students are more likely to respond positively and not display signs of distress, disruption or negative behaviour.

POSITIVE WAYS OF MANAGING THE CLASSROOM

In the spring of 2020, we decided that we wanted to seek out other teachers at our school to discover the classroom management techniques that they use and that are special to our school. In the following, we describe our observations when visiting different classes at the school. The section is divided into upper and lower primary.

Upper classes: Grades 2–5

Greeting the children at the door strategy

We started our observations with the Grade 5 classroom. In the morning, the teacher stood at the door of the classroom as she waited for the children to come in. The teacher used smiles and direct eye contact with each student to build up their trust in their teacher and made sure to greet and welcome each student into the class. With this simple strategy, each student's day started in a positive light.

Rules and routines strategy

As the students began to enter the classroom, they knew exactly what to do without the teacher's assistance. They automatically took off their coats and their bags and hung them on the racks in a specific order, with their bags on the bottom and their jackets on the top. The students made sure that they had their water bottle and their lunchboxes in their hands before entering the classroom. The students who had forgotten to bring their lunchbox or water bottle were stopped at the door by the teacher. The teacher gave them a gentle reminder with hand gestures and the students would immediately turn around to retrieve what was needed.

In the classroom, the students placed the lunchboxes and water bottles in a designated area. After that they put the chairs down quietly without a sound and transferred the pencil tins from the cupboard onto their desks. After these tasks were completed, the students checked the daily programme on the board and started to take out the appropriate materials for the first lesson. The teacher had still not given them any instructions, only welcomed them to the classroom with a simple good morning greeting. It was easy to see that the teacher had put a lot of effort into the students' well-being that was hand in hand with her classroom management techniques. Providing that structure that includes rules, visual schedules, classroom job charts and sticker charts to encourage and motivate work completion helps children become more independent. Children feel secure and comfortable when they have routines which allow them to cope more effectively when something stressful is occurring as they still have consistency in their day-to-day routines.

Positive reinforcement strategy

Only after all students had arrived in the morning did the teacher walk back into the classroom with a smile on her face. She slowly walked over to her desk observing the morning activities and emotions in the class. The children were busily engaged in some task either independently or in a small group. Again, as the teacher sat down, she said good morning to the class, and all the students looked up towards her and then continued the busy work that they were completing. The teacher praised the successes in the classroom in the morning and commented on many things throughout the morning, for example:

> *Sam, I love how you're sitting there nice and quietly. I can really see that you're engaging with what you are completing.*

> *John, I love that you are sitting up nice and straight and looking at me to show me that you are ready to begin.*

> *Emma, I can see by your handwriting that you are putting in a lot of effort into making sure that it's neat and legible.*

> *Susie, I love the way that you were sitting there and patiently waiting with your hand up to tell me that you are finished. I already know that you're finished; however, it was nice to see that you didn't run up to me quickly and tell me that you're finished, well done.*

Praising students for jobs well done motivates and improves academic and behavioural performance as well as inspiring the class and raising students' self-esteem. At the same time, it is a great way of reinforcing rules and values the teacher wants to see in their class. Therefore, the students are more likely to repeat positive behaviour in order to seek the teacher's approval.

Adding this comment within your teaching could automatically redirect the student who is being disruptive by hearing the praise of another student. When the other student hears and sees this praise happening to another child, they might also want the positive attention and change their behaviour quickly. It is important to note that if the child does change their behaviour after you have praised another child, take that as an opportunity to positively reinforce their positive behaviour. Make sure they know that what they are doing is the right thing.

Shout out box and wall strategy

After the Grade 5 classroom, we went to see the Grade 4 classroom across the hall. As we walked in to observe, we noticed a box at the front of the room. The teacher had a positive shout out box in the classroom focusing on positive rather than negative behaviour. The students were encouraged to write down the names of the students who worked hard or were a great teammate on a piece of paper and put it in the box. At the end of the day, the teacher read the names out loud and the class discussed how great this person had been during that day. The room also had a wall designed for a little *'hall of fame shout out'* where positive comments to praise an individual or a group of students were displayed. This was a visual reminder of all the positive things going on in the classroom each week.

> ***Variation***: *Have a jar or a nice bowl and ask the children to fill it with pompoms or marbles anytime they see someone being friendly or helpful towards his/her peers. A soon as the jar is full, you could reward the children by playing games, singing their favourite song or going to a nearby playground.*

Counting backwards strategy

During our time in the Grade 4 classroom, the teacher used two different strategies to grab the attention of students. The first one for the morning was counting back from five slowly, clearly and loudly: *'Five, four, three, two, one'*. As he was saying this slowly, the students reacted instantly and finished their sentence and turned to show attention to him. The teacher really emphasised each number to give the students the time to finish their task at hand.

The light on strategy

The second strategy the Grade 4 teacher used was to engage the students by using a light he had on his desk. The teacher turned on the light which was placed in a strategic position to make sure that it was visible to all students. In both of these strategies, the students were given time to finish what they were saying or doing, after which they turned to listen to the teacher without him having to say the classic phrases of *'Be quiet'* or *'No more talking'*.

The secret garden strategy

After Grade 4, we continued our observation journey to the Grade 3 classroom which was very neat, tidy and neutral and had plants galore. In the corner, the teacher had created a so-called *'secret garden'* filled with grass, sticks, lights and plants (see Figure 3.1). The Grade 3 teacher explained that the idea of creating a secret garden in her class was inspired by the Reggio Emilia approach (Edwards, 1993; Thornton and Brunton, 2014) according to which the quality of the setting in the students' stations plays a crucial and indirect role on students' learning and behaviour. The secret garden was placed right at the entrance area on purpose so that it would welcome students immediately as they stepped into the classroom.

> **Variation**: Create a quiet and relaxing place in your class, using natural plants to facilitate privacy, self-reflection and retreat where the children can think, dream or watch.

Figure 3.1 The secret garden from Grade 3

Labelling strategy

All the drawers and cupboards in the Grade 3 classroom were labelled and looked tidy (see Figure 3.2). The teacher explained that the labelling was done by the students, and actually, they had come up with this idea in the beginning of the school year, by answering the question: '*How can we efficiently organise our classroom?*' Labelling the classroom helps organise the study space so that the students know where things belong if they need something and it guides them to put things back in the right place promoting responsibility. It is a great way to share and work together.

Figure 3.2 The drawers are all labelled

Fairy lights strategy

Finishing up in this classroom, we moved on to the next and headed towards Grade 2. They were in the middle of silent reading. The main lights of the classroom were off and only tiny little fairy lights were on with soft music playing in the background. Soft lights cast warmth and a cosy feeling; therefore, the emotional distance between home and school is reduced considerably. There was a calming energy about the room that provided the students with a stress-free, relaxing environment to learn in.

Home languages strategy

In Grade 2, we witnessed how the use of home languages manages a group of children in order to get them ready for the lesson. Our English language acquisition specialist entered the class, greeting various children in their home languages. In an instant, the children's attention was directed to her and the class was ready to start. As teachers in an international school, in our lessons, we need to consider the variety of cultures or the diversity of languages spoken in the class of our students. Very often there are children at the very beginning of learning the school language of instruction, English. In order to promote a safe and welcoming environment for these students, the teachers learn basic words in a variety of languages such as *'hello'*, *'thank you'* and *'good morning'*, to make sure that the child feels part of his/her community.

Early years: kindergarten and Grade 1

Teaching social stories strategy

Going down the stairs, we entered the part of the school with kindergarten and Grade 1 classes. The first class that we observed was a Grade 1 classroom. There during quiet time, the children were exposed to social stories read by the teacher. She used social narratives to help the children to develop their social skills, routines, appropriate behaviour or transitions. The desired social behaviour is modelled and supported by visual clues to help children understand and relate to the social situation. This strategy can be a powerful way to remind the pupils of what a desired behaviour should look like. The students love being exposed to social narrative books and they are very effective in changing behaviour.

The restaurant strategy

During eating time, the class was transformed into a restaurant. The children were getting their lunchboxes and water bottles and were sitting at their design group with a battery-operated candle. This moment is seen as social interaction. As soon as the candle was on, the students lowered their voices and started eating; however, they quietly exchanged ideas among their group members. Often during lunch time, the teachers also read stories that are related to the unit or that have social characters.

Singing strategy

Next, we went to one of the kindergarten classrooms where the children were preparing for their outside playtime. It can be a challenging task as the children need to change their indoor shoes to outdoor shoes, put on their jackets, waterproof trousers, hats and gloves and get ready for a fun winter day. The whole situation could quickly transform into chaos; however, the early years teachers apply different strategies to manage their students in an efficient way. In this moment, the teacher was singing the following song the kindergarten teachers had invented together: '*Change your shoes, change your shoes song, it's nice to see Giulia ready, it's nice to see Maheera ready, change your shoes*'. This song has as main goal to regulate children behaviour in a positive and fun way, reinforcing the tasks that the children need to perform at the time.

Technology strategy

While observing the early years classrooms, we noticed that one Grade 1 class was returning from its physical activity. In order to speed up the process of changing from their sport clothes into school clothes, the teacher started to play a unit related song on the smart board. It is important to acknowledge that students are very interested and engaged in using technology. This creates many amazing opportunities for the teachers to benefit from integrating some forms of technology in the classroom and to make teaching and learning more effective.

Technology is one of our school's vision and mission pillars; therefore, it is widely used across the levels for different purposes and in different moments of the school day. When the teachers integrate technology into their lessons, the students show higher levels of interest and motivation in the subjects they are studying and demonstrate a better learning behaviour. The teachers are using technology to support and review the difficult concepts and to enhance the traditional way of teaching by keeping the students more engaged.

An important part of lessons is reflection and feedback, and teachers can use technology to facilitate this. Reflection is often quite difficult for children to comprehend and understand how important it is for growth and engaging in learning. Technology is a different way to connect to the students in an interactive and positive way.

Rules and class routines strategy

The kindergarten classroom has a lot of rules and routines that all the students are aware of. The teacher explained that the first weeks of school are the best time to create and teach rules and class routines. These practices help students to feel safe and take ownership, if they are created together with them, as the students need to understand what is included in the rule. Displaying visual and age appropriate classroom rules, and going over them on a regular basis, promotes responsibility among the young students. Students aged four to six may need additional instructions and reminders to make sure that the rules and routines are completely understood and memorised. Giving brief and concise instructions rather than exposing out students' minor misbehaviour also helps reduce disruptions in the classroom. For example, during our observation, when a student misbehaved, the teacher quietly advised the child that it is disturbing for the other students and for the child's own learning as well. The teacher also praised and reinforced the students' good behaviour when they followed the rules appropriately.

Buddy strategy

Going down the corridor to another kindergarten class, we were introduced to a different but efficient strategy called '*buddy strategy*', that is, sending the children to prepare for outside playground in pairs. The buddy has the responsibility to make sure that their own partner respects and follows the instructions given as well as gives a helping hand with zipping the jackets or tying laces. This strategy is also widely used during fire drills, as it is a quick way to identify if all the children are present for the fire drill procedure.

Exit ticket strategy

In the same kindergarten class, we observed the '*exit ticket*' strategy as part of their positive classroom management strategies. An exit ticket can be one or two questions or problems for students to answer quickly at the end of class. Exit tickets are a conscious way to institute an expectation that the students need to be focused and pay attention during the lesson so that they can complete the exit ticket. This strategy also slows down the torrent of children going to the outside areas, as the children need to show patience for their peers waiting in the line.

Shout it out versus whispering strategy

We all have some eager learners in our classroom who tend to blurt out the answers straight away. In this kindergarten classroom, the teacher used two strategies called '*shout it out*' and '*whispering strategy*'. The former one means that the teacher lets all the students tell the answer all at the same time by saying '*Shout it out*', and then continuing '*I really tried to understand your answer, but it was very noisy; now if you know the answer, raise your hand*'. In this way, all the children have the opportunity to give the answer, and by saying '*raise your hand*' in the end, you will remind them what to do. In the whispering strategy, in turn, the teacher asks the students to whisper the answer in another child's or teacher's ear. This strategy ensures that the classroom remains silent.

Overlapping or multi-tasking strategy

This strategy is used on a regular basis across the Grade 1 level, and it allows efficiency, empowerment and ownership of the student's own learning. We witnessed one of the Grade 1 teachers using this strategy. The class was divided into stations or working groups with different tasks and activities. Having the children in small groups allowed the teacher to easily access every student and to provide specific support if needed. This approach is based on the belief that students are responsible individuals who can assess and correct their own learning behaviour. It also gives the students the opportunity to know better their group members, to support and accept each other and to resolve different opinions in a positive manner. The main role of the teacher is to create meaningful activities that give the pupils control of the work they are doing in order to avoid disruptions in the form of the students asking for clarification.

The glitter strategy

We continued to yet another kindergarten class. There the teachers, together with their students, had created a bottle containing glitter of different colours and water. The glitter represents children's feeling and emotions. When the children are a bit restless and disturbing the class activities, the teachers will shake the bottle, explaining that the students' feelings and emotions are now in a confused state, just like the glitter. The children will watch how the glitter settles down again on the bottom of the bottle, and in this way, their feelings also will calm down and they will relax. For young students, it is the perfect way to explain such abstract and intangible concepts such as feelings and emotions and to visualise and make them concrete to the students.

Relaxation strategies

In this kindergarten classroom, slow and relaxing music is played in the background during many moments of the day such as snack, lunch, quiet time or silent reading time. The relaxation response is a natural and protective tool of the body against over-excitement and stress that children can experience in the school. In this kindergarten classroom, one of the moments of the day is quiet time which is scheduled after lunch time when the children feel a little tired and sleepy. It is seen as a moment when the children should relax and try to find their inner peace and balance. However, it is challenging for 24 children to be all quiet at the same time for at least 15–20 minutes. In order to prevent wiggling among the children, the teachers ask them to get in a comfortable position and do breathing exercises. The teachers talk to the students in a quiet voice, asking them to feel different parts of their body, starting with their toes and ending with their facial muscles. The teachers explained that many times the children fall asleep during these quiet times. The relaxation music is flowing and it is continuous, having a low rhythm, low-frequency beat and cyclical patterns. After the relaxation sessions, the children feel their bodies relaxed, their breathing is slowing down and they feel calmer. It is also very important to teach our students ways of relaxation so that they can use them in stressful situations without adult assistance. As the main purpose of using relaxation techniques is to promote the positive behaviour of our students, these strategies are also very beneficial for improving school performance. They help the children to stay calm during a conflict and stress situations, decrease hyperactivity, increase concentration and encourage listening skills.

> ***Variation***: create a set of individual activities that promote fine motor skills such as beads, small spools with thread or puzzles for quiet time moments.

'Get your wiggles out' strategy

Due to the young age of the children in kindergarten (ie four to seven), active play is essential for their physical and social developmental process. Besides being a fun and creative activity, it is also an important teaching tool. Through play, children learn how to interact with others and develop critical lifelong skills. In the kindergarten classroom we were observing, when the children were hyperactive, the teacher said the magic words '*Geeeeeet your wiggles out*', after which the children gathered on the carpet and the game started. First, the students breathed deeply five times, followed by a sensory-rich movement activity: '*Let us chase the squirrel*'. These activities help children with their balance and gross and fine motor skills, and improves their social skills as they need to collaborate and compromise with others, share and show empathy, solve conflicts and respect rules. The game session ended with a relaxation breathing exercise following the pattern: '*relax–move–relax*'.

CONCLUSION

One of the key components of teaching is effective classroom management. The main goal of the different approaches presented in this chapter has been to promote a positive classroom management that will stimulate children's learning and development (see Table 3.1). The listed strategies have been adapted to fit and to respond to different classroom sizes, age groups and behavioural patterns. This is the set of procedures

Table 3.1 Positive classroom management strategies in a nutshell

Upper classes	Lower classes
Greeting the children at the door	Teaching social stories
Rules and routines	The restaurant
Positive reinforcement	Singing
Shout out box and wall	Technology
Counting backwards	Rules and class routines
The light on	Buddies
The secret garden	Exit ticket
Labelling	Shout it out vs whispering
Fairy lights	Overlapping or multi-tasking
Home languages	The glitter
	Relaxation
	Get your wiggles out

and strategies that help the students to pay attention, stay on the task and not disturb their peers. Working with young students is a continuous process that includes planning, organising, developing rules and routines as well as creativity. Younger students naturally require more observation, but regardless, classroom management is an important aspect of any successful class. The aim of efficiently planning and organising the classrooms is to prevent the disruptions from occurring in the first place. The idea is to avoid problems rather than having to respond to them.

The small things that you might change as a teacher can help to promote a successful learning environment. These small things include greeting students when they come into the classroom, having beautiful cosy spaces for the students to feel calm and giving them feedback that is meaningful. They include setting expectations and routines during the day that the students are familiar with and can recognise what action they need to take. They include being there for the students when they need you to be there. The learning environment you create as a teacher has a direct correlation to behaviour and managing the classroom. It changes the way you, yourself, as a teacher might feel, reflect and react as well as your students in the room.

A teacher is a '*magician*', always ready to use '*magic tricks*' with his/her students. The strategies presented in this chapter are only a few examples used by the teachers at ISUtrecht in order to maintain a creative and responsible working place for the students and for the teachers. As teachers in a modern-day society teaching within the PYP, we feel the need to explore other ways as well. Building relationships, sharing a bond, being respectful and caring as well as showing kindness and willingness to learn opens up a whole new side to positive management strategies. However, we wonder whether it is really classroom management that teachers should be talking about or should we as modern teachers begin to change the term? The model strategy used in one classroom may not be as effective with a different set of students. Think about the flow of your classroom and the needs of the children in it, and then decide what model would most effectively manage the classroom.

Reflective questions

1. Have you tried out any of the strategies described in this chapter? If yes, how did they go?
2. What are your classroom management strategies and solutions for promoting a successful learning environment?
3. Which strategy would you use to control disruptive behaviour in a classroom without disrupting the lesson?
4. What strategies would be effective to handle mixed-ability students in learning English as a foreign language?
5. How do you use technology in your lessons?

REFERENCES

Cologon, K (ed) (2014) *Inclusive Education in the Early Years: Right from the Start*. South Melbourne: Oxford University Press.

Cuttance, P (2001) *School Innovation: Pathway to the Knowledge Society*. Canberra, Australia: Commonwealth Department of Education, Training and Youth Affairs.

Dewey, J (1916/1966) *Democracy and Education*. New York: Macmillan.

Edwards, C P (1993) *The Hundred Languages of Children: The Reggio Emilia Approach to Early Childhood Education.* Norwood, NJ: Ablex Publishing.

Ford, E E (1999) *Discipline for Home and School: Book Two, Practical Standards for Schools.* Scottsdale, AZ: Brandt Publishing.

Ginott, H G (1972) *Teacher and Child*. New York: Macmillan.

Glasser, W (1998) *Choice Theory in the Classroom*. New York: Harper Perennial.

Gordon, T (1974) *Teacher Effectiveness Training*. New York: Wyden.

Hattie, J A C and Timperley, H (2007) The Power of Feedback. *Review of Educational Research*, 77(1): 81–112.

International Baccalaureate (nd) *The IB Learner Profile*. [online] Available at: www.ibo.org/benefits/learner-profile/ (accessed 12 September 2020).

Killen, R (2016) *Effective Teaching Strategies: Lesson from Research and Practice*. 7th ed. Melbourne: Engage Learning Australia.

Skinner, B F (1954) The Science of Learning and the Art of Teaching. *Harvard Educational Review*, 24: 86–97.

Sullo, B (2011) *Choice Theory*. [online] Available at: www.funderstanding.com/educators/choice-theory/ (accessed 12 September 2020).

Thornton, L and Brunton, P (2014) *Bringing the Reggio Approach to Your Early Years Practice*. New York: Routledge.

4 Collaboration

María Campos Ippólito

INTRODUCTION

I want to start this chapter by encouraging you to ask yourself the following question: *'Would you build 20 houses exactly the same way no matter their location or structure?'* Of course, for you, your way of building a house is the most appropriate one. You made it yourself based on what you know about houses. However, sometimes you may need to build a house in a specific location that does not match your expectations and you start struggling with the project. Maybe you then start to look at other builders and see things you have never even thought of that may work for that specific house. You then start opening your eyes and trying to incorporate, for instance, a new way of combining colours in the house or a new way of taking better care of the floor so that it does not get scratched that often. You get inspired by someone else's idea and start refreshing yourself. When other builders come and visit the house that you have built, they look around and, in turn, get inspired from you to incorporate some of the elements of your house in their own designs. While exchanging ideas you may start to realise how you can complement each other as housebuilders. Eventually, you may start building houses together. Maybe you are in charge of the paint, while your partner is in charge of the furniture. You know you are both working with the same goal in mind, to create a unique house adapted to its needs.

The above metaphor also applies to teaching. You can probably manage your class by doing the same things year after year on your own, but is that the ideal way? Do you want to teach every year the same way? What if the children in your class come from a different culture than yours and their way of learning is different? Would you still solve problems the same way as you did before? What if it does not work? Is it then the children's fault? You may have enough experience and resources to handle different types of situations but if you want to develop and go far and beyond, you need people, you need to collaborate.

This chapter focuses on the importance of collaboration and argues that while you are sharing and collaborating with other staff members, you are building a reciprocal trust and relationship that helps you to develop professionally. After briefly reviewing the theory on collaboration, this chapter explains the benefits of collaboration. The chapter uses the International School Utrecht (ISUtrecht) as an example and describes the different forms of collaboration there and how everyone works together in order to provide a holistic and authentic education for each student. At ISUtrecht, we are all open to hear about all those different ways of teaching, always under our shared values of providing the students with the resources to be lifelong learners and worldwide citizens.

WHAT IS COLLABORATION?

Thousand et al (2006) relate the journey towards collaboration back to 1994 when the United Nations Educational, Scientific and Cultural Organization supported the practice of inclusive education for students with disabilities. This inclusive education consisted of collaborative planning between teachers, subject area teachers, school staff, peers, parents and families, all working together with the well-being of the child in mind. Referring to the metaphor of the house, all parties involved built a house together taking everyone's perspective into account and enriching each other's ideas. The focus then was on *what* the children had to learn, while now the focus has shifted more towards *how* we learn. In today's schools, '*pupils need to have learned to be tenacious and resourceful, imaginative and logical, self-disciplined and self-aware, collaborative and inquisitive*' (Claxton et al, 2011, p 2). This does not only apply to the students but also to the teachers. The students' learning focus on how they learn can also benefit the teacher since now the teachers need to focus on '*how we think, how we collaborate and how we self-manage which helps us become more mindful, effective learners*' (Murdoch, 2015, p 96).

Thousand et al (2006) have reviewed studies of collaborative partnership and co-teaching in different schools. The findings showed that collaboration is beneficial not only for students but also for teachers. Among the benefits were, for instance, '*decreased referrals for behavioural problems [...] improved academic and social skills for low-achieving students, improved attitudes and self-concepts reported by students with disabilities, and more positive peer relationships*' (Thousand et al, 2006, p 240). In general, students realised that they received more teacher time and attention, while the teachers felt that they grew professionally, received more personal support and perceived a greater sense of community. In addition, the teachers felt happier and less isolated (Thousand et al, 2006).

Kath Murdoch (2015) describes the developing learning assets in the enquiry classrooms and explains how we need to be researchers, thinkers, self-managers, communicators and, of course, *collaborators*. She connects the skill of collaboration with values such as empathy, compassion and reliability. She also gives examples on how we can encourage this from a young to a high age and how to include these learning assets in the classrooms making them meaningful, for instance, by taking turns, sharing, debating, giving feedback, encouraging, consulting, participating, compromising or working in teams. The above skills are applicable in the classroom and during outside play, at school or at home, in the kindergarten classroom or at university, as a teacher or in any other job.

WHO SHOULD BE INVOLVED IN THE COLLABORATION PROCESS?

In order to create authentic learning, all the different parties involved in the children's education need to work together. Similarly, a house is not built with only one person, we need architects, designers, builders, painters, electricians, plumbers, etc. Before the start of any project, it is important to know the main goal of the project, how the work is going to go and who is responsible for what. At ISUtrecht, we work as a community in which we all have responsibilities in order to provide the best education for our students. Within the community, there are several roles interconnected between each other. We all work within the following core elements which illustrate how we collaborate. These elements are reflected on throughout the chapter when describing how these types of collaboration work in practice.

- **Trust and respect:** are the basis of every staff member at school.
- **Connection and reciprocality:** can be shown in the way some teachers plan within their grades creating lesson plans for each other.
- **Shared values:** we model our values to the children so that they would learn them and implement them in their behaviour. These values include the learner profile, co-operation and positive feedback which is linked to being a lifelong learner.
- **Reflection and improvement:** these elements are shown in our open-door policy described in the co-operation between leadership, teachers and parents, but also in the way the teachers create the curriculum, reflecting on the units already taught and improving them every year.
- **Lifelong learning:** we are open for improvement, open for feedback and open for other teachers to come to observe us. We have the opportunity to get professional development from the teacher next door. We participate in professional development and share our learning with the rest of the staff members.
- **Egalitarianism:** this extends from the students to all the staff members and the parents. We all have a voice and everyone is acknowledged. In lesson plans, the students' interests are taken into account. In leadership meetings, feedback from parents and teachers is considered. Parents, teachers and students are also represented in senior management meetings or in advisory bodies such as the Division Council.

In Figure 4.1, all the parties are represented and connected. Within each of them, there are subgroups who also collaborate. Our shared purpose is the student which is presented in the middle.

From all these different types of collaboration in our school, this chapter focuses on the ones related to teaching and students' learning. In other words:

- collaboration between all teachers from the school;
- collaboration between teachers and leadership team;
- collaboration between teachers and parents.

In the next section, you learn about the interconnectedness of the groups and how they support one another.

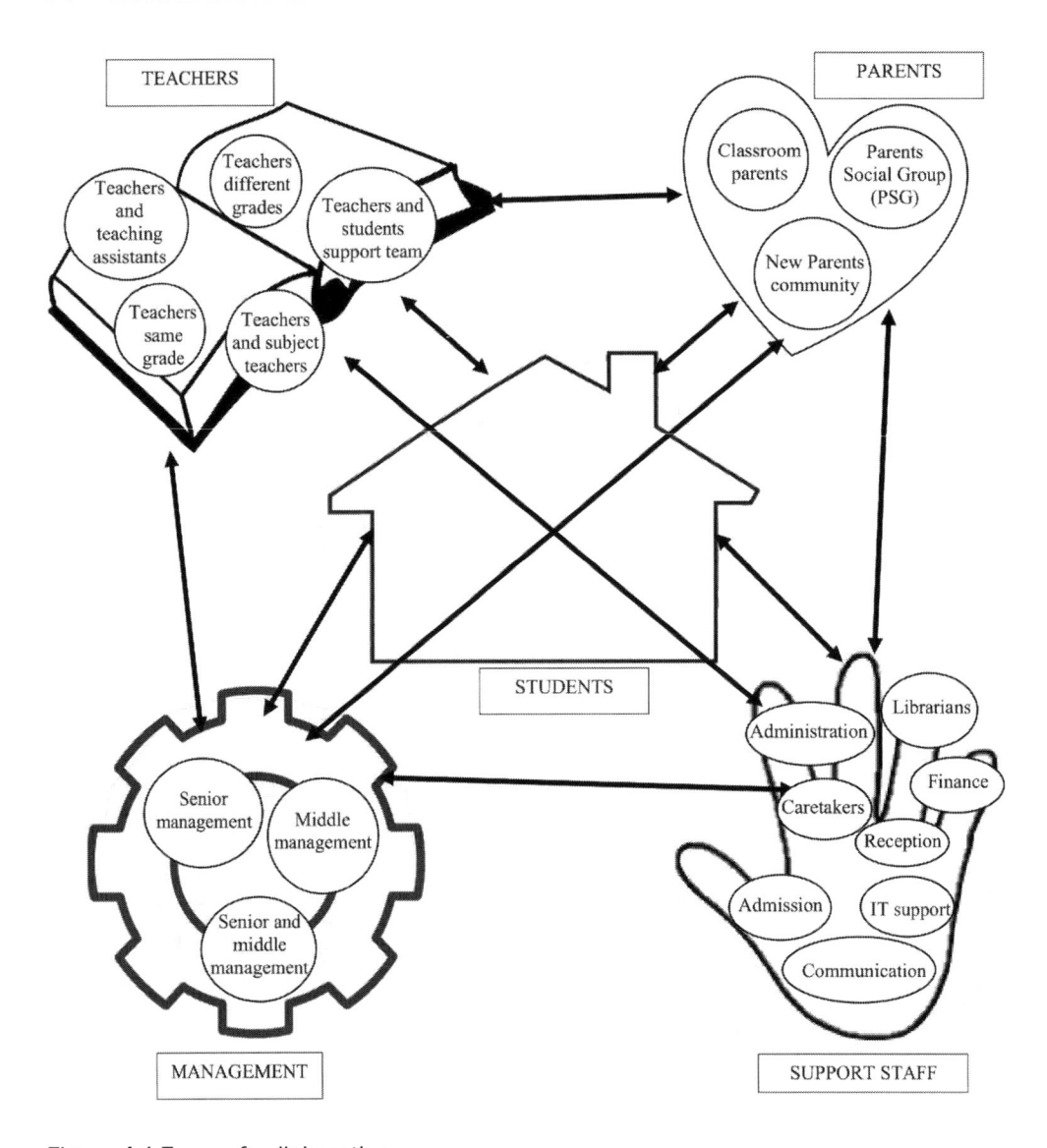

54 TEACHING AND LEARNING IN INTERNATIONAL SCHOOLS

Figure 4.1 Types of collaboration

HOW DO ALL THESE GROUPS WORK TOGETHER?

The following practical part is broken down into four sections: *collaboration between school teachers, collaboration between teachers and leadership, collaboration between students* and *collaboration between parents and school*. The first section starts by describing the collaboration that occurs in the classrooms between the teachers of the same grade level and how they carry out their collaborative planning sessions. The section also gives an insight into the kindergarten classes and how they work together with a teaching assistant. Then collaboration between all the different teachers at the school is outlined. The second section, which focuses on management, explains how leadership collaborates between their teams to take care of the present and the future. It includes the collaboration between the leadership teams and the teachers to make school decisions and to create an environment of continuous development and trust. The third section deals with the collaboration between students and explains how different age groups work together. Finally, the fourth section discusses the collaboration between the parents and the school since parents have a pivotal role in the school community.

Collaboration between school teachers

Before starting to write this chapter, I interviewed several teachers to find out their opinion on what collaboration means for them. They all agreed on collaboration being the only way to succeed as a teacher. They saw collaboration as the key to provide the best learning experiences to their students and to feel supported by their peers. Some of the teachers explained how collaboration gives them the feeling of being trusted and being able to trust. It gives the power to everyone to have a voice and to be supported. Everyone is welcome to generate new ideas and provide and receive help.

Planning sessions between teachers from the same grade level

The units we teach are not set in stone. We review them every year to improve and adapt them. Therefore, to the question posed in the introduction '*Would you build 20 houses exactly the same way no matter their location or structure?*', our answer is no. There may be things that you planned but that did not work while you taught them, so they need to be adapted. Furthermore, every year new students come in the class with different skills and interests, so you need to amend your unit to provide your students with the education they need. These adaptations in the units of enquiry are done by the classroom teachers from the same grade level together with the programme leader in their weekly planning meetings. These meetings are meant to discuss the lessons the grades are currently teaching and will teach in the weeks to come.

There are many different ways the teachers collaborate in these sessions. Some teachers prefer to sit together and build the different sections of an enquiry unit but then divide the lesson planning. The teachers share a level of trust which allows them to work individually on the area they feel more comfortable with, whether it is language, mathematics or unit, and create the lesson plans for the rest of the members of their team. After they have all finished, they share their plans with each other and make the adaptations necessary for differentiation in their classrooms.

The teachers will start by deciding what main unit concepts they want the children to understand. They then create the central idea, lines of enquiry and key concepts, and in other words, the main topic of the unit, subtopics and the key concepts such as form, perspective, function, connection, responsibility, causation, change and reflection (see Chapter 6 for a more detailed discussion on concept-based learning). Then, they will determine the learning outcomes, and decide on the assessment, transdisciplinary skills and learner profile (ie values to be taught). Furthermore, teachers brainstorm ideas for constructive learning experiences that start with a provocation and build up to going further as well as discuss differentiation. To finalise the unit plan, they will write the report template. The unit is built in different weeks as it progresses, which allows reflection and room for adaptations if necessary.

There are other teachers who do everything together, ranging from unit development to lesson plans. In kindergarten, for example, the units and the learning experiences are developed and created together. The first learning experience discussed is the hook which is the name given to the first activity of the unit which catches the children's attention and makes them wonder what the unit is about. Sometimes, all the teachers have the same hook and sometimes the hooks differ depending on what will excite the children the most. After this provocation, the students take different directions as they make different connections. Having a bank of learning experiences allows the teachers to make the teaching student-oriented. The planning meetings take place in a different kindergarten class every week. The meetings start off with five minutes of sharing and sparking. In these five minutes, the teachers of that class share their experiences on how the unit is going and the things they have been doing with the children. This allows other teachers to bounce off ideas or to take some for their own classrooms.

In our kindergarten classrooms, we have children from the age of four until the age of six. The main goal for this two-year cycle is to build a solid base for the children to feel comfortable in their learning environment. The children need to create strong relationships with their peers and teachers and look at their classroom and school as their safe place where they learn and have fun surrounded by their friends. In order to guide the holistic development of a child, we use an observation diary which contains several different areas of development such as: *self-image, how the children see themselves, relationships towards adults and other children, play development, independence, gross and fine motor skills, drawing development, visual and auditory perception, oral language development, body, spatial and time orientation, early literacy and numeracy* and *logical thinking*. The areas of development look at a child from the age of three and a half until the age of seven. These areas are normally related to the age; however, children develop individually, which means that we need to provide each child with different type(s) of support.

In order to provide the children with what they need, the kindergarten teachers work together with a teaching assistant who stays in the classroom during the morning. The role of a teaching assistant is to support the children in their learning and to work hand in hand with the classroom teacher. The assistants know exactly what is going on in the classroom since they know the children, have access to all the lesson plans which are shared in online platforms and also plan together with the teacher. This provides the assistant with enough information to be that extra teacher the children need in kindergarten.

The main role of a teaching assistant is to help the teacher and the students in the lessons. This can be done in several ways. For example, most of the time the teaching assistant is making notes and documenting what the children say. This documentation is really important since it helps the teacher to see children's interactions and it gives clear examples on how their learning is growing which will be used in their progress reports. When necessary, the teaching assistant also participates in the lesson. Together with the teacher, the assistant can introduce a concept with a role play or, in order to differentiate and give a more personalised lesson, the teacher and the assistant can divide the classroom into two separated groups to teach the same concept in different ways.

After the carpet time where topics are being discussed, the children move to what we call stations. The stations are activities where the children need to collaborate with the resources displayed to show their understanding of the lesson. Sometimes, the stations are chosen for them and all the children have the same task. In kindergarten, the stations are always play-based. The children can choose between different activities such as role play, drawing, construction, puppets, crafting or playdough. In these stations, they have the freedom to show their understanding of the lesson through play. In order to be able to support all the groups, the teacher and the teaching assistant walk around the classroom observing the children's play and intervening when necessary. These techniques allow differentiation and more personal support for children who need extra help or extra challenges. Since kindergarten has no English language acquisition (ELA) teacher, those children who come to school with insufficient English proficiency are still getting the support they need with these stations and the collaborative work of the teacher and the assistant.

Collaboration between all the different teachers at school

We teach by always showing the purpose of learning, making it tangible and authentic for the children. This will help them to see for themselves the importance of learning and how they could use that in real life. For the type of differentiation and integrated education this chapter describes, all the teachers need to be interconnected to make the learning as accessible as possible. The students use the same learning techniques throughout their school journey. Every time they use those techniques, they become better at them and at applying them in different contexts. Furthermore, by communicating between grade teachers, one gets to know one's students in a much deeper way. One knows what the students have previously learnt and what the next step should be. This section explains how all the teachers from different grades plan their curriculum vertically and how specialist teachers and student support teachers collaborate with the classroom teacher to plan the unit and lessons.

Imagine yourself working on the transdisciplinary theme '*How people express themselves*'. You are a Grade 5 teacher and you plan to teach persuasive writing by teaching students about social media and the messages from advertisements. However, your Grade 5 class knows everything about the way companies convey messages in advertisements and how they are used to make people buy their products. Now what? You need to adapt your language learning outcomes and challenge your students with maybe other types of persuasive writing such as essays, speeches or debates. Within the enquiry programme, teachers always plan their lessons according to their students' prior knowledge. Imagine then the benefits of being aware of what your students already know even before getting to know them.

At ISUtrecht, our curriculum is yearly reviewed not only horizontally but also vertically. Together with the teachers from the previous and the next grade, we compare our learning outcomes and build our curriculum according to it. In other words, at the end of the year, Grade 2 teachers will sit with Grade 3 teachers in order to share what the focus was in each of the transdisciplinary themes as well as what they learnt regarding language and mathematics. So, for example, under the theme of '*Who we are*', Grade

1 students learnt about healthy choices. This learning will be connected and further developed in Grade 2 when they learn about body systems.

This type of curriculum planning allows for better differentiation and personalised education. This is also encouraged and supported by our philosophy on working in phases rather than within set grade goals. We plan our units depending on the phase our students are in at both language and mathematics learning, or in the different areas with regard to kindergarten. We follow the *First Steps Curriculum* which is based on a learning continuum.

> *It recognises that not all students learn in the same way, through the same processes, or at the same rate. A teacher collects data in order to identify where on those continuums a student is positioned to better design appropriate learning experiences. These experiences are designed to move the student from one development phase to the next. In this way, the learner is able to build on established skills and understanding, while being supported to meet appropriate challenges to extend their learning.*
>
> (ISUtrecht, nd, p 1)

In other words, one year your students may identify the purpose of a text but they do not know how to select a publishing format that best suits purpose and audience. In this case, you may need to teach them about web pages, slide shows or posters. You build your lessons according to their understanding. However, the next year you find your students to be already at the next level of the use of those strategies, but they do not know how to reflect on or proofread their own writing and their spelling needs improvement. We also need to bear in mind that each student is at a different stage of learning; therefore, the support provided also differs. For a deeper explanation of this, see the *First Steps Literacy* and *Mathematics Maps of Development* (Department of Education WA, nda; Department of Education WA, ndb).

Through collaborating with the teachers from the previous grade, we start building an overview of what our next school year planning is going to look like, and most importantly, we start getting to know our future students in order to be one step ahead on their learning styles and interests. Referring to the house metaphor at the start of the chapter, you already know the structure of the house, so you can plan ahead what the next steps are and what you need to prepare, instead of having to start from the foundations of the house because you do not know what the previous builders did. In this way, we are making learning more meaningful and authentic since we as teachers show we care about the students' needs and that we are there for the students as facilitators, not dictators.

Classroom teachers collaborating with subject area teachers

All the different areas from our learning are interconnected and integrated into our unit. We do this in order to have an authentic education where the children are engaged in the lessons and can get the most out of them since what they are learning is seen as something useful and something that they will need in their daily lives. This interconnected learning is supported at ISUtrecht by all the teachers from the same classroom. This includes the classroom teacher, specialists, ELA teachers and student support teachers.

The specialists are subject area teachers who come to the classroom to teach their subject. We have specialists for music, physical education, drama, Dutch language acquisition and visual arts. Some of the specialists teach in kindergarten throughout the whole year and some teach only in certain units. Music, physical education and Dutch language acquisition are subjects that have a fixed schedule no matter the unit we are in. Visual arts and drama, in turn, are included in our schedule when we are teaching a specific unit. At the end of an academic year, all teachers sit together to plan the units for the next academic year. As explained at the beginning of the chapter, this is the moment when teachers from different grades come together to do their vertical planning. Furthermore, the teachers decide in which units they are going to collaborate with the specialists to integrate their subject into the unit. For example, in kindergarten, the unit under the theme of '*How we express ourselves*' focuses on visual arts. This means that the art teacher collaborates with the kindergarten team to plan the unit hand in hand. The central idea, lines of enquiry and assessment are created together matching and supporting each other.

The unit having a specific subject focus does not mean that the rest of the specialists are not doing something related to the unit. It rather means that the other specialist teachers are doing the same unit but with a different approach and with their own assessment. At the end of the unit, both the specialist and the classroom teachers will sit together to write the report comments which will be given to the parents as a whole.

Due to ISUtrecht being an international school, some children come to school with little English skills. In order to support their learning and well-being at school, the classroom teacher works together with an ELA teacher. The ELA teacher has a 45-minute timeslot within their schedule to meet with the grade teachers in order to plan their language lessons. They collaborate to decide upon the language goals of that week and how the ELA teacher is going to work with the students. This is sometimes done by taking the students out of the classroom or by providing the students with extra support in-class. The grade teachers together with the ELA teacher look at the contents of the lesson and later on the ELA teachers modify the lesson to adapt it to the needs of each student.

Students may have difficulties with learning such as concentration problems, dyslexia, poor comprehension skills or processing issues. Therefore, the student support teachers collaborate with the classroom teacher and set goals for specific students (see also Chapter 2). These goals can be related to students' skills, understanding of the unit or other needs the students may have. Both teachers make a plan for the students and review it every six to eight weeks. This support can be given in the classroom with the rest of the students or outside the classroom, depending on the lesson. The student support teacher sends feedback to the classroom teachers who will then communicate it to the parents.

Collaboration between teachers and leadership

This section explores the importance of a good leadership team to support the teachers and ensure their well-being within the school since this will ultimately benefit the students who are our first priority. I describe the techniques used by the management team in our school to promote open communication, motivation and development in the teachers.

The teachers at ISUtrecht believe that collaboration is what keeps professional development alive and is teachers' key to success. They would not be able to teach in such an effective way if they had to do it on their own. Collaboration both helps and challenges you to keep growing professionally and personally. It incites you to try new things your colleagues have suggested, things you would have never thought of yourself. At our school, we have an open-door policy that provides us with a range of learning experiences. It allows open communication which connects with the feeling of being supported by our leaders. Studies have demonstrated that it is important to take care of teachers' well-being due to its effect on children's education. For instance, Spilt et al (2011) present several studies that show evidence of how children's socioemotional adjustment and academic performance are affected positively or negatively depending on teachers' stress levels. Teachers' stress is often related to the lack of team or leader support (Borg et al, 1991). Additional factors connected with teacher stress include the support one gets from one's colleagues and the recognition for one's work (Cross, nd).

Table 4.1 demonstrates how the ISUtrecht leadership team and teachers create a sense of community which minimises stress in the work environment by using professional training and development, communicating policies openly, listening to all opinions and input, giving and receiving positive and constructive feedback to improve themselves, and collaborating. Most of these elements were mentioned in the policies recommended by the UK National Union of Teachers for teachers' well-being (Cross, nd).

Table 4.1 Collaboration between leadership and teachers

Senior management	**Middle management**
Head of school	Primary Years Programme leader
Deputy heads of school	Early years co-ordinator
Primary Years Programme (PYP) leader	Teacher mentor (supports new teachers with teaching duties not related to curriculum. For example, getting used to the school schedule, time management, parents' confidence or even a balance between personal and professional life)
Middle Years Programme (MYP) leader	
Diploma Programme (DP) leader	

The communication between these two groups flows in both directions. The decisions made in each of them are communicated to the other and then to the staff members. Middle management meet every week in order to discuss staff issues. They are the ones who discuss what teachers need and think of ideas on how to support the teachers for them to grow professionally and to be happy at school. One of the techniques used for teachers to receive feedback on their teaching or on a specific skill they want to improve on is the teachers' observations led by middle management. Each teacher has an observer to whom they need to send their lesson plan in advance and the area of development on which they want to get feedback. After the lesson, the teacher reflects on how it went and receives constructive feedback on how to improve.

The power of modelling and showing in your behaviour what you want your students to copy is applicable to learning in so many different ways. Regarding feedback, if you promote it in your teachers, they will learn from it and promote it in their classrooms which will ultimately teach the students an important skill (Dontigney, nd). Another purpose and benefit of giving positive feedback is to motivate your team members. With motivation, the quality of their performances will rise up since they will be confident and encouraged to give their best. Positive feedback also helps with correcting and improving one's performance. Other benefits of positive feedback mentioned by Sturgess and Higson (2013) are related to developing skills and understanding of what you are doing and showing people that you value them.

Our mentor looked into everybody's schedule searching for the timeslot when teachers had a specialist and could be outside of the classroom. In those timeslots, she wrote the teachers who were available in their classroom to go and be observed by others. This time frame was integrated within our school time for us to observe our colleagues and learn from them. This idea was brought to us as a way to learn from each other and appreciate the number of wonderful teachers we have in our own school. After observing someone, we took a picture of them and put it on the Wall of Fame, a wall meant to showcase the amazing things teachers do in their classrooms. This wall is now full of pictures of teachers in their daily routine with a nice message which describes what the teacher showed in the class. The wall also elucidates the various skills the different teachers have, some of which they may have been unaware of themselves (see Figure 4.2).

Figure 4.2 The Wall of Fame

Last but not least, to add the cherry on top, our mentor introduced us to another activity in which we got a big poster on which we needed to put our strengths and the strengths of others. This was meant to show people's skills as a *'dictionary'* on who to consult if you need help with something specific. So, for example, if you need help with differentiation or concept-based teaching, you could turn to the teachers who in the poster were indicated as being good at those. Moreover, each teacher is able to see the positive things others think of them.

Apart from these observations and techniques which help us grow professionally, teachers also get professional development in the form of a course or a workshop. This topic is also discussed by the middle management. They will look at people's needs and provide teachers with a course they would benefit from. Sometimes, the process works the other way around. That is, if the teachers find a course that they think would help them in their career, they present it to the leadership team who will decide on it.

All these techniques are a reflection of our school philosophy of being lifelong learners. The students also learn from their teachers how to be lifelong learners. Teachers, much like students, construct meaning together on what education is about. By wanting to grow professionally, they are modelling the way children should learn, with an open mind that sees how many things there are in the world for us to learn about and how there are no limits to learning.

Senior management also meets every week to discuss the scoop of the school, where the school is moving towards, school policies, long-term planning, etc. In these meetings, the students and teachers are represented by their programme leader. When an agreement is being made, the programme leader brings it to the middle management who will then discuss what is the best way to implement it in primary taking into consideration the workload of the teachers and the timing. In general, staff members are quite involved in bureaucratic issues such as policies, school agreements, professional development, curriculum or budget. As an example, the teachers are given the freedom to decide what they really need for the classroom and what materials would help them to teach with good quality. Teachers are given a certain amount of money to spend throughout the year. Regarding this, the teachers collaborate within their grade in order to decide what are the things they really need taking everything into consideration such as field trips, resources and teachers' books for professional development.

Collaboration between students

Kath Murdoch (2015) describes how and why we use enquiry in today's classrooms (see also Chapter 7). She gives examples on what elements we need to see more in the classrooms and what we need to move away from. In this comparison, we notice how we need to see more continuous learning instead of intermittent and more differentiated instead of homogenised teaching. Enquiry is transferable and not fixed as well as student-centred instead of teacher-centred. These elements are the base of the vertical planning described earlier. However, there is one more aspect that needs to be highlighted, that is, enquiry is more collaboration and less competition. Research has shown how mixed aged classrooms remove the competition from the classrooms by creating a spirit of collaboration where students learn through teaching and leading other children and through being able to trust their peers who will support them in their learning. This fosters a sense of community and uniqueness which benefits the children's motivation towards learning and blossoms their self-esteem. There is evidence that mixed aged classrooms can be beneficial for the children in both their academic and social development (Vine Academy, nd).

Our kindergarten classrooms are the only ones from our school that follow a two-year cycle allowing children from four years old to six years old to grow and learn together. The other grades are aged-based. However, this does not prevent them from interacting with other grades. There are multiple situations in which students from all the different grades go to different classrooms to either present something or do activities together. For example, the whole school knows about the Grade 5 exhibition week when all the grades are welcome to learn from Grade 5 in their area of expertise. On a weekly basis, there are several grades being mixed together as reading buddies. Some kindergarten classes have the pleasure to be read to by the Grade 3 students while the little ones are eating their snack. Every session takes about 20 minutes and starts off by letting the children have the freedom to choose who they want to read with. In the same scenario, Grade 4 students read to Grade 1, while Grade 2 students read with Grade 5 students. There are also students from secondary who volunteer once a week to support kindergarteners. They come in the morning, while the kindergarten students are arriving at school and playing in their morning stations. The secondary students, aged between 14 and 16 years old, walk around the classroom looking if any children need their help in the stations.

Collaboration between parents and school

Another big part of our community is formed by parents and support staff who are also represented in the meetings from both management teams. As mentioned before, in order to create authentic learning, all the different parts involved in the children's education need to work together. Parents are strong members of our community who contribute to students' well-being in many different ways. They receive weekly emails from the teachers explaining what the learning of that week was, and giving some tips on how the children can apply their learning at home. By creating a connection between school and home, we are once again reinforcing the importance of authentic learning for our lifelong learners.

The way parents collaborate in the classroom is through organising volunteers for field trips or outdoor activities, coming to read a book during library time to the kindergarteners, decorating the classroom for special events or helping in the organisation of festivities. Each classroom has a classroom parent who is the connection of communication between the teacher and the rest of the parents from the classroom.

Apart from the classrooms, the parents have their own organisation, Parents Support Group (PSG). The group is administered by a chairperson and several committees which support the school in many ways such as organising cultural festivities like Sinterklaas (ie Dutch festivity) or events like the ArtBurst (ie the school's art day), together with after school activities, or social events for parents. Parents' input is more than welcome; therefore, the PSG sometimes gives feedback to middle management who then brings it to senior management. There is another school organisation, Division Council (DC), which is formed by three parents, three staff members, a DP student and the head of school who attends meetings as a representative of the school boards and in an advisory capacity. The discussions from the meetings are then shared in senior management by the head of school, and also to the teachers by the staff members present in the DC meetings.

ISUtrecht has a big sense of community and one of our goals is to make everybody feel welcome. Our mentor helps new teachers, but new parents also need help. This is done through one of the parents' groups called the New Parent Connectors (NPC). This group is also run by volunteers who want to help new parents in settling in the new school and the new country. This is organised by nationality so that these new parents can express themselves in their mother tongue and get a feeling of home.

CONCLUSION

Education has greatly evolved and adapted to the times. It is no longer limited to a book, and a class with students who are supposed to learn the same things in the same way and where there is no room for creativity is seen as outdated. In Kath Murdoch's (2015, p 96) words: *'Teachers now have a much greater responsibility to help students build a repertoire of skills and dispositions that enable them to more effectively locate, access, understand and critique idea, as well as design, create and share their own'*. As teachers, we have a big responsibility on our hands since the world around us has become so big and complicated that we need to be ready to understand it. We need to teach the children to be ready for it. The world is accessible, changing and interconnected. Through collaboration, one feels supported to face those changes, learn about them and work together with one's colleagues to create a unique and authentic learning journey for each student.

> ### *Reflective questions*
>
> 1. What forms of collaboration do you have in your school? Do you see your school as a collaborative workplace?
> 2. Do you have an open and transparent leadership who shares their way of working and goals and takes care of your well-being?
> 3. How is the atmosphere of collaboration among the teachers in your grade level? Is it supportive or competitive?
> 4. Are you open to receive new ideas from colleagues, to try new techniques or new ways of teaching in order to improve professionally and cover your students' needs?
> 5. How do your students collaborate? With whom do they collaborate? Do you teach your students how to collaborate?
> 6. How are parents involved in your school? What is their role in the school community?

REFERENCES

Borg, M G, Riding, R J and Falzon, J M (1991) Stress in Teaching: A Study of Occupational Stress and Its Determinants, Job Satisfaction and Career Commitment among Primary Schoolteachers. *Educational Psychology*, 11(1): 59–75.

Claxton, G, Chambers, M, Powell, G and Lucas, B (2011) *The Learning Powered School: Pioneering 21st Century Education*. Bristol: TLO Limited.

Cross, D (nd) *Teacher Wellbeing and Its Impact on Student Learning*. [online] Available at: www.research.uwa.edu.au/__data/assets/pdf_file/0010/2633590/teacher-wellbeing-and-student.pdf (accessed 12 September 2020).

Department of Education WA (nda) *First Steps Literacy*. [online] Available at: http://det.wa.edu.au/stepsresources/detcms/navigation/first-steps-literacy/ (accessed 12 September 2020).

Department of Education WA (ndb) *First Steps Mathematics*. [online] Available at: http://det.wa.edu.au/stepsresources/detcms/navigation/first-steps-mathematics/ (accessed 12 September 2020).

Dontigney, E (nd) *The Advantages of Positive Feedback*. [online] Available at: http://smallbusiness.chron.com/advantages-positive-feedback-18135.html (accessed 12 September 2020).

ISUtrecht (nd) Mathematics Learning in the PYP. [online] Available at: www.isutrecht.nl/wp-content/uploads/2018/10/ISUtrecht-PYP-Math-syllabus.pdf (accessed 12 September 2020).

Murdoch, K (2015) *The Power of Enquiry: Teaching and Learning with Curiosity, Creativity and Purpose in the Contemporary Classroom*. Northcote Vic: Seastar Education.

Spilt, J L, Koomen, H M Y and Thijs, J T (2011) Teacher Wellbeing: The Importance of Teacher–student Relationships. *Educational Psychology Review*, 23: 457–77.

Sturgess, A and Higson, P (2013) *High-impact Interpersonal Skills: How to Be a Persuasive Leader*. London: Apex Leadership Ltd & Book Boon.

Thousand, J S, Villa, R A and Nevin, A I (2006) The Many Faces of Collaborative Planning and Teaching. *Theory Into Practice*, 45(3): 239–48.

Vine Academy (nd) *Benefits of Mixed Age Classes*. [online] Available at: www.vineacademy.com/benefits-of-mixed-age-classes/ (accessed 12 September 2020).

Part 2
Progressive pedagogical approaches

5 Play-based teaching and learning

Elvira Oskam, Jennifer Diepman and Marianne Lauritzen

INTRODUCTION

At International School Utrecht (ISUtrecht), we make use of play-based teaching and learning from kindergarten up to the Middle Years Programme (MYP). We adhere to the definition of play by van Kuyk and Groot Koerkamp (2002), according to whom play should always have a child's voice, choice and ownership. When children play, they do not think in goals like adults. They play with a pursuit of personal gain in a social and stress-free setting. This definition is a strong starting point, because it means that play is flexible and is not always set in a certain way; having multiple ways of play keeps the learning ongoing and gives the children the opportunity to show their learning that fits their interests and capabilities. In the end, it is all about students' agency over their learning and for us teachers to let go and see how we can provoke children in their play to reach a higher level of play and understanding of their world.

In this chapter, we explore the theoretical underpinnings of play-based teaching and learning, describe various types of play and provide examples of play. You learn about how we facilitate play-based learning at ISUtrecht and what this looks like in kindergarten, the Primary Years Programme (PYP) and also in MYP. We hope that this chapter inspires teachers to come up with ideas to implement certain elements in their lessons for learning through play.

THEORY

Play development

A child develops play over the course of their overall development. Play is interconnected to the rest of the child's development and should never be viewed as a separate component. Emotional and social states are always deciding factors on how well children play. The largest part of their play development happens in the first seven years of their lives. After the play development becomes stronger and their play deepens, the focus and perspective of the children will change depending on their life stages. Table 5.1 shows the shift in emphasis for each life stage.

Table 5.1 Forms of play during different life stages

Life stage: early years (up to 7 years old)	Life stage: primary years (7–11 years old)	Life stage: secondary years (12+ years old)
Emotional: Very egocentric, importance to learn boundary of good/bad and real/fantasy.	**Emotional**: Less egocentric, more aware of others. Values and beliefs system grow.	**Emotional**: Altruistic, working on talents becomes a bigger part of a person.
Social: Interacts by choice, often personal gain. Short and few 'good' friendships.	**Social**: Interacts by choice, less personal gain. More 'good' friendships and mingle in with the group. Peers become of bigger importance, but family is still the most important.	**Social**: Interacts by choice, which becomes more complex. Struggling balance between mingling with/acceptance within the group and excelling in a talent. Peers often become most important, often loosen themselves from family values.
Translation in play: A lot of analogue play, testing boundaries within play. Children can lose themselves in the 'make-believe' world they have created.	**Translation in play**: Start with digital play, explore the social value of it. Understanding that the real world is different from the imaginary world.	**Translation in play**: Serious gaming, also online. Understanding that the digital world and analogue world are connected. Analogue play is to strengthen talents.
Focused phases within play: Solitary play Onlooker play Parallel play Associative play Co-operative play	**Focused phases within play:** Co-operative play Collaborative play	**Focused phases within play:** Co-operative play Collaborative play

(Adapted from Spel deel 1 Theoretisch Kader, nd)

Phases and forms of play

In this section, you get a brief introduction of the different phases and forms of play children engage in, and the importance of the development of their ability to play. Children develop the different phases of play in a chronological order. Table 5.2 opposite gives an overview of the different phases of play and their associated age.

All children begin with solitary play, which is considered the lowest level of play, and after some time and practice, they gradually develop a higher level of play. Through this process, the child will eventually develop the skills and understanding they need to take part in co-operative and collaborative play, which are considered the highest levels of play one can achieve. Towards the higher grades at school, the children should show higher levels of play, especially since the group sense is becoming stronger and their learning involves a lot more collaborating in groups.

Table 5.2 Phases of play associated with different age groups

Phase of play	Description	Associated age
Solitary	Plays alone. Focused on own work.	<4
Onlooker	Watches others play. Takes in what others are doing.	≃4–4.5
Parallel	Plays next to others, while remaining focused on own work.	≃4.5–5
Associative	Plays next to others, while sharing materials and ideas.	≃5–5.5
Co-operative	Plays together, input and responsibility may vary per child.	≃5.5–6+
Collaborative	Plays together, equal and essential input and responsibility.	≥6

Bob Hughes (1996) describes 16 forms of play that we also use at ISUtrecht, which you can see in Table 5.3. When in the younger years, the children use these different forms of play in the analogue world; the older children will shift more towards the digital world. Being able to play in the analogue world is crucial, because during this play, the children fully experience their world and their limitations. Developing an image of everything in and around their world can only be done through making use of their senses. The more the senses are triggered and used, the more grip children will get, and the better they will be able to apply their skills in various situations, whether the situations are real or imaginative.

Table 5.3 Bob Hughes' (1996) 16 forms of play

Form of play	Description
Rough and tumble play	Physical vigorous play, such as play fighting and chasing.
Symbolic play	Using objects, actions and ideas to represent other objects, actions and ideas, such as making sand cakes and pretending to eat them.
Socio-dramatic play	Acting out imaginary situations in imaginary places, such as pretending that a room is a hospital, pretending to be a doctor, tending to sick toys.
Creative play	Modelling and painting (arts and craft), expressing themselves while developing manual skills.
Social play	Two or more children interacting with each other through structured play where rules are set or discovered together, such as playing hide-and-seek or playing house.
Communication play	Playing using words and gestures, such as singing and miming.
Dramatic play	Taking on specific roles and acting them out, dramatising situations that go along with the roles they chose.
Locomotor play	Activities that involve moving from one place to the other, such as skipping, jumping and running.

Form of play	Description
Imaginative play	A type of role playing where children act out situations they have had or that they are interested in.
Exploratory play	When children use their sense of smell, taste and touch to explore the world around them, such as squishing mud with their hands, or smelling and tasting a leaf.
Fantasy play	A type of non-realistic play where children take on different roles and act out situations.
Deep play	Play that allows the child to experience risky or life-threatening situations to develop survival skills and conquer. Such as lighting fires, making weapons or facing their fears such as heights or snakes.
Mastery play	When a child is learning a new skill. Using trial and error, repeating an activity over and over to get better at it.
Object play	Playful use of objects, such as building blocks, cars and dolls.
Role play	Acting out a different role, pretending to be someone else. Practising understanding how other people think and feel.
Recapitulative play	Play that allows the child to explore ancestry, history, rituals, stories, rhymes, fire and darkness.

Learning environment

It is important for children to be able to manipulate things around them to get a better sense of the world during the early years life stage and to reconstruct and explore concepts during the life stages after. To make sure that this child development happens at school, it is crucial that the children are exposed to a learning environment that drives their need to take part in play-based activities.

In light of this, it is good practice to give the children agency in the development of their learning environment when possible (see Chapter 1). We encourage the children to tell us what the classroom should look like, which tools they need and what needs to be developed. Because the children learn about their world, their learning environment should align with that. An example of this is when our students learn about science in the early years. In this case, we set up a lab in the classroom by letting our students explore what real scientists do at work and which tools they need in their jobs. We let the students craft imitations of actual tools, for instance, making magnifying glasses out of cardboard and cling wrap, as well as letting the children use real magnifying glasses to explore the world around them. Through the process of learning about science, the children are introduced to more content and produce more content themselves as well. This results in the learning environment physically changing throughout the unit depending on the knowledge the children gain. Often, we start with a simple display and the children will share what needs to be added or adjusted and how different learning stations can be combined, and the teachers help facilitate the exploration and guide the children through the learning processes.

Guiding play

The main responsibility for teachers, once children are playing, is observation. Looking at how children play, with whom they play and how the play develops, helps the teacher gain insight into a child's development. Based on this understanding and how well the teacher knows the students, the teacher can decide to intervene or let the children keep on playing. When it is necessary to intervene, it can be done in various ways. At ISUtrecht, we use an observation form as a tool, which you can find in the appendices. We use the form for our observations, because play cannot be seen separate from the situation the children are in, and it is important to dedicate proper attention to this important part of the student's development.

There are several roles one can take on while observing the students in their play, and we make a distinction between observing younger and older children. In the early years observation form, we use the terms *audience*, *actor*, *props manager*, *stage director* and *script writer*. We use the following for working in the primary years observation form: *audience*, *player*, *journalist*, *lawyer* and *coach*. However, the terms used are referring to the same observation roles a teacher can take on. The different observation roles can be described as follows.

- *Audience*: coming very close and observing the play; the children know that you are watching.
- *Actor/player*: becoming part of the play; the children tell the teacher what to do and what rules they have for their play.
- *Props manager/journalist*: asking questions (why and how) or adding materials to provoke the children.
- *Stage director/lawyer*: taking the lead instead of the children, telling them what to do and explaining the rules.
- *Script writer/coach*: changing the hierarchy established by the children, giving other children opportunities to take the lead in the play.

PLAY-BASED LEARNING IN THE EARLY YEARS

ISUtrecht implements play daily in our lives (see Figure 5.1). We use stations for both the guided sessions and the free sessions, in kindergarten and Grade 1. These stations can be traditional like a construction station and a drawing station, or more contemporary ones such as photography, science lab and shadow puppetry. This depends on what we want the students to learn during a unit or subject strand.

Recently, we started writing play plans for the units taught in kindergarten. Since learning environment can be viewed as the third pedagogue (Thornton, 2014), we need to think critically about how we arrange the classroom, and which tools we make available to our students. This play plan is written before the unit starts and reflected on during and after the unit. When observing our students, we can see what they do and what they learn while playing in the stations and compare it to what we planned; did the stations facilitate the desired result? Were the students really practising the skills we planned for them to practise, and did they adopt the intended knowledge?

Figure 5.1 Early years student building a cake out of sand

In the kindergarten classes, the children had a unit on '*How we organise ourselves*' with the subheading '*Community helpers*'. In the first week, the children went on different community walks around the school and made maps using magazine images, book images and drawings. First, they started with the buildings, then after another walk, they added the roads and finally added people as an essential part of their community maps. The classroom setup in the second week of the unit on community helpers changed and was quite bare. Tables were in upright position and only had a paper stuck to the front with a door drawn on it, a label and a sign, such as fire station, grocery store and library. Before the children walked in, they were asked to look what the teacher had done and what it could mean. Once they understood the signs, they started role play using imaginary play. Hosing down a fire was done by using their hands as the sprinklers. When reading a book, the students used their hands to pretend to read and, for buying food, the gesture of exchanging money was quickly used. In the meantime, a child found a bag with dress-up clothes and a pile of boxes with food and he asked if he could put the food in the grocery store. He was given that freedom and the play turned into general exchange of money, to looking at the item and saying a price. The 'firefighters' were suddenly recognisable, because they decided all red clothes should be for that station.

After letting them play for another 25 minutes, the children discussed the question that was given before entering the class. One of the children replied that this is a community. When asked why the teacher did that, another child responded that it helps them learn and understand what it is like to be a community helper like a firefighter. Throughout the remaining weeks of the unit, the children built on the existing materials and crafting items that were missing but essential. Through research they learnt that, for instance, the job of a firefighter is more diverse than just putting out fires. They learnt that in a shop, there is a system in place for weighing and buying items and they crafted scales and added a cash register with pretend money. They interviewed a doctor and a librarian to improve their play and added more resources like a patient form for the hospital and a scanner with computer in the library. Through the research, their play became more realistic and lasted longer. The children who understood the importance of working together and who also had developed the skills to partake in co-operative and collaborative play started working together during their play. At the end, the class reflected on the play and the children mentioned that they wanted more time to try out more stations. This resembled the reflection of the teachers. The environment was changed to challenge them in their play. The goals and skills practised in the stations could be referred to the play plan. See Table 5.4 for an extract of the play plan, created by our early years co-ordinator.

Table 5.4 Unit play plan

Station: Hospital	Unit play plan	Station: Library
Knowledge:	**Unit: Community helpers**	**Knowledge:**
L – Reading: Relies on copying and approximation to compose a spoken language.	**Main knowledge for these stations:**	**L – Reading:** Relies on copying and approximation to compose a spoken language.
L – Listening and speaking: Asks questions about signs, pictures and labels.	**L – Reading:** Recognises significant environmental print.	**L – Viewing and presenting:** Makes use of images to read simple picture books and signs. Makes meaning from personally significant multimodal texts. Displays viewing behaviours. Recognises common signs and symbols used in the environment. Recognises familiar symbols in relation to codes and conventions.
Understands simple and familiar questions.	**L – Listening and speaking:** Assumes a shared background between speaker and listener.	
Responds to spoken texts in own personal way.		
Communicates own needs.	**SS – Resources and the environment**: Gives examples of ways in which people co-operate in order to live together peacefully.	
L – Writing: Reacts to written text in their environment.		
Role plays writing for a purpose.	Practises citizenship skills.	**L – Writing:** Reacts to written text in their environment. Role plays writing for a purpose. Asks questions about printed words and symbols.
Asks questions about printed words and symbols.	**SS – Social organisation and culture:** Recognises that everyone has particular interests and abilities.	
SS – Resources and the environment: Recognises that their actions affect others.		**SS – Human systems and economic activities:** Identifies the difference between wants and needs.
	Identifies people who are responsible for helping and caring for them at home, at school and in the community.	
SS – Human systems and economic activities: Identifies the difference between wants and needs.		
	SS – Human systems and economic activities: Gives examples of rules and identifies their purposes.	**Skills:**
PSPE – active living: Recognises that acting upon instructions and being aware of others helps to ensure safety.		**Communication:** Reading, writing, non-verbal.

PSPE – Interactions: Asks questions. Reaches out for help when it is needed for themselves or others. Skills: Self-management skills: Healthy lifestyles, spatial awareness. Communication: Listening, speaking, reading, writing, non-verbal. Research: Formulating questions.	Main skills for these stations: Social studies: Identifies roles and responsibilities in society. Social skills: Accepting responsibility, respecting others, co-operating, group decision-making, adopting a variety of roles, resolving conflict. Thinking skills: Comprehension, application. Self-management skills: Codes of behaviour.	Add-ons: M – Data handling: Looks at physical displays of familiar data and says which is most or has more. Sorts and arranges data they have collected into familiar groupings. Counts when asked to say how many in each group in a data display.

PLAY-BASED LEARNING IN THE PRIMARY YEARS

Children of all ages are happy when they are engaged in play that interests them. New knowledge can only be added to already existing knowledge. A play-based form of learning allows older children to play in a familiar way while gradually adding new concepts through experimentation. Students can already have familiarity with the items that they are playing with as well as the form of play. Many students know what building sticks, clay and blocks are, yet they can use them through play-based learning to discover something that they did not know before. Also, most students already have previous experience with building a new construction, taking part in role play and using technology to develop a creative idea. The children then know how the form of play normally is played (ie dramatic play), yet the play can be open-ended. This gives the students the possibility of variation in their play, where they get to act out situations as they discover them, resulting in learning new things that the children would not be able to predict beforehand. This can also be exciting for educators because they then get to see what is happening at that moment in the classroom when the children are fully engaged in fun play-based learning experiences. At this point, the educator can make use of all their roles as an observer while watching how the students act out their parts in the play in the different situations they are creating.

Role play and acting out scenarios are forms of play-based learning that are easily accessible for all age groups. This is applied in most units or themes as well as various subjects such as language, mathematics, science, geography and history. Learners create the scenarios to act out themselves or the teacher provides the framework for the role play. Through role play, students consider the emotions and opinions of others, even if these ideas are opposite to their own ideas. This develops their sense of perspective, consideration and open-mindedness. Role play is also a great way to build confidence when students are well prepared for their performance and classmates are supportive as good listeners and are given the opportunity to give positive feedback.

An example of using role play in a storytelling unit is when students in Grade 2 were asked to create their own stories and then act them out using props to make the characters come to life. This interaction in groups can also be a way to address social issues if necessary. Students had to work together and help one another in order to create their group assignment. If students did not agree on their storyline or how to act it out, then they needed to learn how to discuss the development of their story and play in a polite way. Sometimes, group members acted inappropriately with each other. If the teacher believed that students just needed a reminder about how to interact with each other, he or she simply asked the students how they would like to discuss the issue if they thought about it again.

Another example of role play was done in Grade 4 by having students take on the role of scientists who needed to do research about living in outer space. Because science is evidence-based, students reported their findings in a presentation to the class. They researched topics such as how they would get water, oxygen and food to where they need to go in outer space. They did mathematical equations to figure out how many light years they would need in order to travel. Classmates acting as scientists asked the students questions to engage the entire class.

In Grade 4, students were also assigned the role to host a sustainable development investment convention. During this convention, these entrepreneurs presented their innovative solutions to real-world problems. They had to do research in advance to develop the product. Also, the product had to be marketed. Students discovered how the process developed as it unfolded before them.

When studying products and services, students also created their own product that many consumers would like to purchase. When learners were given the freedom to experiment with different materials and come up with their own tangible product, they were able to get more out of the activity than if they were only to write up a report. Examples of these products were cars, T-shirts, plants and books. Afterwards, students reflected on their product and the process they went through in creatively coming up with their idea.

A lesson that involves creative skills or building has more impact on learners than simply reading, writing or even drawing. When students made constructions using materials to experiment with, they were able to make discoveries while building their projects. When offering construction as a form of play-based learning, it is important to have different options for the students to build with. Students also used modelling clay, building sticks and magnetic stick block toys to experiment with. They created their own construction materials by using cardboard and papier-mâché as well. Recycled materials were also a good option for students to use because they did not cost any money. Students used building blocks made up of wood, foam and plastic for these constructions.

When asked to construct in a lesson, the assignment was to come up with a specific final product or model that could represent a subject that students are studying and it could also be open-ended. In Grade 2, students built body systems such as the muscular or respiratory systems. In upper primary, students were asked to experiment and come up with a product to market and sell to investors. A goal was given in advance, for example, that they had to represent what they learnt about the topic in a creative structure; however, the experimental path that they took in order to reach that goal was full of choice and the result was unknown. Learning through building helps students to retain the information better than only reading facts in a book.

Learning more about nature and natural disasters in Grade 4 was reinforced by asking students to create buildings that should be able to withstand a specific type of natural disaster. Students needed a thorough understanding of the potential effects of the natural disaster on buildings before beginning. Through their experimentation, they then tested out an idea and adjusted their idea if it did not work out as planned. If their structure came down too easily, for example, they changed an aspect of the structure. One group decided to build more walls, for example. Finally, the group had to decide on the strongest structure. This type of group work also practises teamwork and is a great way for teachers to observe this social development.

Learning about mathematics in a play-based environment also creates a more interesting lesson than learning about measuring or equations purely out of a book. Converting various measurement scales in an environment of play also links this topic to real-life examples more concretely. Students were given hands-on manipulatives and various measuring tools to use through trial-and-error to make mathematical discoveries, for example. When students were studying algorithms in mathematics, they experimented with patterns in a game of Yahtzee and dominoes rather than only doing mathematical problems in a book. In a group, students took turns playing various roles. Some students rolled the dice, while some put the dominoes on the table and a couple of students wrote down the results for everyone to study later. Simply playing a game is different than play-based learning because students experiment more in play-based learning. In a simple game in which students can win or lose, there is more focus on simply winning and learning facts. Any time students learn through true play-based learning, it makes the subject more interesting because they have an active role in the choices and outcome of the learning process. This makes their learning more relevant to them because they were a large part of the process.

Imagining mathematical constructions and how specific mathematical concepts link together physically is beneficial to do in a constructive environment. Offering choices and allowing for experimentation is key, as always. Students have constructed building structures for mathematics using blocks, 2D shapes and 3D shapes. When students were given the freedom to think about mathematical structures and were able to be creative, it was more interesting and became easier to conceptualise these mathematical concepts.

Technology can also be an integral part of play-based learning. In Grade 4, students experimented, using design tools on tablets, in order to choose which graphic image they would produce. This allowed learners to explore various ideas creatively. This activity is also used for a variety of subjects, such as language or a specific unit. Students also used tablets to take photographs of objects that they believed display various forces. Examples of this were when they took pictures of parachutes that were thrown outside and floating boats made of modelling clay. Students also used tablets to make creative videos, promotional videos, podcasts and presentations; do research; and use creative platforms to express their ideas and reflect on their work.

The specialist

Specialist teachers give instruction in the arts, language, computational thinking and physical education (see also Chapter 4). The specialists also play an important role in giving students freedom of choice to experiment and learn from play-based learning. Examples of learning through play in the specialists' lessons can be role play, using language while constructing an object, acting out scenarios and making unique creations in the arts.

In a foreign language lesson like our Dutch lessons, teachers and students played an active role together in shaping vocabulary development. Students were encouraged to take on a role of someone in particular, such as a store clerk or captain of a sports team. When students mispronounced words or did not use proper grammar, the teacher repeated the sentences and they stated it properly in a way that kept the flow of the conversation going. This type of language correction keeps students confident and encourages them to try and speak as much as possible in the foreign language. During free play or when students were asked to construct an object, they were asked to focus on using a foreign language as they were playing. This was based on a theme and the students had word cards on hand that they could choose from to talk about. After students were done with free play or constructing an object, the students were asked to describe what they did and these answers were given in the foreign language.

In a physical education lesson, play-based learning occurs when students discuss team tactics and which position everyone will stand in. In advance, they would have already learnt about the variety of choices they have to choose from. They then discover what effect their final choice had on the play and they reflect on this later. This learning is open-ended in the regard that students will not know what the result will be. Even though a goal may or may not be made, the discussion itself and the trial-and-error process of discovering the effects of various tactics is not right or wrong. This strategising and collaboration definitely encourages teamwork as well.

During drama, early years students use role play to further develop their characters and discover how scenarios will play out. Students are given a box of scenario-specific props, and then the teacher gives students the freedom to play freely with the attributes and then discuss what they discovered afterwards. The drama teacher receives inspiration for the characters from the students and then helps the students to develop the characters further. Students have the freedom to improvise within the parameters of the assignment to see where the play takes them.

In a music lesson, students are already active by playing an instrument or singing, but they also create music within a framework, such as a chordal or a rhythmic pattern. Students come up with their own creations through experimentation. They are given a variety of instruments as well as a list of genres to choose from and then they discover which musical choices they like best through experimentation.

Just like the classroom teachers who create play-based learning lessons, specialists also make their lessons engaging and interactive through play. Many of the above ideas can also be transferred to other subjects as well.

PLAY-BASED LEARNING IN THE MIDDLE YEARS PROGRAMME

One might think that the play-based approach to teaching and learning is only applicable to primary school, but that could not be further from the truth. Learning through playing is essential in many subjects in MYP as well. The playing, however, looks a bit different in

MYP, where learning goals are more pressing, than it does in the early years where there is more time to explore and have free play. When given the chance, adolescents display a large degree of playfulness and creativity. As a teacher, it is very important to make use of this to enhance learning.

Current approach in science

In the science classes during MYP at ISUtrecht, we have a strong focus on practical activities. Often, the teacher will present the basics within a topic, and afterwards, the students are required to make hypotheses within the topic at hand, design their own lab experiments and use them to investigate their own hypotheses. When the students make the designs themselves, they will generally not be limited in what materials they can use, as long as it is within a reasonable price range and that the experiment is possible to perform at school within the time frame they are given. With this type of freedom, the students are given the opportunity to use their creativity and imagination to their fullest to come up with variables they can use to achieve different results. The students are given ample time to play around with ideas and discuss them with their peers and their teacher, to finally decide on an approach they would like to attempt in an actual experiment. This approach is making use of the students' innate ability to imagine things, and their curiosity to discover new things. Because this is in MYP, and not early or primary years, the play has to be framed within a specific learning goal, and it can, of course, be challenging to find the optimal balance between accommodating playfulness and enabling the students to learn what is required. At ISUtrecht, we believe that allowing the students to design their own lab experiments is one of many ways of doing this.

When the students use their own designs to perform lab experiments, they get to 'play around with materials' to see how they interact or to achieve different results with their own goals in mind. By using this approach, the students also get to experience what it is like to do hands-on research, which can be viewed as a sort of role play. The students have to take on the role of a scientist: acting differently than they usually do, by assuming a more serious approach to their work, being careful and precise in measuring materials and results. They also have to practise being careful when handling the different tools and equipment and they are using different words than usually when describing their process and results. They need to be more analytical and critical of their own work, in addition to actually wearing the costume of the scientist: the lab coat and safety goggles.

The students do not only get to perform their own experiments and learn from them, but they also get to observe their peers perform experiments that differ from their own. That way the students get a broader perspective within the topic as well as getting new ideas or approaches they can use the next time they investigate independently. This is not much different from what happens when young children play together and learn new games and skills from each other. By using this approach, the students make their own personal learning experiences and their own discoveries rooted in their own curiosity and interests, which we believe will enable the students to gain long-lasting knowledge and understanding, as well as achieving a high level of motivation and independence during class.

The future of play in the Middle Years Programme

Using their imagination, playing around with their own ideas and pretending to be a scientist are all part of the way a young adult plays, but it is perhaps not what young adults themselves would call 'playing'. In our day and age, computer technology is providing us with more possibilities to enhance learning than ever before. We have access to almost any type of information with just a click of a button, and we have endless ways of entertaining ourselves using our newly invented digital devices. With this technology comes a different type of play: *gaming*. Young adults are often very engaged in computer games and can spend hours on end playing games and interacting with their friends in a digital environment. At ISUtrecht, we see this as an opportunity. What if the students were given the chance to dive into the digital world of gaming and at the same time achieve learning goals? What if playing a fun and engaging computer game could help the students pass exams?

At ISUtrecht, we are trying to keep up with recent developments within computer technology, because we see how many doors it can open if applied correctly in the school environment. You can read more about our approach to this in Chapter 9, where we go into depth about *computational thinking*, and how we combine playing and coding as early as kindergarten and Grade 1.

One of our current goals on MYP, however, is to dive into the educational world of *virtual reality*: a technology that gives you the opportunity to go to the other side of the world, or into outer space and back without even leaving the room (see Figure 5.2). All you have to

Figure 5.2 MYP students using virtual reality during their science lesson at ISUtrecht

do is put on a headset and let yourself be amazed. With hand-controllers in addition to the headset, you also get the ability to interact with the virtual environment, using your whole body to move around and using your controllers to grab things as if they were in front of you.

Using this technology, we can have a whole class dive into a virtual version of the Atlantic Ocean to observe the plant and animal life there one lesson. In another lesson, the students might be able to combine atoms to make molecules using their own hands as if the students themselves were shrunk to the size of protons or quarks. The possibilities increase greatly when the walls of the classroom and sizes and distances no longer limit us, and the students will get to fully use and enjoy their innate curiosity and playfulness in a wide variety of ways both outside and inside the virtual world.

CONCLUSION

There are many ways educators can encourage creativity through engaging play-based activities. This is not only exciting for students, but it can also create a great opportunity for teachers to make observations during the entire process. Assessments can be made during free play as well as guided play and the topics which are assessed can be either decided on in advance or assessed from a longer list which stays relevant throughout the school year. Play-based teaching and learning is a win–win situation for both students and teachers. Students need prior information such as basic vocabulary, information or skills. If materials are new, let students play around with them and let them discover any limitations. Consider their emotional and social state of mind before delving in deep, because this affects how a child will play and how a group of players respond to learning. Research and reflection are a big part of play and should always be integrated to help advance the play and the environment. Finally, remember that play is fun, but also a serious way for learning.

- Play is not limited to a certain grade or subject.
- Emotional and social states of mind come before academics.
- Use the environment as your third pedagogue.
- Give students control of what they need for their play.
- Stand-alone lessons teach specific skills and support play.
- Technology can enhance play; embrace this and make use of it.
- Add materials or resources if you see that the students are ready for the next step.
- Do research in the meantime and evolve the stations along with the play.
- Teachers model play-based learning through their discoveries and teachings.
- Reflect on play and use these elements for future play.

Reflective questions

1. How do you facilitate and encourage the various types of play in your own classroom?

2. How can you set up your classroom in a way that fosters the students' need to partake in play-based activities?

3. How can you maximise your effectiveness as an observer during your students' play and discovery?

4. What types of activities can you develop that encourage creativity with various materials?

5. Which play-based activities could you include in your teaching to help your students develop their interpersonal skills?

6. If you teach adolescent students, how can you ensure that their playfulness is preserved and encouraged in their lessons at school?

REFERENCES

Hughes, B (1996) *A Playworker's Taxonomy of Play Types*. London: Playlink.

Kuyk, J J van and Groot Koerkamp, T (2002) *Piramide, Spelboek*. Arnhem: Citogroep.

Spel deel 1 Theoretisch Kader (nd). [online] Available at: www.slo.nl/downloads/archief/Spel_deel_1_Theoretisch_kader.pdf/ (accessed 15 April 2018).

Thornton, L (2014) *Bringing the Reggio Approach to your Early Years Practice*. London: Routledge.

Appendix 1: Unit play plan template

Station:	Station:	Station:
Knowledge:	Knowledge:	Knowledge:
Skills:	Skills:	Skills:
Add-ons:	Add-ons:	Add-ons:
Station:	Unit play plan	Station:
Knowledge:	Unit: [Name of unit]	Knowledge:
Skills:		Skills:
Add-ons:		Add-ons:
Station:	Station:	Station:
Knowledge:	Knowledge:	Knowledge:
Skills:	Skills:	Skills:
Add-ons:	Add-ons:	Add-ons:

Appendix 2: Form for play observation for early years

Form for play observation – early years

Child:	Date:
Date of birth:	Age:
Prior knowledge provided:	Goal of session/lesson:

Setting: The children have free play/guided play/structured play during XXX (enquiry stations/free play/golden time). The child is playing alone/together; his/her input is by XXX. He/She takes/shares/shows no responsibility during (most of) this session. The environment contains: XXX.

Type of play:

Rough and tumble play	Symbolic play	Socio-dramatic play	Creative play	Social play	Communication play
Dramatic play	Locomotor play	Imaginative play	Exploratory play	Fantasy play	Deep play
Mastery play	Object play	Role play	Recapitulative play	Digital play	

Shown level of play:	Desired level of play:	Guidance:
• Onlooker play • Solitary play • Parallel play • Associative play • Co-operative play • Collaborative play	• Onlooker play • Solitary play • Parallel play • Associative play • Co-operative play • Collaborative play	Audience, actor, props manager, stage director, script writer I said/did XXX ⇒ The child now does XXX

Photo/description before	Photo/description after

Appendix 3: Form for play observation for primary years

Form for play observation – primary years				
Child:			**Date:**	
Date of birth:			**Age:**	
Prior knowledge provided:			**Goal of session/lesson:**	
Setting: The children have free play/guided play/structured play during XXX (enquiry stations/free play/golden time). The child is playing alone/together; his/her input is by XXX. He/She takes/shares and shares/shows no responsibility during (most of) this session. The environment contains: XXX.				
Type of play:				
Rough and tumble play	Symbolic play	Socio-dramatic play	Creative play	Communication play
Dramatic play	Locomotor play	Imaginative play	Exploratory play	Deep play
Mastery play	Object play	Role play	Recapitulative play	
				Fantasy play
				Social play
				Digital play
Shown level of play:		**Desired level of play:**	**Guidance:**	
• Onlooker play		• Onlooker play	Audience, player, journalist, lawyer, coach.	
• Solitary play		• Solitary play	I said/did XXX ⇒ The child now does XXX	
• Parallel play		• Parallel play		
• Associative play		• Associative play		
• Co-operative play		• Co-operative play		
• Collaborative play		• Collaborative play		
Photo/description before			**Photo/description after**	

6 Concept-based teaching and learning

Eryn Wiseman, Kelsey Middleton and Sridevi Brahmadathan

INTRODUCTION

Concepts in education are not new; they have been taught for decades, just not in primary schools. It seemed that concepts were something only more mature minds could cope with. You needed the basics to think about concepts. Nonsense, of course. When an infant first decides to put something in their mouth or pick something up to examine more closely, they are developing their conceptual understanding of that item, its place in the world and what it means to that child. Every child that partakes in learning mathematics is developing their understanding of the concepts of number and operation, moving from the concrete or symbolic to the abstract.

Teaching conceptually is not really new either; different approaches have been described by Maria Montessori, Jean Piaget and Benjamin Bloom. Then more specifically, and more recently, by Lynn Erickson, Ron Richart and the dynamic duo of Wiggins and McTighe. Concepts have been defined in various ways by the above-mentioned scholars. The most used definition of a concept comes from Lynn Erickson and was first published in 1995. She now defines concepts as mental constructs drawn from a topic or process that transfer to new situations and contexts (Erickson et al, 2017). In order to help us recognise concepts, she also provides the following characteristics of a concept. A concept:

- *is identified by one or two words (nouns) or a short phrase;*
- *is abstract (to different degrees), timeless and universal;*
- *has examples that share common attributes;*
- *transfers across new situations and contexts;*
- *can be micro (specific) or macro (broad).*

(Erickson et al, 2017)

Figure 6.1 attempts to replace the model described by Erickson et al alongside the International Baccalaureate (IB) model of concepts. Carla Marschall and Rachel French (2018) build upon Erickson's original definition to explain that macro concepts are broad disciplinary or interdisciplinary concepts and are used to add breadth to an enquiry while micro concepts are specific and disciplinary. The IB names seven key concepts: *form, function, change, connection, causation, perspective* and *responsibility*. From the above definition, these are macro concepts. All other concepts are called *related concepts* in IB jargon. To illustrate all of the above: *decisions* is a concept; it is intangible and therefore

```
          Macro concepts
     Transdisciplinary in nature

IB-related concepts                    IB key concepts
All other concepts                     7 specific concepts

          Micro concepts
       Disciplinary in nature
```

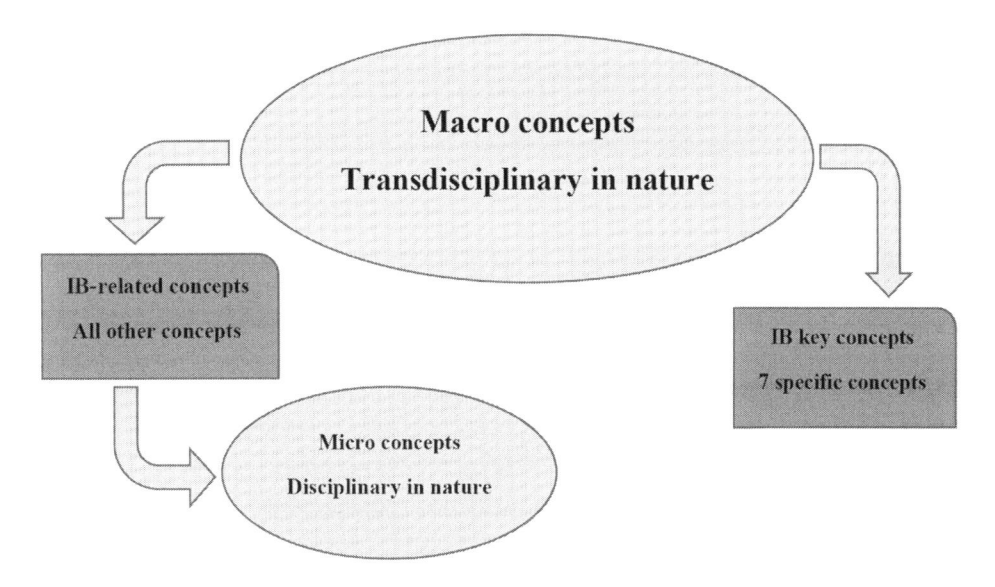

Figure 6.1 Macro and micro concepts

abstract, it is timeless, has multiple examples and is transferable. It is a related concept and would usually be defined as a macro concept as you can look at decisions and decision-making across the disciplines.

In this chapter, we provide an understanding of how concepts can be used to strengthen a school's curriculum. We also provide snapshots of how teachers can use concepts in their daily practice. In the final part of this chapter, we explore some of the challenges of teaching with concepts in the lead.

A PERSONAL LEARNING JOURNEY

Author 1 of this chapter first encountered concept-based teaching and learning when she went to work at an IB world school. She started learning about how to use and think about concepts in the classroom. It was challenging. It required another layer of thinking when she was planning, teaching and assessing. But she could see the absolute value of this as an approach in this age where traditional information, otherwise known as facts, were available at the touch of a keyboard.

However, the author always felt something was lacking with the key concepts as the only concepts to teach through. They are, as mentioned before, hugely broad and therefore hugely applicable, but at most times, she often found them too broad. When approaching a topic through these lenses and nothing else, she lacked the depth in the subject area and the rigor within the discipline. The IB has a list of what they term related concepts but provides little support as to how these fit within its framework, nor how to use them. So, it was up to the educators to educate themselves on this matter.

The author's most effective education came when she was introduced to Lynn Erickson's work. She started reading Erickson's books and finally was able to join a workshop. This is where her eyes were opened to the need for more specialised concepts within a subject area. If an educator does not use subject-specific concepts, they will lose the coherence and understanding necessary to be successful within that subject. What she also learnt is that the subject-specific concepts also grow more specific, as one specialises within that subject area.

WHOLE SCHOOL ALIGNMENT

If in pre-school and kindergarten, learning about animals and plants in life science can be enough, in lower primary, the students will need more and could explore more disciplinary concepts such as *offspring*, *features* and *variation* in the life sciences. Then, as a student moves up in the grades, the conceptual understanding goes deeper into the discipline, introducing more subject-specific concepts. However, the key concepts are still extremely important as a lens through which to focus the enquiry and to transfer across the disciplines. One year a class might enquire into the life sciences through the lens of *form* and *change*, while another year might focus on *connection* and *responsibility*.

At the International School Utrecht (ISUtrecht), we have been working to achieve this conceptual growth. One area that we have had quite a bit of success in this is in the transdisciplinary theme of '*How we organise ourselves*' (see Table 6.1).

Table 6.1 Conceptual understandings across grade levels

Grade level	Conceptual understandings	Depth of conceptual understanding explained
Kindergarten	People make significant contributions to their community. People participate individually and collectively in response to community challenges. Rules and authority figures provide order, security and safety in the home, school and larger community. Good citizens act responsibly with the interest of the larger community in mind.	You see that the concept of a person or people is expanded to include the community, authority figures and citizens.
Grade 1	Goods go through a process before a consumer can buy them. The needs of the consumers determine the provision of goods. Consuming a good is always a choice. The process of production relies on occupational skills.	Here people are described in the role of a consumer, deepening the concept of what a person or citizen is, and expanding our role in the community.

Grade level	Conceptual understandings	Depth of conceptual understanding explained
Grade 2	Individuals and groups of people share and borrow from others to form a community. Cultures, traditions and religion bring diversity to a community. The number of people, use of space and types of buildings determine the type of community. A community has both private and public spaces.	Here the concept of people is deepened into individuals and groups. The roles in the community are also expanded to include cultural contributions.
Grade 3	Limitations force us to make a choice. The choice of one product results in the loss of another choice. Consumers trade for goods. Information is an important part of making a choice.	With this unit, we revisit consumption and make it personal, namely how to make good consumer choices. This combines the responsibility of the community to the consumer with the responsibility of the consumer to act appropriately, bringing both sides together.
Grade 4	Communities develop products and services in order to fulfil their needs and wants. A marketplace brings opportunities and challenges. An economic system needs decision-making and responsibility. A product or service needs development and marketing.	This unit looks at economics from a producer's point of view instead of a consumer, as Grade 3 did. We delve deeper into the economic way of thinking.
Grade 5	People make decisions in order to function as an effective community. Roles in a group are dependent on each other. Consequences are directly linked to how a decision-making system is organised. Each person within a group is accountable for their choices and the impact of their contribution.	At the end of primary, students are introduced to the ideas of leadership and government with this unit, bringing their understanding of a community to its pinnacle.

This theme focuses on community systems. The learning in kindergarten starts with a unit where students are challenged to understand that people make significant contributions to their community. Within this unit, students learn how to become a good citizen through participation, understanding why rules are important and acting responsibly. In Grade 1, the students move into the field of economics with the understanding that goods go through a process before a consumer can buy them. While this does not explicitly lead on from the prior unit, the idea of people as consumers is a deepening understanding of our role in a community. Students explore community and personal needs, the skills required to provide for these needs and that consumers always have a choice. In Grade 2, we return to the community in a wider sense: a city, with students understanding that cities are designed and structured to meet a purpose. Here students build on the understandings established in kindergarten, adding the idea of diversity, traditions and culture, as the need for public and private spaces. In Grade 3, we revisit the economic side of our community to understand that consumers are responsible for making informed choices when purchasing a product or service. Students are introduced to the personal side of economics by exploring advertising, choice and finance. Grade 4 remains in the realm of economics, while understanding communities develop products and services in order to fulfil their needs and wants. Here, the ideas introduced in Grade 1 are deepened into specialisation within an organisation. The concept of decision-making is introduced, and the idea of responsibility is expanded upon from kindergarten. Finally, Grade 5 works towards understanding that people make decisions in order to function as an effective community. More community roles are introduced in this unit, including leaders and decision-makers, and responsibility is expanded to include accountability.

Another aspect of our school that is driven by concepts is our curriculum documents. Over the course of our existence, we have been steadily moving towards curriculum documents that describe learning as developmental phases, rather than grade-, year- or age-level outcomes. In more traditional scope and sequences, each grade has a set of skills which the teacher endeavours to teach the students and the students endeavour to master. There is generally also a list of facts that the students must memorise, or at least be familiar with. Once the student has acquired that knowledge and mastered those skills, then the student is deemed ready to progress to the next grade. If they have not done so, the consequence is often retention. If a student does so quickly, acceleration is suggested so that the student receives more facts and skills and does not stagnate in the grade already mastered.

A very broad and relatively simple understanding in life science is that most living things need water, food and air. This can be taught by studying plants, animals or humans, it does not really matter which. The facts of studying each can lead to this understanding, but it is when you ask students to transfer the understanding that real concept formation occurs. A student can choose to study their pet bird and learn all about what a bird needs to survive, but the challenge is to ask: *Is that only true for birds, or other animals as well?*

During or after the study of their pet, the student might understand something like: '*Animals eat plants or seeds for food*'. So, the next challenge is to transfer to other animals: '*What do they eat?*' They might then broaden their understanding to: '*Animals eat plants, or other animals, for food'*. Now, to transfer to plants: *'What do they "eat"'?* After that study, a student should now understand that plants and animals both need to take in air and water and animals need to take in food. In addition, plants need to take in light. This is basically the broad idea we wanted them to understand.

These three understandings, leading to the one big understanding, would constitute the first phase of life sciences and when those ideas have been understood, the student is developmentally ready to move to the next phase in scientific understanding. Though this is somewhat simplified for this example, this is our approach.

PLANNING FOR CONCEPT-BASED TEACHING

In order to plan for a concept-based unit, it is vital to decide which concepts will drive the unit and how the teacher will support the students in developing their understanding of those concepts. This is the goal of concept-based education: a deep understanding of the concepts that we will be confronted with in our daily life. So, if we know what our goal is and work back from that, then the planning is backwards by design. As explained by Grant Wiggins and Jay McTighe (2005) in their book *Understanding by Design*, the basic steps are as follows.

1. As stated above, the teaching team identifies the goal, in other words they state what the learners should know, understand and be able to do after instruction.

2. Then the team needs to determine what types of assessments and engagements would serve as evidence of whether students have achieved the desired outcome. They also need to determine how and on what they will give feedback.

3. Finally, the team plans and develops said engagements, including the scaffolding needed to ensure success.

(McTighe and Wiggins, 2005)

The following examples of each step illustrate this process.

Identifying the goal

When starting the planning of a brand-new unit, we ask ourselves first: *What do we want to teach about?* That becomes a brainstorm of ideas, words, topics, books, clips, quotes and anything else that inspires the teachers about the unit. Then the team analyses the ideas, tickling out the driving concepts, main pieces of knowledge and key skills, these last two often driven by the school's curriculum. Once that has been determined, they start to write generalisations.

Generalisations are statements of conceptual relationships and are the fundamental guide for learning in your unit. These statements include driving concepts that you want to develop with your learners. At Primary Years Programme (PYP) schools, you usually have one broad, overarching generalisation that becomes your *central idea* and this is supported by *lines of enquiry*. At ISUtrecht, we write our lines of enquiry as generalisations as well, but this is not common practice at most IB schools.

Determining assessments and feedback

Students can provide evidence of their learning in a variety of ways. It is important to allow students freedom through enquiry with solidly planned lessons that allow them to dig deeper into the concept they are exploring. This allows them to do their own thinking and learning, promoting student agency and making deeper connections.

One tool to use is *Visible Thinking* routines from Project Zero (nd). These provide an excellent set of routines for students to scaffold their thinking in an organised way and allow them to think on a deeper level and enable them to develop their own understanding of a concept (see Figure 6.2).

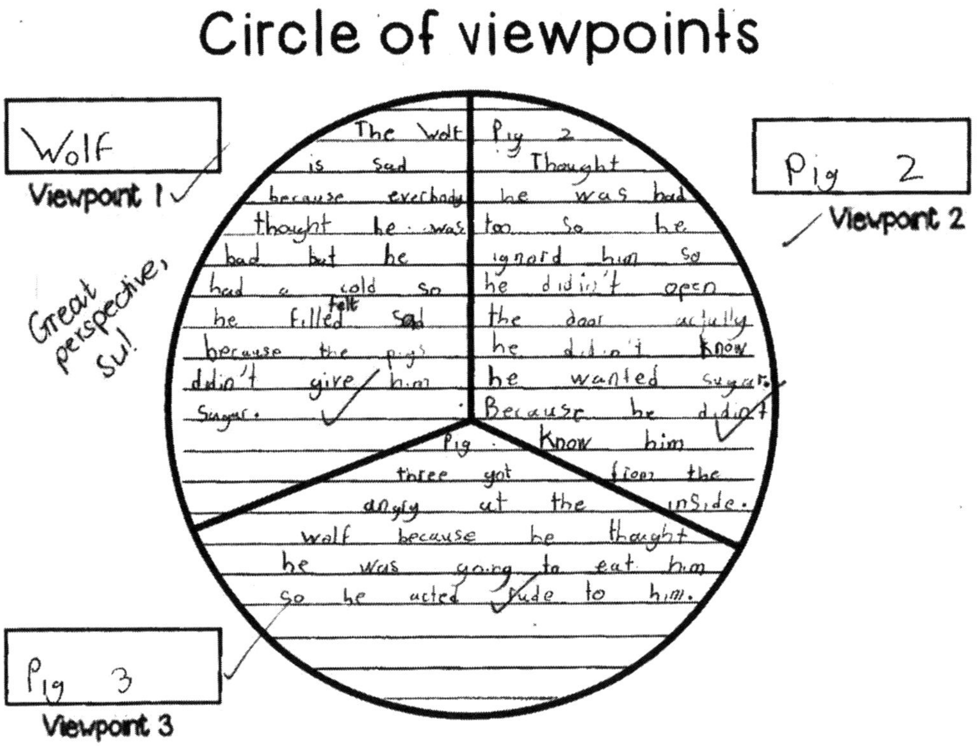

Figure 6.2 Circle of viewpoints

We used this routine to show our understanding that each character has their own perspective or opinion and that we sometimes only see one side.

Another way of collecting assessment data is to ask students to explain their learning. So, as teachers, we often look to see if a child can place pen to paper to assess their level of understanding. Time spent asking probing, provocative questions in the beginning, middle or end of any unit will give a good gauge of where the child is at in the learning journey. This allows you as a teacher to then adjust and revise what it is you are teaching. The concept can be threefold.

1. What do my children know?
2. What do they have misconceptions about?
3. What are they still not sure about?

Simply asking these questions can go a long way to enhancing the learning and building of concepts in your classroom. These reflections can take the form of a journal, log or just a collection of sticky notes (see Figure 6.3).

Figure 6.3 Field trip understandings

Graphic organisers come in very handy as a tool for collecting data on skills and knowledge, and, depending on how and why you are using them, can also be used to assess understanding (see Figure 6.4).

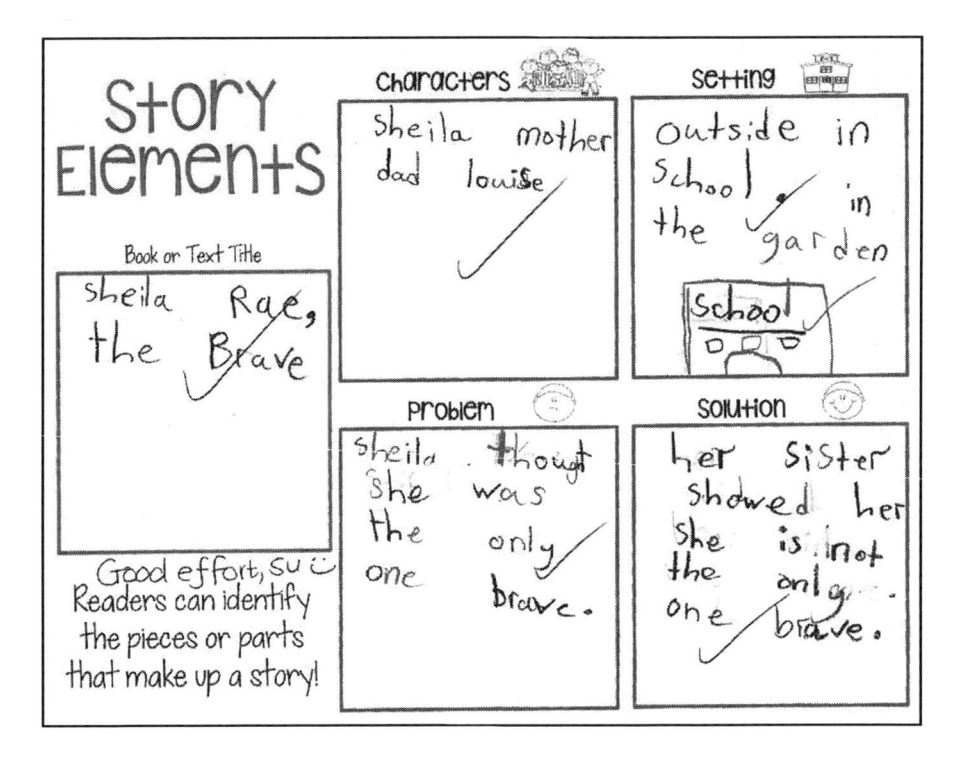

Figure 6.4 Story elements graphic organiser

One final way of assessing student understanding is recording students' generalisations. Through scaffolding and organising, the teacher guides students to come up with their own statements to describe the relationships between concepts. Both students and teachers can then refer to this growing understanding throughout the unit (see Figures 6.5 and 6.6).

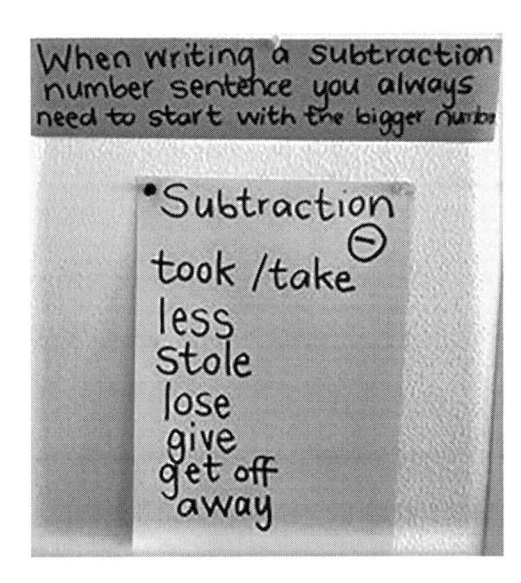

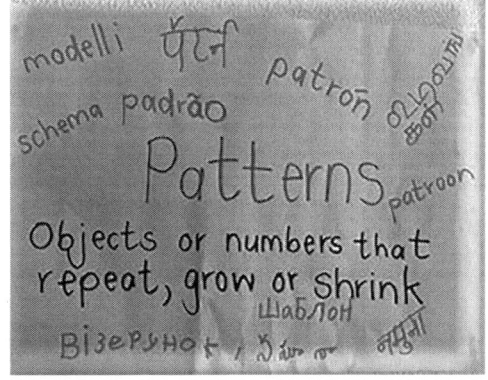

Figures 6.5 and 6.6 Mathematical understandings

Developing engagements

When starting off a unit using concepts, it is vital to gauge how much the students already understand about the driving concepts. This can be done in many ways but most important is for students to define the words, describe connections between concepts and show some affinity towards the ideas. Following that introductory set, the teaching team needs to have some way of introducing new concepts or deepening current understandings, while addressing any misconceptions noticed. Table 6.2 clearly lays out a set of steps a teacher could use to help students develop their conceptual understandings.

Table 6.2 Effective concept formation practices

Practice	How to use
Provide a clear definition*	Although definitions may vary or be unavailable for particular concepts, concepts that are socially constructed often have an accepted meaning, for example, *family, community*, etc (Keil, 1992). Where possible, provide students with a clear definition to support their exploration of factual examples. Students can improve upon these definitions over a unit.
Start with the 'best' examples	When introducing a new concept to students, use the most *obvious* examples to highlight attributes of the concept (Jonassen, 2006; Markman, 1991). Providing students with exceptions to the rule should come only *after* a concept has been initially formed.
Use examples and non-examples	Ask students to compare a number of examples and non-examples of a concept, including those that are less obvious (Markle and Tiemann, 1970; Tsamir et al, 2008).
Stress relevant attributes	Direct students to relevant attributes of a concept during sorting or grouping activities to ensure that they do not focus on irrelevant ones (Keil, 1992). For example, *number of sides* is a relevant attribute of a triangle, but size is not.
Compare and contrast using factual and conceptual examples	When exploring a concept, invite students to explore examples and non-examples at the factual and conceptual level. For example, migration can be developed by looking at various migration case studies (factual), as well as by comparing migration to the idea of a journey (conceptual).
Promote a culture of sustained thinking	When engaging students in discussion, make use of wait time and stick with a chid until thinking is clarified and reasoning has been provided (Durkin, 1993; Ingram and Elliot, 2015). Plan questions in advance to eliminate 'rapid fire' questioning, which can discourage student sharing and risk taking.

*In deductive concept formation activities.
(Marschall and French, 2018, p 108)

A useful concept formation strategy was provided by one of our former colleagues. He came up with a very effective routine he dubbed the *concept crunch*. He quickly discovered, in Grade 2 initially, that, for students to really understand the purpose of our enquiry, and their role in it, they needed practical and meaningful connections to the key and related concepts. Since each line of enquiry was explicitly linked to at least one concept, he felt that students needed opportunities to build bridges between life as they saw it and the content in their enquiry. So, concept crunch was born – necessity is the mother of invention and all that. They worked in the Grade 2 planning team to come up with a variety of engagements, from simple sorting activities and role playing to open-enquiry prompts and activities that organically stemmed from the interests and/or questions of individual students; putting the students in situations where they could teach each other was also an integral component. It worked well in Grade 2. The teacher then moved to Grade 5 and saw that the concept crunch worked again, ergo every grade level could benefit from this. The teacher would simply have to establish and push the boundaries to suit their students.

Many of the engagements described above already incorporate enquiry and other approaches to teaching. Although it is possible to teach a concept-based curriculum without enquiry-based approaches, the two marry so well, they are hard to think of separately (see Chapter 7 for enquiry-based teaching). A teacher should vary their choices for a balance across the teaching continuum (see Figure 6.7).

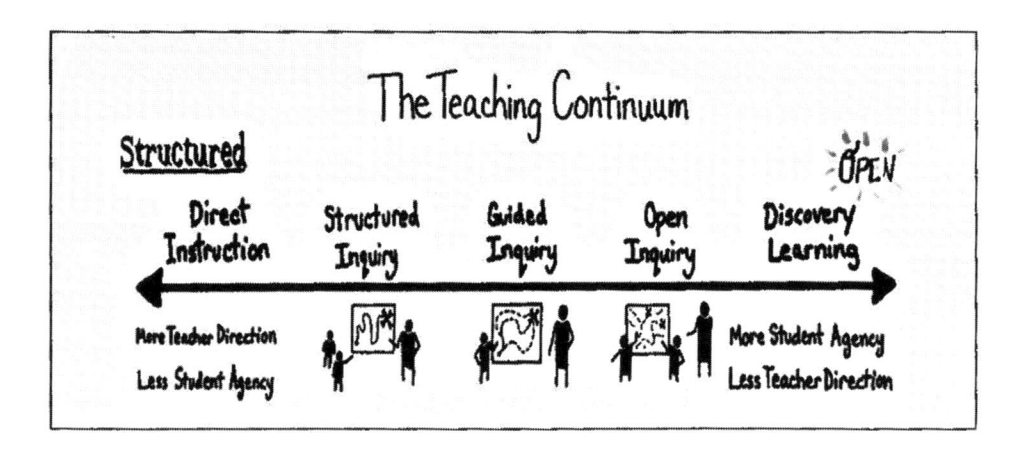

Figure 6.7 Approaches in the teaching continuum
(Marschall and French, 2018, p 8)

The teaching continuum provides an excellent illustration of a variety of teaching approaches within a concept-based classroom. It is a structure designed by Rachel French and Carla Marschall that guides you through a variety of ways to approach teaching your concepts. Within conceptual teaching, you move away from the 'teacher-centred' approach, to a more guiding or partner role for students.

It is a teacher's job to scaffold and model meaning for learners through a variety of teaching engagements. The aim of this is to increase student agency and decrease teacher direction, allowing the teacher to become more of a facilitator for students'

Concept-based teaching and learning

journey of learning. Teachers often have the misconception that enquiry teaching is removing all teacher-directed moments, and for a teacher having taught and schooled through the 'traditional system', this can be particularly scary. However, meaningful enquiry is a mixture of approaches including direct teaching moments.

The approaches depicted in the continuum are as follows.

- *Direct instruction* – The direct modelling or frontloading of information without scheduled time for enquiry into the topic. This is at one end of the teaching continuum and is a very structured part of learning. It is essentially teacher-driven with very little input from the students. As mentioned above, there are moments for this within a concept-based classroom.
- *Structured enquiry* – This is a situation where the teacher sets up specific activities for children, determines how long they will be at each station and what concept he/she wants the students to explore.
- *Guided enquiry* – Here, the teacher is responsible for providing a topic, and the students can come up with their own understandings and solutions.
- *Open enquiry* – This is a scenario whereby the students determine the questions, purpose and solution for the enquiry. The teacher is there to provide a mentor role.
- *Discovery learning* – Teachers will model an example for students and then students will demonstrate their understanding of concepts through exploration and completing experiments of their own without guidance from a teacher. This is also sometimes called genius hour, passion projects or 20 per cent time.

The following tables are example lessons for concept development. Table 6.3 is a lesson plan of a unit on city planning and Table 6.4 of a unit focusing on the concept of decision and how decision-making is important to function as an effective community. As the students proceed with the tasks, the teacher will take a note of the different strategies and arguments used by the students to make a decision.

Table 6.3 Grade 2 lesson on city planning

Grade 2 **Transdisciplinary theme:** How we organise ourselves **Unit:** City planning		**Targeted generalisation:** A community has both private and public spaces.
Guiding questions: • What are examples of public spaces? (factual) • What are examples of private spaces? (factual) • What makes a space public or private? (factual)	**Knowledge and skills:** • Learner knows the meaning of 'public spaces'. • Learner knows the meaning of 'private spaces'. • Learners provide own definition for the two ideas.	**Assessment:** Anecdotal notes of group thinking process. Learners use 'what makes you say that' routine to record thoughts.

→

• Can a space be both public and private? (debatable) • What spaces are public and private around our school? (factual) • How should public and private spaces be treated? (conceptual) • Why does a community need both types of spaces? (conceptual)	• Learner can give examples for both concepts and record their understanding. • Learner is co-operative within a partnership/group setting.	**Concepts:** function public space private space

Introduction:

Learners need to define:

1. public spaces;

2. private spaces.

They first work individually to come up with a definition for each word and then pair up and create a combined definition for both concepts. Then they can pair up with another pair to make a group of four and re-tweak their definition. This builds conceptual understanding and helps to challenge misconceptions. Learners can read one another's definitions.

Main lesson:

Using the list brainstormed in the previous lesson (ie *things we need in the city to survive*), learners classify public and private spaces. Learners can work on their own, in pairs or in small groups. Groups visit each other's work and use the routine '*what makes you say that*' to discuss and justify reasons for their thinking. The teacher is facilitating the discussion, asking questions and helping to address any misconceptions the learners might have.

Plenary:

Learners generate a group definition, with examples that will go up on the unit wall. Students leave the room with the following question to ponder: *Can a space be both private and public? Explain why.* (This will be the opening to our next lesson on this line of enquiry.)

Table 6.4 Grade 5 lesson on decision-making

Grade 5 **Transdisciplinary theme:** How we organise ourselves **Unit:** Decisions		**Targeted generalisation:** People make decisions in order to function as an effective community.
Guiding questions: • Do you like making your own decisions? (factual) • When do you think that it is a good idea to tell a person what to do? (factual) • Do you like it when people tell you what to do? (factual)	**Knowledge and skills:** • Learner knows that every community makes decisions.	**Related concepts:** decisions need want

• Is decision-making difficult? (conceptual/debatable) • Were your decisions based on emotion or reason? (factual) • Was it easy to come to a unanimous decision? (factual) • How did you come to a decision? (factual) • How do we take decisions? Is there a set process? (factual)	• Learner demonstrates how decisions are made in groups.	**Key concepts:** function

Introduction:

- Do you like making your own decisions?
- When do you think that it is a good idea to tell a person what to do?
- Do you like it when people tell you what to do?

Children are expected to give varied answers and examples. Start noting down their ideas on the white board.

Main lesson:

After the discussion, children watch the Sesame Street video www.youtube.com/watch?v=0NpQronsFic

Children are asked to list the different decision that Georgie made.

- How did Layal help Georgie make a decision?
- Is decision-making difficult?

Learners use the thinking routine '*think, pair, share*' to answer.

The teachers guide the discussion by asking '*How do we make decisions in a group?*' To further the discussion, the teacher divides the class into groups of five and introduces a scenario where the groups have to make decisions unanimously.

Introduce 'plane' scenario:

You are all on a plane that has crashed in a jungle. The plane will explode in ten minutes and you have time to take three of these items from the plane. If they do not make a unanimous decision, the aeroplane will crash and they will have nothing at all.

After ten minutes, the class generates thoughts on how groups make decisions.

24 empty glass bottles 12 plastic bottles of water Five warm sweaters A box of matches	First aid kit Radio An axe A gun with 20 bullets A bag with five big blankets	A bag with ten magazines Inflatable life raft (four people) Insect spray Sewing kit Flashlight

Plenary:

Children identify needs and wants as factors affecting decisions and the importance of roles in a group to make decisions. Children continue this lesson to consider the role of emotions in decision-making.

Once students have had time to develop their understandings and examine relationships between concepts through exploring different case studies, scenarios and factual examples, it becomes time to plan for them to transfer and generalise. Helping children to make deep connections that promote transferable understanding reflects the main ideas and reasoning behind concept-based education. This allows learners to formulate their own grasp on something, allowing for misconceptions to be addressed and then a deep connection to a concept to be concluded. The idea is not to teach content for the sake of teaching content, but to really equip learners with conceptual understandings to use their skills for a multitude of opportunities.

THE CHALLENGES TO TEACHING CONCEPTUALLY

Teaching through this method brings immense value for students but poses certain challenges for the teacher. An anonymous author wrote, '*Don't miss out on something great just because it is difficult*'. This sums up concept-based teaching. Although it takes a lot of effort and hard work to plan, assess and assist in the transfer of knowledge for your students, the results are often surprising. However, there are distinct challenges that one can face and finding solutions can take collaborative planning and learning from others who may be experts in specific fields.

The following are some challenges the teachers at ISUtrecht came up with when teaching conceptually.

- Many parents struggle to accept, understand and support this way of teaching; educating them can be difficult and time-consuming.
- Similarly, learners take time to adapt to this way of teaching especially when they come from a more traditional system; this also requires much teacher input.
- Students still acquiring the language of instruction struggle to make meaning of their learning at the beginning of the school year and this can lead to frustration on their part.
- Concepts can be very abstract, and learners can struggle to understand them at first; this results in initial teaching tending to be more explicit rather than enquiry-based.
- The conceptual lens that you are teaching through can be extremely broad and this can be challenging for the teacher to always plan appropriate learning engagements.

The quotations below from teachers further illustrate the challenges of teaching conceptually.

> *Modeling and teaching the kids HOW to think conceptually in the beginning of the year is key. In the beginning when I get students, they have just been told what to do their whole life and some have never had to think on their own. Starting the process of thinking, showing them to think conceptually at the beginning of the year is a lot of work, but as the year progresses, you can really see that a lot of them are starting to think conceptually.*

The biggest challenge for me when I teach conceptually is making sure that I have touched enough all of the topics necessary, such as skills and other content. There needs to be a balance between how much time is spent on exploring the concept and how much time is spent on other content and skills. I find it necessary to keep a very structured plan as to how much time I spend on all topics to make sure that each topic is covered properly.

Making sure the concepts are broad enough and remembering to always make connections to the big picture with the kids.

I find concept-based teaching to be a very nice idea in practice, though the implementation of it on a daily basis is challenging. I find it hard to link a full series of lessons together that will always ensure the optimum learning process for students. I find that the easiest way to combat this is to constantly ask guided questions to students to lead them to this greater concept meaning.

THE VALUE OF TEACHING CONCEPTUALLY

Despite the challenging nature of implementing a concept-based curriculum, the benefits far outweigh the challenges. In most schools, but especially in international schools, the students arrive with completely different educational backgrounds. At our school, a class of eight year-olds may have students that have followed formal schooling for four years already, and some that have only been attending school for one year. Some countries or schools may teach reading from the age of three and others start at seven or eight. Topics in science and social studies vary enormously. So, we need to accommodate that variance as flexibly as possible. At ISUtrecht, we believe that the traditional front-loading approach to teaching is not the best way to meet our students' needs. This is one of the reasons we teach using a concept-based approach.

Another reason why this approach is valuable is that we do not need to dictate a set of facts that must be known. With our growing access to information, there are simply too many facts to teach and our curriculum can become 'crowded' and teachers feel that they need to scramble to cover all the facts. Conceptual understanding can come through many different facts, and most importantly through transfer from one situation to another. This shifts the time to deep discussion and sharing of ideas.

A third, and connected reason, is that citizens in the twenty-first century will need to participate in intercultural communication, critical thinking, technological integration and so much more. Our students rely on us to prepare them for these new expectations and needs. As Lynn Erickson puts it:

Conceptual thinking requires the ability to critically examine factual information; relate to prior knowledge; see patterns and connections; draw out significant understandings at the conceptual level; evaluate the truth of the understandings across time or situations; and, often, use the conceptual understanding to creatively solve a problem or create a new product, process, or idea.

(Erickson, 2006, p 19)

With anything, there are always challenges and the light at the end of the tunnel. Below are some examples of personal experiences from some of our teachers about their experiences teaching conceptually.

I enjoy concept-based teaching because it focuses on what we really want students to take away from the message, rather than a lot of busy work and spoon feeding. It also keeps the topics relevant.

Concept-based teaching challenges learners to broaden their understandings and grow their interests in what they actually want to learn, not just what the textbook prescribes.

I enjoy teaching this way because you are able to link different skills in a number of different ways, and also teach different skills through these concepts. For example: Research skills, communication skills and thinking skills.

This way of teaching allows students to learn a concept through a variety of lenses, broadening their interest, application and transfer of knowledge.

CONCLUSION

Concept-based teaching encourages authentic learning opportunities for our students that focus on the big picture and making meaning of their world and the problems within it. The traditional idea behind content-driven engagements has shifted due to our ever-increasing access to information at our fingertips. This approach to teaching encourages students to become lifelong learners as well as global citizens who make a difference, however small. They are able to transfer their skills and understandings within a variety of situations and display conceptual values that they live out, not just read on the classroom wall.

This way of teaching requires flexibility to meet the needs of the students where they are at. Planning is key and displaying a very good understanding of the concepts yourself as a teacher really aids in the transfer of excellent conceptual understanding. The idea of making learning meaningful, and not just because they need to learn something, is at the core of concept-based teaching. We hope that this chapter has convinced you that although there can be challenges to this approach, there are also positives that can certainly start to outweigh the difficulties that one might face.

Reflective questions

1. How would concepts fit into curriculum mapping?
2. What value would a concept-based curriculum have over the more traditional approach with regard to:
   - reducing the stress of needing to 'cover' everything;
   - helping higher level thinking;
   - creating connections;
   - sharing diversity and human commonality;
   - supporting multi-age groupings.
3. How could a teacher change a more traditional theme into a concept-based unit?
4. How could you use generalisations with younger students?
5. How do thinking routines support conceptual understanding?

REFERENCES

Erickson, H L (2006) *Concept-based Curriculum and Instruction for the Thinking Classroom*. Thousand Oaks, CA: Corwin Press.

Erickson, H L, Lanning, L A and French, R (2017) *Concept-based Curriculum and Instruction for the Thinking Classroom*. Thousand Oaks, CA: Corwin Press.

Marschall, C and French, R (2018) *Concept-based Inquiry in Action. Strategies to Promote Transferable Understanding*. Thousand Oaks, CA: Corwin Press.

McTighe, J and Wiggins, G (2005) *Understanding by Design*. Alexandria, VA: ASCD.

Project Zero (nd) *Visible Thinking*. [online] Available at: www.pz.harvard.edu/projects/visible-thinking (accessed 12 September 2020).

7 Enquiry-based teaching and learning

Anne Brandwagt and Brian Lynam

INTRODUCTION: WHAT IS ENQUIRY-BASED LEARNING?

Before starting, it is important to understand the pedagogy, which has been defined as *'any conscious activity by one person designed to enhance learning in another'* (Watkins and Mortimore, 1999, p 3). Stemming from this, an enquiry-based learning therefore draws on pedagogy which is based upon certain teaching and learning methods. It develops student-centred research and investigation and student autonomy and offers a platform that stimulates discussion and collaboration among peers, all of which fall neatly under the principles of constructivism. This type of learning is viewed as a social process in which a common goal and exploration of ideas is conducted through interacting experiences and language (Cross, 1996).

Enquiry-based learning is a key component of modern educational practice across many international schools and educations. A keen practitioner of enquiry-based learning is Kath Murdoch, who proposes that

> *inquiry teaching has often been described using the metaphor of a journey. It's like travelling with your students to a destination that I, as the (active) guide, can see at least some of the tips of the trees, the church spires – I have some markers on the horizon. Gradually, the view reveals itself to my fellow travellers. They don't all see it the way I do, and they don't necessarily see it the same way or at the same time as their companions do, but we have some common understanding and are enriched by our diversity. And we learn a lot along the way. As an inquiry teacher, you lead and guide, but you must also be prepared to be led and be guided in turn.*
>
> (Murdoch, 2015, p 16)

As proponents of enquiry-based thinking and learning at International School Utrecht (ISUtrecht), we also believe that the very journey and guiding process makes even the true definition of what makes the most effective enquiry-based learning an ongoing process. The best definition that encompasses our core beliefs about the enquiry process is best encapsulated by the old proverb *'Tell me and I forget. Teach me and I remember. Involve me and I learn'*. This is the attitude that we aim to foster in our school environment and teaching practices. In later parts of this chapter, we directly outline how these enquiry-based learning beliefs and principles manifest themselves in the overall planning and learning process, the strategies we find the most effective to maximise active student participation and how to optimise the learning environment (ie classroom setting) to allow students develop their thinking skills.

There are many benefits to enquiry-based learning, which we feel are increasingly important to children in the age of technology and change today, where future employment opportunities may require skills and thinking capacities that were not needed, or indeed promoted, since the industrial revolution of the 1800s. At ISUtrecht, we believe that the children of tomorrow need to be flexible, creative and resilient towards the future challenges that will inevitably come. With this in mind, our belief is that an enquiry-based learning provides a platform for the students to develop these key skills. At ISUtrecht, we have seen success in these aspects as well, such as our students' ability to research and plan the unit together, inventing products and being entrepreneurs and taking ownership of their learning.

DIFFERENT TYPES OF ENQUIRY

Trevor MacKenzie (2018) explains when students choose how they would like to show their learning, delve into their strengths, interests, and learning styles, amazing things are bound to happen. In his book, he describes four types of enquiry: *confirmation enquiry*, *structured enquiry*, *guided enquiry* and *free enquiry* (see Figure 7.1). His advice is to not throw your learners into the deep end of the enquiry pool without empowering them with the types of student enquiry first.

Figure 7.1 Types of student enquiry

Structured enquiry

In terms of structured enquiry, this is centred on the idea that the teacher is in complete control of the classroom environment, that is, the resources, research questions, learning engagements and assessment criteria. There is little or no room for student input into the enquiry process.

Controlled enquiry

In a controlled enquiry lesson, the teacher decides the essential questions for students to delve into and organises various resources to be utilised in the enquiry classroom. Students' use of resources is limited and controlled, yet students are responsible for making their own findings on the research questions.

Guided enquiry

In the guided section of the enquiry process, the teacher allows student ownership by providing a small selection of research questions that they choose to enquire into accordingly. The students will select the resources to locate the answers and decide how they will present their findings.

Free enquiry

In the free enquiry process, students are in charge of their own research questions, select the resources to be used in the journey and create their own end products. The role of the teacher is to support and facilitate the students in their enquiries. Once a student enters the free enquiry stage, in order to be successful, it is expected that they are familiar and skilled with all the previous elements of the enquiry process. This will allow them to be more comfortable and confident as true enquirers and maximise their learning experience.

In addition to the above, Natasha Hutchins inspired us by creating an easy to use tool that gives examples of the enquiry cycle aligned with Kath Murdoch's (2015) model. We recommend a visit on her website www.prodivame.com/pd-bites/making-sense-of-inquiry-cycles where the enquiry cycle can be downloaded.

WHY IS ENQUIRY-BASED TEACHING IMPORTANT FOR CHILDREN TODAY?

The education of children, and indeed young adults today, is occurring in a technological and fast-paced society, faced with challenges and uncertainty that require innovation, resilience and engagement. Traditional educational systems, driving the industrial and corporate systems that have allowed civilisation to prosper, are now creaking under the weight of their own limitation, creating the ever-increasing need for creativity, problem solving and autonomy. It is partly for these reasons, and our own personal beliefs, that learning is always most effective when pursued under the ideals of curiosity and passion, which have influenced our own reasons to adopt enquiry-based learning. Combined with this, is the added confidence of an accepted International Baccalaureate (IB) model of enquiry that allows for these ideas to be structured and implemented across the globe, creating a platform for the development and improvement of enquiry-based teaching ideas and routines.

There are many reasons to follow an enquiry-based learning approach. All students have unique talents and abilities that should be nurtured and developed in the classroom, and through providing the environment that allows students to explore these passions, this talent is given the opportunity to prosper, rather than being curtailed. Students thus become empowered as their decision-making skills are utilised, as they exercise choice and actively use their voice to provide direction for their learning. This is achieved through providing multiple learning opportunities that promote this learning culture in the school environment. An enquiry-based approach also leads to students becoming more excited about their class and learning journey. For students to start the day feeling enthusiastic about what learning fruits that day may bring, is a great motivator and regulator of students' passion and energy. In addition to this, given the enormous impact of technology on society, the vast availability of knowledge and the role of the teacher being transformed from purveyor of knowledge to a facilitator of learning, it is now essential that the curiosities of students are fostered and actively guide their own individual and collective paths. It is their ideas and curiosity that will lead to the most productive and rewarding places.

At ISUtrecht, we believe that students' own resilience and perseverance needs to be strengthened in the classroom, through regular moments for reflections and self-thought. With this in mind, the classroom space is filled with opportunities for learning and growth, with an in-built positive mindset that allows students the comfort of failure to project growth. An enquiry-based model also strengthens student research skills and knowledge. The advent of *fake news* and the vast bank of online resources available to learners is both an opportunity and a threat for educators. While it is now very easy to direct students to find and research their own information, for instance, through Wikipedia and Google, the quality of such information is unreliable and potentially fraudulent. Enquiry-based learning is important as learners quickly gain digital literacy skills, such as using a school online library and checking the quality of sources used in their research. Students should also realise the importance of such research, as it gives credibility and depth to their own works. As students are given more space and time to internalise and make connections between concepts, whether this is at an individual or group level, students achieve a greater overall sense of meaning and a clearer mental picture of their journey. Rather than the memorisation of facts before clear understanding, by linking their innate understanding of key information, a superior ability to recall, recollect and reuse vital statistics is created.

We firmly advocate at ISUtrecht that students need to harness the ability to question and think critically. Our students should be encouraged to ask questions and be given the time and work space to actively ponder and question ideas and concepts they have encountered in their learning journey. It is vital that this skill is practised, as it is the very component that is being slowly eroded in a digitalised and social media-driven world. Aligned to this, it is also recommended that students take ownership of their own learning in class, which allows them to adopt their own goals and work towards achieving them. The class should also have the flexibility for students to revise their own targets and reflect on their progress, which is in itself an important skill for later life. It is tempting to view the twenty-first century world as a global environment in a permanent flux of environmental dangers, political and economic threats and ecological disasters, and a myriad of societal concerns, yet the necessity of the voice of tomorrow is that it approaches these problems with a critical mindset and one that is backed up with actual practice. An effective problem-solving approach may contribute to providing the innovative and creative solutions that will almost certainly be demanded in the coming future. A classroom that is designed for students to communicate and collaborate while tackling ideas and challenges is a healthy one.

USE OF ASSESSMENTS

Assessment is a key feature of enquiry-based learning. At our school, we assess children on the following four different levels.

1. I can't think of anything. I don't get it. I don't have any ideas about this.
2. I have a couple of ideas, but I still need help to think of more.
3. I can do this independently.
4. I can see how all of this connects to other things I know about. I can see the bigger picture and make predictions/inferences based on this and can teach others how to do it.

However, how do you know that you understand something? As a teacher, and this also applies to children, there are certain recognisable criteria that demonstrate true understanding. These may include the ability or willingness to teach someone else about the topic and give multiple examples, being able to explain it in alternative ways or to make links and connections between other ideas and concepts and perhaps most interestingly, possessing the knowledge and awareness of how other people feel, perceive and relate to the topic in question.

At our school, we base our assessment system upon enquiry principles, which include the core belief that assessment information, from the pre-assessment stage through to summative assessment, should guide the classroom planning for that unit. In this way, students are active participants of the learning process, and when the assessment tasks implemented are original and varied, students' knowledge and true understanding can be more accurately gauged.

In the *pre-assessment* stage, teachers can organise stations for the students that allow them to explore and demonstrate their pre-gained knowledge on a particular concept or topic. When this is combined with sorting activities, think-pair-share routine, a colour symbol image activity and even a more formal/informal assessment as deemed necessary by the teacher, a realistic level of each student's knowledge in an area can be achieved.

During each unit of enquiry, *formative assessments* are conducted at regular intervals and at ISUtrecht, these form a major part of our assessment process. Deeper understanding can be made evident when students explain the topic or idea through a classroom expo or gallery walk, a concept map or perhaps an oral presentation, interview or podcast. Throughout this process, the teacher asks regular questions such as '*How does this work?*' or '*What would happen if...?*' Students can also show their knowledge gained through interpreting the information from their own personal lives, such as using freeze frames, art works, constructing metaphors or symbols and writing narratives or poetry. Students can also demonstrate their knowledge through a selection of activities where their application of knowledge, ability to flexibly perceive and hold alternative viewpoints and demonstrate self-knowledge become the drivers of progress. Examples of activities that could be utilised include action projects, campaigns, creating websites/blogs, role plays, circle of viewpoints, debates, simulations and reflective journals/diaries. Other activities that could be included are '*I used to think but now I think*' or paired interviews, yet it is our core belief at ISUtrecht that the best activities depend upon the needs and individual personality of each class and student.

During the *summative assessment* period, students get the opportunity to demonstrate how their understanding of the central idea or concepts has developed by applying what they have learnt in new and authentic ways. A summative assessment should not be seen as the final test; it utilises what the students have gained throughout the unit and provides an opportunity to extend and celebrate the students' learning.

Clarify your learning intentions starting with the why

Why are students asked to undertake tasks? A vague and unclear learning intention can also result in the widely held belief that enquiry is simply a matter of '*letting the kids go*' and allowing them to discover whatever they please, which is certainly not the case. Clarity of intention does not signify holding and implementing a rigid lesson plan that satisfies all achievement standards and learning objectives mapped. On the contrary, clarity begins when we ask ourselves some simple yet powerful questions such as:

> *Why is this important? Why are we doing this? How is this relevant and meaningful to our students? What do we hope students will come to understand? What skills and dispositions do we want to strengthen?*
>
> (Murdoch, 2015, p 144)

When we are clear about what it is we want students to learn, we ask better questions, make more useful observations and provide more relevant feedback.

The feedback we provide to students based on our assessment should be:

- linked to intentions or goals;
- tangible and easily understood by the learner;
- specific;
- able to be acted upon;

- personalised;
- timely;
- ongoing;
- consistent.

(Wiggins, 2012)

Have students help to design assessment criteria

Similarly to Davies and Herbst (2013), we have learnt that *'instead of telling learners what is important, what needs to be done or what 'should' be happening*' (p 19), successful assessment occurs when the teachers and students are jointly involved and engaged in the assessment process. When students feel that they are *'doing the learning*' rather than having the teacher *'doing the learning to them'*, they are undoubtedly more engaged, and with engagement comes increased potential for learning. One way to give students more ownership over assessment in enquiry is to involve them in the development of the criteria by which they will be assessed. For example, students undertaking an enquiry into the questions *'Why do animals get extinct?'* may decide to create some kind of text to inform or advise others how to take better care of the earth.

Before embarking on the tasks, teachers and students work together to build criteria by which the quality of this text will be judged. Whether in the form of checklists, rubrics or capacity matrices, these criteria both guide the students as they compose the text and become a basis for self-, peer and teacher assessment. Work in the field of formative assessment by Dylan Williams (2013) and Anne Davies (2007) suggests strongly that when students are involved in decisions about what is being assessed and how, then the quality of their learning improves.

Activate and analyse thinking and learning

Using the thinking routine, for example, of asking students to identify how their thinking has changed, can give us evidence of growth at the same time as allowing students to recognise and articulate their own progress. There are many ways we can activate and assess prior learning as well as keep on checking on learning during the learning process. Below are some understanding check-up strategies used in our school in different grades.

Think-pair-share

This involves students collaborating together, working towards a common objective or solving a problem. The benefits for students are that it improves their ability to focus on a task and to find solutions to problems. It also encourages students to express their ideas socially and develops their clarity of communication, in addition to motivating and captivating students. For example, pose the question: *'What are some of the things you think we could do to help animals that are endangered?'* Give students some time to think on their own – no talking to others, no hands up. Then have them turn to a partner and share their thinking, and look for patterns and connections. Finally, select a few pairs to share with another pair and again look for connections. The teacher should move among students and listen as they share.

I used to think, now I think

Students are instructed that the objective of this learning engagement is to encourage them to identify their own thoughts on a subject and to observe how these ideas have evolved over time. It can be done at any stage in an enquiry. For example, students can stand in a circle and take turns to share their thinking. Changes in thinking may also be written and displayed throughout the unit.

See think wonder

Students are invited to make a comment on a piece of art, a photo or subject, and to continue the exercise by pondering about what the content may be about, or make a relevant observation. This can be done at any given time in the unit. This activity is most effective when a student combines all three parts in the same sequence, that is, '*I see... I think... I wonder...*'. Another important aspect is that students are able to provide evidence or credible arguments for their observations (see Figure 7.2).

Figure 7.2 See think wonder, by a Grade 1 teacher

Agree/disagree

This allows students the opportunity to form an opinion when confronted with some controversial statements or facts. They can form a line, make a human graph, go to corners of the room or use any other means by which they can identify and then justify their point of view. Their justifications can give you an important insight into their understanding and any misconceptions.

Thumb actions

This is an activity that is very quick and effective and provides very immediate feedback for teachers. The students are invited to use their hands to demonstrate how strongly they feel about their level of understanding of a particular topic. Upward facing thumb means '*I am confident!*', horizontal thumb '*I need some more guidance*' and downward facing thumb '*I don't understand, I'm confused*'.

Kahoot!

One of the most effective collaborative games available using technology is 'Kahoot!'. This is a learning program where students can design, share and complete online quizzes, and is a great, free resource for educators. These games are an excellent way of sharing information in groups, as the participants respond to questions in real time and the results are available for viewing on a shared screen. They can also produce an excellent learning dynamic and atmosphere in class, whereby students are both stimulated and engaged in a learning topic, yet deepen their social bonds and group togetherness. The creation of this space allows students to learn and gather information from an expert. The experts are not only teachers but also students who are empowered to share. You can assess individuals by listening in and observing while they negotiate (Kahoot!, nd).

CSI – colour, symbol, image

Students are asked to think about a particular topic or idea to work on. Once their attention is on the topic, a colour, symbol or image is then chosen by the students that best represents that idea. There are no wrong answers and it is an ideal opportunity for the students to share, expand and utilise concepts and ideas. Once the colour, symbol and images are shared among the class, students can discuss the reasons for their choices which provides a great platform for understanding. A CSI routine can also be utilised as part of a final assessment.

Question me the answer

Small groups of students are created, and each is given a key word that is linked to their learning for that particular day or learning sequence. The students then think about a question that would give the same answer. Once this is done, the question is then posed to the class to check whether the response given is the same as their previous word.

Make a connection

An excellent measure of student thinking is being able to connect ideas and experiences with other similar concepts and potentialities. The associations students make will then allow them to hold a superior perspective on the subject, with deeper connections and thoughts. Teachers are responsible for asking probing questions to students such as '*Is there anything else this reminds you of?*', '*How is this similar to…?*' or '*Is there anyone who can make a connection to this idea?*' Once this is done, students can then share their thoughts orally or through images and diagrams.

What makes you say that?

This thinking routine helps us justify our reasoning with evidence. This strategy is used a lot in our kindergarten classes, when digging deeper into ideas. For example, when provoking the students at the beginning of a new topic, we might set up the classroom with loose parts or artefacts for them to explore. We then ask them to tell us what is going on. A question that we will ask once they have told us what is going on is '*What do you see that makes you say that?*' By asking the students this question, we are building on their ability to describe what they see and build on their explanations. Another example is that recently, when enquiring into light and colour, we looked at how artists manipulate light and colour to express their own ideas and feelings. As part of our enquiry, we explored and reflected on different types of art done by several artists including Mondriaan, Kandisky and Picasso to mention but a few. We challenged the students to tell us what kind of feeling(s) they think these artists are expressing through their work. We asked the question '*What makes you say that?*', as a tool to weave into discussion, so as to get the students to give evidence for their assertions. The students not only had the chance of sharing their interpretations of the feeling being expressed but they also understood that we all have different perspectives.

3, 2, 1 thinking routine

This thinking routine involves 3 thoughts or ideas, 2 questions, 1 metaphor or simile. It is used at the beginning of a new topic to activate prior knowledge. This routine helps students develop questions and make connections through metaphors.

Compass point

Compass points allow students to give a response using the points of a compass. Each point encourages them to provide feedback in a slightly different way. It can be used at the end or beginning of a lesson. It is an example of formative assessment that allows the teacher to gauge the needs of the learners.

- N – What do you **n**eed to know?
- E – What **e**xcites you?
- S – What might be a **s**trategy, **s**tance or **s**uggestion for moving forward?
- W – What are you **w**orried about?

Include self- and peer assessment

It is highly valuable to teach students how to self-assess rather than assume that they can simply do it. It is important to promote independence and responsibility which fosters a sense of ownership of learning. In order for self-assessment to be productive and successful, we believe that just having the students involved in the assessment process, so that they can have an input into the success criteria, will make their learning goals clearer and give them more responsibility and ownership over their learning. We make the link between the success criteria and self-assessment by ensuring that the process begins at the start of the lesson or learning sequence, through discussing the learning objectives and how the task could be developed. The idea being, once students know what they are being assessed on, the standards required and how it could and should appear, then they will have a better assessment of their own learning and progress.

In the plenary phase, we ask the class how helpful it would be to look at the checklist to assess their learning progress and gauge performance. Often, most students find this to be a useful exercise, because students might forget what they had completed and have the opportunity to look at it again. Students benefit from this understanding and process from an early age, showing clear benefits to formative assessment, and particularly one that is self-piloted.

At ISUtrecht, we have seen that peer assessment is very useful and effective, since all students agreed that they enjoyed having the chance to check their work, and indeed, all made certain changes or improvements at various stages. This shows that the questions and opinions from other students strengthened their understanding of the learning objectives.

HOW TO PUT THEORY INTO PRACTICE?

At ISUtrecht, our classrooms and teaching methods in both early years and upper primary are designed to promote enquiry-based learning. In what follows, we explain how to implement enquiry-based learning at both stages.

Early years

In the early years, we use Kath Murdoch's (2015) enquiry cycle on our walls. This wall grows and changes throughout the unit based on what we do. In our classrooms, you can find different enquiry tables with interactive engaging activities and questions which encourage the students to explore the different materials displayed. We also use different thinking strategies across the room and have an '*idea wall*' where the students put their ideas up and suggest how we should learn certain things (see Figure 7.3).

In our classrooms, you can find mathematics and language stations provided with open-ended activities and a lot of loose parts that allow the students to enquire into mathematics and language concepts. Each lesson starts with a provocation that gets the children thinking about their learning and stimulates subsequent questions. In the early years, we use lots of provocations on tables that allow students to ask questions, think

Figure 7.3 Idea wall, by a kindergarten teacher

and discover. Students work in collaborative groups that are often led by a key question. Almost every lesson, the students have moments in which they discuss a key question with each other in different ways, such as a strategy mentioned before like think-pair-share. Collaboration is encouraged as students are encouraged to first ask a friend before asking the teacher. On our walls, there are lots of child-made resources that give students agency and ownership over their own learning and understanding. We also implement a *'wonder wall'* on which children can place their questions that can be updated. In the early years, we work with a flexible seating plan whereby students occasionally choose their own place. If the children work together, they mostly work in clumps, in which students are free to make groups of their choice (eg bigger than two, smaller than six). The lessons are designed around student–student interaction instead of teacher–student interaction.

Upper primary

Upper primary teachers believe that it is important to have classroom displays created by the students themselves. We use wonder walls to record students' wonders, as well as reflection walls with sentence starters (see Figure 7.4).

Our upper primary teachers design interactive walls whereby children ask and answer questions with their peers, particularly useful for mathematics or language. In some of

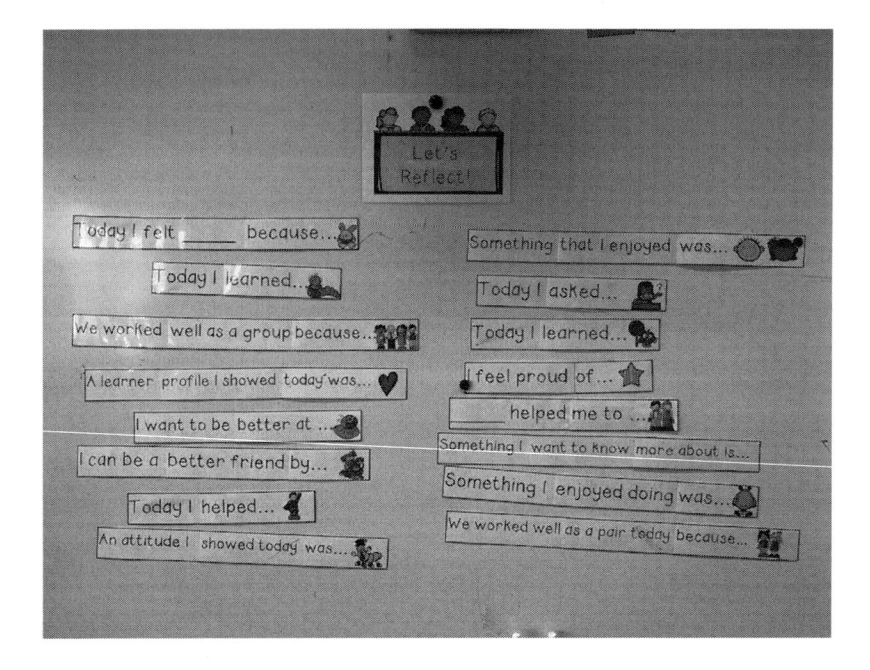

Figure 7.4 Reflection wall, by a Grade 2 teacher

the classes, the daily schedule is led by questions of what will be covered during that time period, for example: *'What is the relationship between area and perimeter?'* In our classrooms, we use statements of who the students are as a learning community and learner profile detectives (see Figure 7.5).

Figure 7.5 Learner profile detectives, by a Grade 4 teacher

All classes have a class library thematically linked with the unit. Strategies that our teachers use for student–student interaction are, for example, think-pair-share, group/clump work, turn-and-talk and paired activities like reading and research projects. The students have lots of ownership over their own work and reflect on collaboration through video. It is very important to model effective collaboration and teach how to give and receive feedback. Teachers are using the ladder of feedback to co-construct feedback for each other's learning. We promote flexible working spaces for the students to freely choose where they would like to sit. Students are challenged to try and problem solve by themselves, then encouraged to 'ptyask three before me'.

Above we have outlined some common strategies to implement an effective enquiry learning process in our school. Each individual teacher plans and selects resources and engagements that best suit his/her personality and learning objectives throughout that unit. At ISUtrecht, we deliberately vary these activities between our classes and grade levels and actively share best practices during collaborative planning (see also Chapter 4). We find that once our students have reached the end of the Primary Years Programme, they are capable learners who have developed a good understanding of all aspects of the enquiry process. This allows the majority of students to be successful in their further educational journey, as they are flexible and independent learners and thinkers who have gained understanding and personal growth in all the enquiry stages.

CONCLUSION

At ISUtrecht, we steadfastly believe that enquiry-based teaching and learning is the best way to prepare our students for the future. The core skills that they develop at our school, their ability to problem solve and be independent thinkers and their confidence, empathy and curiosity, help prepare them for the individual uncertainties and global challenges that lie ahead. We have outlined and explained what enquiry-based teaching is and what it may look like in the classroom, the strategies to best implement it, and how best to manage an enquiry-centred classroom, whether this be through practical examples or student-led assessment. There are many ways to conduct enquiry-based teaching in a classroom and throughout the school, and at ISUtrecht, we believe that the most important factors to achieve this are an openness to new ideas and a willingness for both students and teachers to evolve and improve through the appropriate support, mechanisms and feedback.

Reflective questions

1. How do you question your students? How can you change your way of questioning for the students to get more ownership of their learning?
2. Which strategies in this chapter did you really connect with? How can you use this in your own classroom?

3. Would you be open to taking the risk and not planning your full lesson in order to allow the students more freedom and independence in their own questions and research instead of the teacher's pre-planned expectations?
4. How can you implement elements of the enquiry cycle in your teaching?
5. Can you think of some thinking routines you already use in your teaching and adjust them to become more enquiry led?

REFERENCES

Cross, M (1996) *Teaching Primary Science: Empowering Children for Their World.* Melbourne: Longman Australia.

Davies, A (2007) Involving Students in the Classroom Assessment Process. In Reeves, D (ed) *Ahead of the Curve: The Power of Assessment to Transform Teaching and Learning.* Bloomington: Solution Tree Press.

Davies, A and Herbst, S (2013) Co-constructing Success Criteria: Assessment in the Service of Learning. *Education Canada*, 53(3): 16–19.

Kahoot! (nd) [online] Available at: https://kahoot.com (accessed 12 September 2020).

MacKenzie, T (2018) *Inquiry Mindset: Nurturing the Dreams, Wonders & Curiosity of Our Youngest Learners.* Irvine, CA: EdTechTeam Press.

Murdoch, K (2015) *The Power of Inquiry: Teaching and Learning with Curiosity, Creativity and Purpose in the Contemporary Classroom.* Northcote Vic: Seastar Education.

Watkins, C and Mortimore, P (1999) Pedagogy: What Do We Know? In Mortimer, P (ed) *Understanding Pedagogy and Its Impact on Learning.* London: Paul Chapman.

Wiggins, G (2012) Seven Keys to Effective Feedback. *Feedback for Learning*, 70(1): 10–16.

Williams, D (2013) Assessment: The Bridge Between Teaching and Learning. *Voices from the Middle*, 21(2): 15–20.

8 Transdisciplinary teaching and learning

Katharina Scherpel and Raakhee Ramaiya

INTRODUCTION

Before delving into the chapter, a question you might want to ask yourself is: *'What is the task of education and the role of a school?'* The following scenarios are examples of different types of education. While you are reading, reflect on your thoughts on them.

Scenario 1: A child enters the classroom and the teacher informs the students that they will be doing a mathematics activity. On the board, the teacher writes down the following question *'Which is the healthiest drink?'* On the desks, the teacher already laid out a variety of drinks such as water, juice and soft drinks and a few bags of sugar. She also reminds students of the resources they have access to in class such as kitchen scales, measuring jugs, filters, funnels, calculators and unit-related books on food. Child A is fascinated by the variety of resources and begins ordering the drinks by looking at the amount of sugar in the ingredients. He chooses to work some parts alone and some parts by collaborating with his peers. He also starts to experiment by measuring the amount of sugar to visualise the amount in each drink. He begins to calculate the effect that amount of sugar will have on a body by using the information from the unit books. This activity takes him the entire session and he still has questions and wonderings to further his understanding.

Scenario 2: A child enters the classroom and sits at her designated desk. The teacher hands out a worksheet and gives the students a short explanation on what is expected. It is the exact same question as the one in scenario 1. The children have to work on their own to complete the multiple-choice worksheet. The teacher collects the worksheets and grades them. The students are given 20 minutes to complete the worksheet. The teacher then moves on to another activity and, yet again, hands out a worksheet for the students to complete. After break, the students are given back their mathematics worksheets which have now been graded. They are asked to check where they made errors and are expected to make better choices the next time they do the worksheet.

In some educational institutes, the school focuses merely on the result through standardised testing and making students memorise numerous amounts of information as knowledge. In other educational institutes, schools may choose to find a curriculum which balances both standardised tests and the individual learning journey. The International School Utrecht (ISUtrecht) is a school that works within the framework of the Primary Years Programme (PYP). *'The PYP transdisciplinary framework focuses on the development of the whole child as an inquirer, both at school and beyond'* (International Baccalaureate, nd, para 2). At ISUtrecht, we strive for excellent education that is not based on test results. We are aware that the world is changing at a fast rate and as educators we believe that we are responsible to prepare our students for the future using a sustainable approach to education. In other words, *'the PYP endeavours to develop internationally-minded students. We encourage students to become life-long learners and equip them with the academic and life skills to enable them to actively choose to be world citizens'* (International School Utrecht, nd, para 2).

This chapter is broken up into six areas explaining how we implement transdisciplinary teaching and learning in our primary school at ISUtrecht. First, the chapter provides background information on transdisciplinary learning and why it emerged. The next part focuses on the themes which drive the educational programme. After that, the focus is on collaboration and the importance of it. The chapter then demonstrates how ISUtrecht plans the programme to deliver it to their students. Thereafter, included are examples of the classroom environment and how it plays an integral role in showcasing the theme. Finally, the chapter addresses the different approaches to learning, previously known as the transdisciplinary skills.

BACKGROUND

According to Lexico dictionary, the term transdisciplinary means *'relating to more than one branch of knowledge'* (*Lexico*, nd, transdisciplinary). When linking this definition to teaching, it clearly means allowing students to gain new knowledge from a variety of sources. According to Park and Son (2010), transdisciplinary learning is seen to generate the highest level of learning interactively through students' participation towards problem-solving. They state: *'the levels of interactivity also affect student identity and teacher identity in the mode of transdisciplinary learning; teachers become interactive learning designers while students become knowledge producers'* (Park and Son, 2010, p 85). This shows that the role of the teacher is different in a transdisciplinary approach to education compared with mainstream educational approaches, since the teacher does not necessarily have the role of knowledge deliverer and the student the knowledge receiver. Also learning is not driven by a specific subject or topic, but through the participation of the students, relevant issues or problems and new knowledge and understandings as well as combining and linking different subject areas together. Therefore, we can also agree with Wiesmann et al (2008, as cited in Savage and Drake, 2016, p 2) who argue that *'transdisciplinary teaching, learning and research has emerged as a response to the complex problems that exist in 21st century society'*. Nowadays, students can easily access new knowledge through different tools and media, but they need to be able to combine different types of knowledge and apply them to new situations to gain a deeper understanding to help them flourish in our developing and growing world.

Wonderings...

- How can the concept of measurement be connected in a transdisciplinary way under the theme *'how the world works'*?
- What is your understanding of the complex problems that exist in the twenty-first century?

PRIMARY YEARS PROGRAMME, MIDDLE YEARS PROGRAMME AND DIPLOMA PROGRAMME

In 2015, ISUtrecht received the accreditation for the Primary Years Programme (PYP) and Middle Years Programme (MYP) from the International Baccalaureate (IB).

Table 8.1 explains the difference between the three IB programmes. The PYP follows the transdisciplinary approach to learning. The MYP follows an interdisciplinary approach and the Diploma Programme (DP) a disciplinary and multidisciplinary approach.

Table 8.1 Programmes in the International Baccalaureate

Programme	PYP	MYP	DP
Model	Transdisciplinary	Interdisciplinary	Disciplinary-multidisciplinary
Primary organiser	Key elements are: • Knowledge • Conceptual understandings • Skills • Dispositions • Action	Eight subject groups are explored through the global contexts of: • Identities and relationships • Orientation in space and time • Personal and cultural expression • Scientific and technical innovation • Globalisation and sustainability • Fairness and development	Six DP subject groups are supported by the core which include: • Theory of knowledge (DP)

(International Baccalaureate Organization, 2018)

Before looking specifically at transdisciplinary learning, we analyse the difference between the four disciplinary approaches (see Figure 8.1). The disciplinary image represents a traditional approach to teaching and learning where each subject is taught in one way with limited connections to other subject areas and the real world. The multidisciplinary image recognises the real world but both aspects are kept as separate entities. Interdisciplinary learning is when disciplines overlap, for example, in the case of a unit on migration, the history and geography subject areas would be linked. Transdisciplinary learning is when a concept is taught that can be covered across all subject areas and disciplines. Mitchell (2005, p 332) states: '*true transdisciplinarity goes beyond simply drawing together concepts from the disciplines and that it creates new frameworks that break down (transgress) the traditional boundaries of the disciplines*'.

| Disciplinary | Multidisciplinary |
| Interdisciplinary | Transdisciplinary |

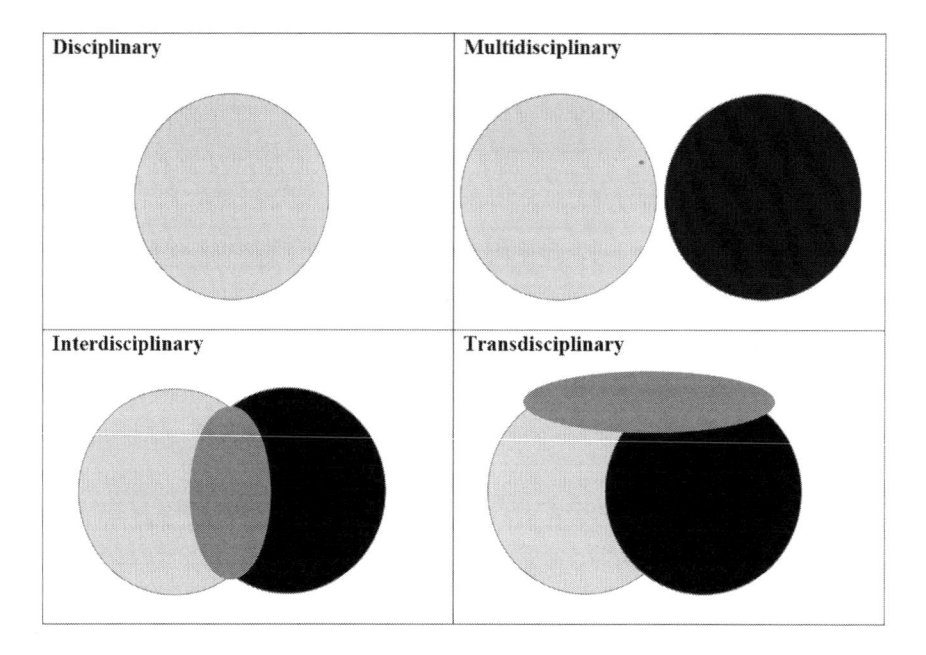

Figure 8.1 The four disciplinary approaches to learning
(Adapted from Carrillo, 2018)

The core of the PYP curriculum is transdisciplinary learning. This chapter therefore explains the teaching and learning behind transdisciplinary learning, focusing on what it is and how it is used at ISUtrecht. We believe that transdisciplinary learning is the exploration of a concept or a problem that integrates multiple disciplines for students to connect new knowledge, build on their skills and create a deeper understanding that connects students to the real world. For example, if the children are learning about a scientific concept like forces, the educator may create a real problem like needing to have an architectural design made up for a playground in a new school. This playground needs to use forces to create movement. In order to create a successful playground, the children have the task to work collaboratively to first design and create a model, and then present their playground model to the director of the school. Within this problem, the educator has been able to teach and expose the children to measurement and shapes to build with for mathematics, procedural writing for language as well as working on skills such as collaboration, communication, fine motor skills and conflict management.

> **Wonderings...**
>
> o Which disciplinary approach do you think your school falls under?
> o What is your understanding of the transdisciplinary approach?

TRANSDISCIPLINARY THEMES

A school year at ISUtrecht is split up into six different units known as the transdisciplinary themes (see Table 8.2). The transdisciplinary themes that have global significance allow students to explore knowledge and create new understanding. The themes allow for

Table 8.2 Transdisciplinary themes

Transdisciplinary themes
Who we are
Where we are in place and time
How we express ourselves
How the world works
How we organise ourselves
Sharing the planet

(International Baccalaureate Organization, 2018)

teachers and students to learn about different subject areas, connect them and learn beyond them. The transdisciplinary themes are authentic, engaging, deep and cohesive which is explained in Table 8.3. At ISUtrecht, every grade level has six different units (except for kindergarten which has five) which fit under each of the themes. Before 2018, the duration of each unit was six weeks long and this was a fixed period. After teaching these units, we realised that some units have content that requires more teaching and exploration compared to other units. For example, in Grade 2, the unit on storytelling was very straightforward and easy for children to understand with little teaching when compared to a unit on life cycles for both plants and animals. Therefore, since the academic year 2018–2019, teachers can choose how long each unit will last. These vary now between four and eight weeks. The length of each unit is decided when each grade-level team collaborates and creates the year plan for their grade level. The length of a unit can depend on a variety of factors such as the central idea, lines of enquiry, concepts and learning outcomes.

Table 8.3 Holistic learning

Learning …	How
Extends the international dimension of the PYP	The themes have global significance – for all students in all cultures and places.
Is authentic and engaging	The themes address contemporary challenges surrounding environment, development, peace and conflicts, rights and responsibilities and governance.
Is deep	The themes are revisited throughout the students' primary years so that the end result is immersion in broad-ranging, in-depth, articulated curriculum content.
Is cohesive	The themes contribute to the common ground that unifies the curriculum.

(International Baccalaureate Organization, 2018)

> **Wonderings...**
>
> ○ How would you differentiate between year groups to create units under the theme '*Sharing the planet*'?
>
> ○ What is your understanding of the themes?

COLLABORATION

When looking back at Table 8.2, all subject areas of a transdisciplinary unit are interlinked by a central theme. The fact that they are interlinked means that teachers from different subject areas are asked to collaborate regularly (see also Chapter 4). Transdisciplinary learning requires teachers to collaborate effectively and openly. They must move away from their comfort zone of working individually by sharing ideas with others for the purpose of authentic learning experiences. This benefits the students by building meaningful and long-term understandings. At ISUtrecht, teachers look at a unit of enquiry and connect that unit to themselves, have a discussion of what it means to them and then think about authentic learning experiences to engage the students. While creating a unit of enquiry, teachers are asked to see which specialists will best fit the unit to enhance it. If a specialist is available, then they can be involved in the unit. For example, a unit on cultures would work well with the music and art specialist. Collaboration can vary with a specialist. It takes place often during the unit but especially in the beginning while going through the planning process and towards the end when reporting on the students' learning. However, collaboration within a grade level happens once a week together with the PYP co-ordinator and more often as a team. At the start of a unit, each grade level comes up with a list of generalisations, evidence that is needed from each student and a list of learning engagements that are connected to real-life situations and that make learning challenging and significant for each student.

At ISUtrecht, collaboration is not limited only to the teaching staff but also involves parents and students. Before a unit is started, each teacher is responsible to send out a unit letter with all the necessary information regarding a unit. Parents are encouraged to share their expertise if they have any experience or knowledge about that field. An example of this was when a parent who is also a doctor came and spoke about different body systems with a class who had their unit on the human body systems. After the unit is introduced to the students, each child is encouraged to come up with a question or a wondering about the central idea. These are incorporated in the planning of the unit, including planning with the specialists, to ensure the unit connects to their own interests.

> **Wonderings...**
>
> ○ How do you collaborate at your institute?
>
> ○ How would you plan for collaboration in the classroom?

PLANNING

Planning is a crucial part of transdisciplinary learning since it requires working together with specialists and the grade-level team. It is a process that is ongoing and fluid. Planning at ISUtrecht is forever changing based on new ideas, training courses that colleagues have been on, interests of the children and reflections from the previous years. Once a year a whole school plan is created collaboratively where the themes are aligned with the central ideas, generalisations, inclusion of specialists, a brief idea of the summative assessment and field trips. The purpose of this is to ensure that there are no overlaps with other grade levels which also helps when resourcing for that unit. See Table 8.4 which shows the *'Sharing the planet'* theme for each grade level.

After a professional development course delivered on service learning, the Grade 1 team at ISUtrecht were inspired to plan in a more authentic manner. We collaborate on why a theme has relevance in our own lives. This is the starting point to give the theme authenticity and meaning to our own lives, so we can be fully engaged and inspired to teach and learn with the children. From these authentic sharing moments, we check the previous central idea and adapt it. We lay out a large planner which has subject areas, skills, techniques, research areas, resources and action ideas. As our ideas flow, we fill in the relevant sections and share this planner with our co-ordinator who we collaborate with once a week and we all work together to form a skeleton of the unit of enquiry. We liaise with specialists and highlight the attitudes that we would like to focus on which best suit this unit. We also think about different ways to assess the children for both formative and summative assessments. With younger grades, we start planning ideas with the children as to how they can show their understanding. We help shape their ideas and turn it into a summative assessment. At the start of a unit, we spark students' interest through a provocation and ask the children about their wonders or any questions they have about what we are about to delve into and from this we know where the gaps are in their knowledge and then how to explore the transdisciplinary theme to deepen their enquiries.

The planning process also means that we collaborate with our specialists to see if their area will be stand alone or whether it can be integrated within the unit. Learning areas such as mathematics, language and social studies are all included using a platform for planning across all the PYP. We select the learning outcomes and this is incorporated through the experiences that are co-created through direct, guided or free enquiry (see Chapter 7). Throughout the unit, teachers pose the questions: *'So what? What can be done about this?'* This encourages class discussions to take place.

We also involve our parents as we are a close community school. Parents who are not familiar with the IB may find it difficult to understand why the children do not have stand-alone mathematics block times, for example. However, when they observe the results that their child is learning mathematical concepts in a more authentic manner where they can transfer their knowledge across various areas, they agree that it makes more sense to use it this way in the real world. A unit that is strong in this is called *'farm to us'*, which is connected to money and explores concepts like profit and loss. The attitudes to learning are explored through experiences in roleplay, field trips, drama, stories and case studies. The next step for us as a school may be to explore one transdisciplinary theme for the year to give it more depth and a continuity of learning. For example, the theme *'Who we are'* can look at the unit of enquiry into body systems, human migration and non-verbal communication.

Table 8.4 Unit planner ISUtrecht

Grade	Kindergarten	Grade 1	Grade 2	Grade 3	Grade 4	Grade 5
Unit	Habitats	Extinction	Natural Resources	Water	Changing Earth	Energy
Central idea	Animals depend on their habitat for survival.	When the needs of living things are not met, it leads to endangerment and potentially extinction.	As global citizens, we have a responsibility to sustain and maintain the Earth's resources.	Water distribution differs across the globe.	Natural disasters can be more severe depending on the location of the country and the economic and structural development within the area.	Global citizens make informed choices about the use of limited resources.
Lines of enquiry	• Living things are classified based on their characteristics. • Living and non-living things interact within habitats. • Living things adapt to their habitats. • People's actions impact ecosystems. • People communicate their knowledge through different media. • People interpret and respond to a range of different media. • Life cycles within habitats follow a pattern.	• Human settlements contribute to the destruction of natural habitats. • Conservation is necessary for both humans and animals. • Scientists use the features of living things in order to classify them. • Habitats are inhabited by certain species.	• Every choice we make has a consequence. • Objects can be described in terms of the materials they are made up of and their physical properties. • Water left in an open container disappears but water in a closed container does not disappear. • The Earth's natural resources are classified as renewable and non-renewable. • Many materials can be recycled and used again, sometimes in different forms. • Earth's resources can be found in different places around the world.	• Water undergoes different stages throughout water cycle. • Water cleaning, such as filtration, aids with the regeneration of resources. • Human activity changes the availability of clean water. • New knowledge can lead to better choices about water. • The municipality has created systems to manage water within the community.	• Data gained from past and current events informs future planning. • Natural disasters are caused by geographic factors. • Communities respond to changing environments. • The threat of natural disasters requires emergency readiness.	This unit was the Primary Years Programme exhibition. The Grade 5 students came up with their own lines of enquiry.

> **Wonderings...**
> - Do you plan with your students?
> - Do your students make their own plans?

CLASSROOM

The learning environment plays a vital role in a transdisciplinary approach to learning since the learning environment is often seen as the third teacher. We already mentioned that transdisciplinary learning is the exploration of a concept or a problem that integrates multiple disciplines for students to connect new knowledge and a deeper understanding. This means that a classroom environment needs to represent this understanding of transdisciplinary learning as well. The walls in a more traditional classroom often have stand-alone walls for each subject area such as for mathematics and language with no or very little overlap and integration of other subjects. At ISUtrecht, we encourage classroom teachers to create learning spaces that show the integration of multiple subject areas and disciplines. An example of this is the unit on healthy choices in Grades 1 and 2. During this unit, the Grade 2 language wall showed healthy recipes and workout routines linked to the unit on instructional writing. The language features of an instructional text, such as title, subtitles, list of ingredients and so forth, were identified in a recipe. The mathematics wall showed documentation of children measuring different ingredients using scales when making their healthy meals using their own recipes. Having your learning environments reflect transdisciplinary learning allows your students to make connections between the different subject areas and connections to the outside world.

Another example comes from Grade 3 that had a unit on consumerism and the transdisciplinary theme was '*How we organise ourselves*'. This was an integrated unit; since the mathematics unit was partially on money, the language unit focused on persuasive advertisements and the visual arts unit was on visual language in advertisements. The language wall included different advertisements, the language features in advertisements, and also visual language through the usage of font, pictures, shapes and colours in advertisements which is linked to the visual arts unit and the unit on consumerism. Students were also given the opportunity to Skype with a creative director of a Dutch advertising agency, who was able to explain how art and language are linked in persuasive advertisements. This allowed our students to understand that there is a link between the material covered in class and the real world. Enabling students to interact with professionals is an effective way of transdisciplinary learning. The unit wall included brand named products as well as generic products from the local grocery store. The fact that the prices were included under the generic and brand-named products was a direct link to the mathematics unit on money. These language, mathematics and unit walls allow students to create not only connections between the subject areas but also connections to the real world and develop knowledge and stronger understanding.

Teachers at ISUtrecht are working on integrating the five transdisciplinary skills, now approaches to learning, into their units (see the next section). In order to do this effectively, some teachers are also attempting to organise their learning environment around these skills.

> **Wonderings…**
>
> o How does your environment foster or celebrate students' understandings or interests?
>
> o Is your environment teacher or student created?

APPROACHES TO LEARNING

We are aware that teaching the transdisciplinary disciplines is important, but in order to explore these disciplines successfully, we also need to focus on integrating the skills that go hand in hand with the curriculum. The world around us is constantly changing and as teachers we have the responsibility to prepare our students for the future and to have the necessary skills to thrive in this environment. All throughout ISUtrecht, teachers make use of these skills to boost independence, creativity and the ability to work with others. The skills are according to the International Baccalaureate Organization (2018) *approaches to learning*, formerly known as transdisciplinary skills, and these are skills that are transferable across contexts and subject areas and support purposeful enquiry. The approaches to learning skills are divided into five categories: *thinking, research, communication, social* and *self-management*. Each of these five categories also contains subcategories, known as subskills, which can be interrelated. At ISUtrecht, teachers are responsible in determining the skills their students should work on and integrating these into their teaching. Table 8.5 shows examples of how teachers at ISUtrecht incorporate the five approaches to learning skills into their teaching and learning environments.

Table 8.5 Approaches to learning

Approaches to learning	Ways we implement these at ISUtrecht
Research skills	In Grade 1, during the unit on extinction, the children researched different endangered animals using tablets and unit books and looked for ways of how humans can help these animals. They shared their research with the rest of the class verbally.
Communication skills	In Grade 3, during the unit on traditions and cultures, children created their own new cultures and made PowerPoints to communicate the information with the rest of the class, parents and teachers.
Social skills	In kindergarten, social skills are explored and developed during enquiry stations and free enquiry as well as outdoor learning. In upper primary, children collaborate during genius hour when they choose a topic of interest and do research together.
Self-management skills	In the exhibition in Grade 5, students work on time management and organisational skills by creating their own unit of enquiry.
Thinking skills	During the theme '*Sharing the planet*', in Grades 1 and 2, children are encouraged to take action at school as well as at home to conserve the Earth's resources and look after our environment. Visible thinking routines are also displayed to allow children to follow and reflect on their thinking process.

Previously at ISUtrecht every unit was linked to one of the five transdisciplinary skills. For example, the Grade 2 unit on life cycles focused purely on teaching students the necessary research skills and no other skill was explicitly covered. We have now come to realise that these skills should be interrelated and are transdisciplinary meaning they should not be limited to a specific subject or field. The focus should be placed on teaching the subskills from the five different categories throughout the school year and offering more of an individualised approach. In Grade 3, children write personalised weekly goals connected to these subskills. In order to be successful in achieving these goals, the teacher offers necessary support to these students or encourages other students to model these skills to their peers. These personalised goals can be applied to various moments of the school day and are not bound to a subject area. For example, students who struggle with time management can work on this during lunchtime but also when working on a task together with a group. At the end of every day, the children reflect on their personalised goals and self-assess themselves to see if they were able to work on their goal on that specific day.

> **Wonderings...**
> - Which skills do you think are the most important for children to have?
> - By the age of 11, what do you expect children to have achieved?

CONCLUSION

Based on the information found in this chapter, we conclude that as a school, we have tried and embraced different ways of exploring and delivering a transdisciplinary approach to learning and teaching. Due to the framework of the PYP curriculum changing over time, we as a school also have been adapting to this change and transforming the way we organise our transdisciplinary themes and units. We believe that we have reached this by having staff members that show willingness to collaborate effectively and believe in the transdisciplinary approach to learning. Our goal continues to be to deliver a skill- and concept-based education that meets the needs of our school community. We hope that other educators will also understand the benefits of a transdisciplinary approach to learning and try to implement it in their school. We would like highlight at least the following as takeaways of this chapter.

- Transdisciplinary learning is when a concept is taught that can be covered across all subject areas and disciplines.
- Transdisciplinary learning is seen to generate the highest level of learning interactively through students' participation towards problem-solving.
- There are six transdisciplinary themes within the IB: (1) who we are, (2) where we are in place and time, (3) how we express ourselves, (4) how the world works, (5) how we organise ourselves and (6) sharing the planet.

○ Collaboration, planning, the classroom environment and approaches to learning are integral and crucial factors in making transdisciplinary learning successful.

○ Reflect on the two scenarios at the start of this chapter. Which student had a deeper understanding and hunger for learning more? Which class would you like to be a part of?

Reflective questions

1. Do you recognise a particular type of disciplinary approach used by your school?
2. Can you think of units of enquiry which would fall under each transdisciplinary theme?
3. How would you integrate all other subject areas within a unit of enquiry?
4. How do you plan on sharing the wonderful learning through classroom displays, ensuring connections are made?
5. Why do you think the approaches to learning skills are useful? How would you integrate these in particular units of enquiry?

REFERENCES

Carrillo, J (2018) *Transdisciplinary Education: Learning that Is Authentic and Relevant.* [online] Available at: www.magellanschool.org/transdisciplinary-education-approach-learning-authentic-relevant-real-world/ (accessed 12 September 2020).

International Baccalaureate (nd) *What is the PYP?* [online] Available at: www.ibo.org/programmes/primary-years-programme/what-is-the-pyp/ (accessed 12 September 2020).

International Baccalaureate Organization (2018) *Learning and Teaching.* Cardiff: International Baccalaureate.

International School Utrecht (nd) *Primary Years Programme.* [online] Available at: www.isutrecht.nl/pyp/primary-years-programme/ (accessed 12 September 2020).

Lexico (nd) *Transdisciplinary.* [online] Available at: www.lexico.com/definition/transdisciplinary (accessed 12 September 2020).

Mitchell, P H (2005) What's in a Name? Multidisciplinary, Interdisciplinary, and Transdisciplinary. *Journal of Professional Nursing*, 21(6): 332–4.

Park, J and Son, J (2010) Transitioning toward Transdisciplinary Learning in a Multidisciplinary Environment. *International Journal of Pedagogies and Learning*, 6(1): 82–93.

Savage, M J and Drake, S M (2016) Living Transdisciplinary Curriculum: Teachers' Experiences with the International Baccalaureate's Primary Years Programme. *International Electronic Journal of Elementary Education*, 9(1): 1–20.

Part 3

Developing skills for the future

9 Teaching computational thinking and digital pedagogy

Wychman Dijkstra, Kris Coorde, Ana Yao and Panagiota Fameli Buwalda

INTRODUCTION

This chapter is a representation of the role information and communications technology (ICT) plays at the International School Utrecht (ISUtrecht). We are in the beginning of our digital pedagogy journey. As with almost everything in education such as strategies, views, teaching tactics and lessons, our digital pedagogy approach will too evolve and take other forms with time. However, the aspect that will remain the same is the assumption that the use of ICT in the classroom, the role of computational thinking in shaping the understanding of the world for our students and the digital pedagogy are of great significance. With our school growing and changing, our lessons, our learning aims and online experiences, our technology curriculum, all are evolving too. During the COVID-19 pandemic, the whole school community had to get used to the new reality of online teaching and learning, while ICT skills and the use of online tools were proven not only helpful but also necessary.

According to Blurton (1999, p 1):

> *Information and communication technologies (ICT) are a diverse set of technological tools and resources used to communicate, and to create, disseminate, store, and manage information. Communication and information are at the very heart of the educational process, consequently, ICT-use in education has a long history.*

The role of ICT in education is ever increasing and more and more recognised as an important area of development for students. It is indeed found everywhere in the daily life of a child, at home and at school. As set out in the document beliefs and values about ICT in the Primary Years Programme (PYP) (International Baccalaureate, 2011), ICT offers big, and necessary, opportunities for learning. The use of a set of ICT-skills, such as the ability to use computers and tablets, presentation tools, blogs, learner software (eg mathematics puzzles) or augmented and virtual reality devices, is important and should be a part of any modern curriculum.

This chapter, however, goes beyond the use of those skills in the daily life of a student and takes it a step further. In this chapter, the term '*computer science*' is used as a broader term for anything related to the use of computers and computer technology. We divide computer science into three educational strands:

1. ICT-skills/digital literacy;
2. digital wellness and digital citizenship;
3. computational thinking/coding.

These three educational strands can be taught separately or integrated within the existing curriculum. Moreover, these strands are intertwined with each other as well.

THE THREE STRANDS

What do these three strands stand for? By using a series of questions, an effort has been made to pinpoint the area that every strand covers or deals with. This list of questions is by no means exhaustive; however, it can be used as an indication.

ICT-skills/digital literacy

How does a tablet or a computer work? How do I use presentation software? How do I store and open files? How can I write and send an email? How do I create a certain document? How do I type a report and add pictures? How do I print? How do I use certain apps? How can digital platforms and tools empower teaching and learning? How do I create a podcast? How do I make a video using a green screen?

Digital wellness and digital citizenship

Is the digital world the same as the real world? Are the (social) rules different or the same? How do I keep my files secure? What is a password? Is everything I read online true? Can I use all the information I find? Can I use every picture I find online?

Computational thinking/coding

How do we learn to use computers? How do computers work? How do they think? How can people write software that is fast and easy to use? What are algorithms? What is debugging? What is information? What is logical thinking? How do I divide bigger problems into smaller ones? What is step-by-step thinking?

In the following parts of this chapter, we describe how computer science finds its way into our school. Our focus is mainly on two of the three strands, namely digital wellness and computational thinking/coding, as those two areas have received special attention over the past years. As such, we address ICT-skills/digital literacy comparatively briefly and refer you to the chapter *Rethinking literacy* in this book for more information (see Chapter 10). This short section is followed by a lengthier description of our work in digital wellness and computational thinking/coding. We end this chapter with a general conclusion on computer science in our school.

ICT-SKILLS/DIGITAL LITERACY

ICT-skills refer to relatively modern skills, which a student should develop besides traditional skills; skills that are necessary in order to work with computers, computer programs and digital devices. Digital literacy, on the other hand, is the ability one has to find, evaluate, share and create content using information technologies and the internet. And to add to this definition, it is also the ability to interpret and design communication across many digital forms.

In our school, we make use of tablets and laptops, but also virtual reality and augmented reality devices (see Figure 9.1). We – and this, of course, includes the students – make daily use of various digital platforms. The students use the internet to look up information, create videos using the green screen and some classes make use of blogs and blogposts, or create podcasts. All these relatively new ways of using and creating literacy create a new view on teaching language while also requiring knowledge from both the teachers and the students of how to use all those devices and apps. As explained above, this chapter does not focus further on these important skills which are, however, a part of, or at least complement, what we term, computer science.

Figure 9.1 Students discussing the best coding approach in SAM Labs platform

DIGITAL WELLNESS AND DIGITAL CITIZENSHIP

Nowadays students learn how to make use of a wide range of digital tools in their education. That means they should also be educated on how to use them properly and be aware of the pitfalls associated with them. As in the real world, the virtual world is a social world in which certain ways of conduct are necessary. Technology and the internet have changed our lives significantly. They have created new ways of access to knowledge, have given us new opportunities for learning, have elevated new perspectives and have made distances between friends smaller. This has certainly been the case during times like the recent pandemic where family members, colleagues, communities and whole classes could be connected only online. However, the new technologies have also presented some serious risk factors, to which young children especially are vulnerable. It is the teachers' role to teach children how to use these new devices, how to behave online, what risks there are, what the consequences could be in the real world and to learn to be critical of the information found online. In a world of fake news, plagiarism and blatant spreading of false information, raising awareness is now more important than ever. As such, this is also reflected in the fourth pillar of the ISUtrecht mission and vision statement:

> We use technology in an innovative and sensible way to enhance our teaching and learning. We equally appreciate the value of sensory and tactile experiences. We approach the virtual and real world as one, behaving consistently as we are moving from one to the other.
>
> (International School Utrecht, nd)

Therefore, in the school's curriculum, there is appointed time for digital citizenship lessons in PYP, Middle Years Programme (MYP) and Diploma Programme (DP). We believe in the importance of giving our students the right tools and skills to develop a healthy digital life.

Digital citizenship lessons are always welcomed by our school's students as they provide them with an opportunity to discuss their experiences and thoughts about their digital experiences. One topic that always seems to be burning and ongoing is the amount of media consumption. Parents and teachers often discuss how much screen time is a healthy amount for a child. During the online learning, daily limits were set and advice to the parents was given in order to maintain a healthy online and offline balance. As teachers, we firmly believe that early years and primary students should be developing sensory and tactile skills before spending time with screens. So, in our lessons, this translates into using unplugged or non-screen resources.

At the same time, computers have been used as a very powerful tool for learning and developing skills. A growing proportion of children and adolescents' leisure time is spent with screens, but screen time is not related only to leisure. For example, should a child, who has spent time on YouTube learning how to code or draw, be restricted to a certain amount of screen time? One of our Grade 10 students, for example, has learnt how to code a computer language C++ by himself and now creates games and software. In the past, these skills were for undergraduate university students and IT professionals. Nowadays, with information so vastly available, many learning experiences can be had by much younger students using online content.

Another example is one of our Grade 5 students who learnt how to draw in the Japanese style cartoon, called Manga. This student used YouTube to learn drawing techniques, Pinterest to find examples and tutorials of drawing body expressions and Instagram to collect feedback on how to improve her drawings. Most of the drawings are done on paper, but technology has been used as a learning support. So how should we measure an appropriate amount of screen time hours for these students? What is very important is to teach these, and indeed all, students how to create healthy habits of knowing how and when to take breaks, the importance of spending time outdoors with fresh air, doing sports, socialising with their peers and other activities. It all comes down to finding a balance between mental and physical well-being. In what follows, we describe a few lesson examples that we have taught at our school.

A reflection lesson

Reflection is an important tool in teaching digital wellness. One of the digital citizenship lessons we gave in Grade 7 was a lesson on '*self-reflection of a healthy media diet*'. The first part of the lesson, the students were exposed to content of adults and teenagers being so engaged with their mobile phones and screens that they ignored and are disengaged with friends and activities around them. Raising this kind of awareness makes the students reflect on their own use of digital tools. We were happy to note that quite a lot of the Grade 7 students were aware of the health consequences of spending far too much time on screens and also knew how to use tools on their mobile phones to measure the amount of time they spent on screens. The second part of the lesson required the students, working in groups, to create a piece of self-reflection on their own media consumption. They could choose to express their thoughts in creating a poem, comic, song or story.

Below are two great examples of a song and a poem composed by our Grade 7 students. In the first example, it was very interesting for the students to reflect on how dependent they are on their phones. What became clear from our class discussion was that most of the students know the unhealthy effects of spending too much time on their phone but some do not seem to know how to entertain themselves offline. The poem has a broader reflection of media consumption in our happiness and identity.

Song by Senna and Constanza, Grade 7 students. Tune based on the **Happier Song** *from Marshmallow and Bastille.*

Lately, I've been, I've been using my phone every single day, my phone every single dayyyyyyyy.
When the morning comes, I check my phone to see who has texted and the notifications that I have got.
Every argument every text we can't take back, because all that has happened, I think we all know that our phones are to blame.
Then only for a minute I put my phone down but this just don't feel right to me.
I want to change my habits, I want to see you smile but I'm only looking at my screen.
..

Lately, I've been, I've been using my phone single day, my phone every single dayyyyyyyy.
When the evening falls and I'm left there being bored I rely on my phone to entertain me, oh damn what have I become.
But on my Instagram, I pretend like I'm okay but you don't know my real life, inside I feel like want to die.
Then only for a minute I put my phone down but this just don't feel right to me.
I want to change my habits, I want to see you smile but I'm only looking at my screen.
..
Lately, I've been, I've been using my phone single day, my phone every single dayyyyyyyy.
So, I'll stop, I'll stop. I will stop stop stop. (2x)
Lately, I've been, I've thinking, I'm gonna stop using my phone, I'm gonna stop using my phone.
Even though I might not like this, I think that I'll be happier, I want to be happier.
Then only for a minute I put my phone down but this just don't feel right to me.
I need to change my habits, I want to see you smile but I'm only looking at my screen.
I want to smile again I know that means I'll have to stop.
..
Lately I've been thinking I'm gonna stop using my phone, I'm gonna stop using my phone
So, I'll stop, I'll stop, I'll stooo-ooo-ooop.

Poem by Natasha and Jana, Grade 7 students

Why
Why do we not investigate the world?
Stare at it until we know,
All the secrets it holds.
We don't know true fun
We don't know that happiness is
To play all day long
With kids in a park.
All we do is make kids watch
Stupid cartoons.
We use social media
But is it really social?
Or instead of looking to the soul of a person.
We stare into a coded metal box,
I only have one question,
Why?
What do we gain with this?
What makes us happy?
Is this what we really want??
I guess we'll never know.

Fake news

Our digital citizenship curriculum also includes digital literacy. News and information are so widely available and with so many different agencies and platforms such as Twitter and Facebook providing information that it has become a very serious topic on how to find reliable information or at least be critical of the information a student, or anyone else, reads. In our lesson about *'fake news'*, the students were taught how to distinguish between a fact and an opinion. In this lesson, the students were exposed to two fake videos and to a computer-generated fictional model, who acts as an influencer on Instagram.

The first video was about a type of shoe which could make people walk on water. The video was fake but done in such a professional looking way and using a language of reliable sources and well-known companies that some of the students believed the video to be true. There were two different types of students that initially believed the video to be true: the younger and older grade students who did not spend too much time on social media and YouTube.

The second video came from, what we consider a very reliable agency, the British Broadcasting Corporation (BBC) which has a tradition to create a prank on April Fool's Day (BBC, 2008). The BBC created a video about a new species of flying penguins in a tropical forest. Most of the students could spot this video as fake almost immediately. The students have been exposed to information about penguins and their habitat from such an early age so the video, despite being from a reliable source, could not make it believable.

The most engaged and opinion devised activity for the students was the computer generated (CG) model called Lil Miquela Sousa on Instagram. Most of the students are familiar with the social media platform Instagram and use it on a daily basis. The fake look of the model made the students initially confused and unsure about the Instagram page. Because the model socialises with real people, has music videos and does modelling for real brands, there is quite a lot of confusing information on the web from different sources discussing if Miquela is indeed real or not. Despite the students being shown a video on the making of the Miquela CG model, some of the students were still convinced Miquela was real. The examples from our *'fake news'* lesson show therefore how important it is to teach critical thinking to students.

Safe online talk

At ISUtrecht, we noticed that the students in Grades 4–6 are the group of students who get their first mobile phones and computers. As such we also gave digital citizenship lessons about *'safe online talk'*, aimed at Grade 5 and 6 students. The lessons take a lot of examples from real-life situations. Teachers and parents have been teaching the younger students how to approach, or avoid, strangers. These lessons are the same and can be applied to the virtual world just as well: children should learn not to talk to strangers online, the same as they would not do in real life.

The rules on how to make friends can differ slightly from real versus digital life. Most people do not share personal information in a first encounter with a stranger. But in real life, with time and enough interaction with a person, you can create a bond of trust and make a friend whom you can invite to your house or meet in a social event. In making a friend in the virtual world, this takes much longer and requires extra precaution. You are never sure of the real identity of the person with whom you interact online, and you might never meet or know the real identity of the person.

In our class discussion, our students said that they do interact with unknown people. According to them, social platforms such as Skype, Facetime and WhatsApp are used mostly to contact friends and family members. But there is a grey area when the students interact with strangers. The real-time conversation can occur when they play online games such as Roblox, Fortnite or have chats or make comments using Instagram.

By making students aware of the dangers online, by making them critical thinkers and raising awareness to a fake world online, we hope that in offering the students a digital citizenship curriculum, they will be better prepared for online life. We hope that they can have an informal conversation with unknown people, but be '*virtually smart*' enough to keep some distance and not give personal information too readily. The students need to have the necessary skills and trust in using their '*gut feeling*' about someone or a situation. Once you have enough experience and maturity in the real world, you have enough knowledge to compare and have a gut feeling whether or not an online situation is unusual and unsafe.

Concluding thoughts

Digital citizenship education is essential for any school as students interact with technology daily. Blocking and taking devices away from students is not a very effective solution to keep our students safe. It is very important to keep an open communication channel between adults and young people. Technology is a very powerful and useful tool for teaching and learning, but it requires knowledge and teaching how to use it safely.

COMPUTATIONAL THINKING/CODING

Currently, computational thinking (CT) is broadly defined as a set of cognitive skills and problem-solving processes that include, but are not limited to, the following characteristics (Grover and Pea, 2013; Stephenson and Barr, 2011 as cited in Wikipedia, nd, para 8):

- *Using abstractions and pattern recognition to represent the problem in new and different ways;*
- *Logically organizing and analysing data;*
- *Breaking the problem down into smaller parts;*
- *Approaching the problem using programmatic thinking techniques such as iteration, symbolic representation, and logical operations;*
- *Reformulating the problem into a series of ordered steps (algorithmic thinking);*

Computational and digital pedagogy **141**

- Identifying, analyzing, and implementing possible solutions with the goal of achieving the most efficient and effective combination of steps and resources;
- Generalizing this problem-solving process to a wide variety of problems.

Although it is now a common understanding that students need to develop a full range of ICT skills, the way to do so is not always clear. Before we can start coding, we need to focus on the development of computational thinking skills, for instance, logical thinking, following instructions, problem-solving, trial and error, analysis, prediction and so on. All these skills are used in and can be applied to coding. Computational thinking itself, however, can be taught '*unplugged*', that is, any activities that do not include computers or any other device (see Figure 9.2). We are big supporters of unplugged activities in a world where children grow up with a lot of screen time. A big advantage of using unplugged activities is that children learn CT skills through play, and teaching CT-skills can start at an early age.

Figure 9.2 Students working in collaboration exploring a city mat and beebots

Teaching computational thinking and coding can start as early as kindergarten; programming is a different matter. It is important to note that we do see a difference between the terms coding and programming. Online, in media or in everyday life, these two terms are used interchangeably, but we see programming as writing an actual computer program, whereas coding, like computational thinking, can be done unplugged. Programming makes use of computational thinking when working with and writing a computer program on an actual computer. Programming, using block-based coding as used in Scratch or other coding languages such as Python, JavaScript and SQL, is therefore merely an advanced or next step in the development of computational thinking and unplugged coding (see Figure 9.3).

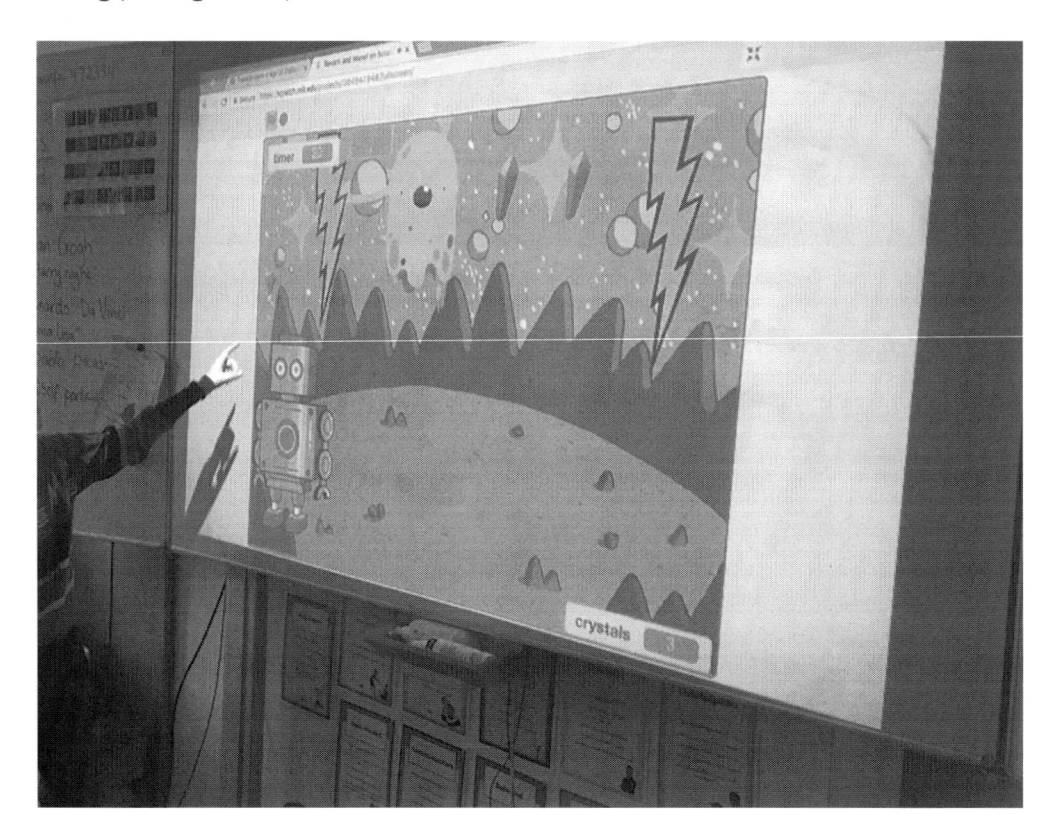

Figure 9.3 Student presentation on a Scratch game design

From the beginning of ISUtrecht, it was apparent that ICT skills were to play an important role in shaping our everyday teaching environment and a big focus was given to investing in the needed devices, boards and tools as well as instilling an ICT-friendly philosophy in the school's teachers, students and parents. In September of 2018, we took a step forward, launching a pilot in kindergarten, Grade 1 and Grade 2 levels, to teach computational thinking and coding. Our goal was to start practising computational thinking and coding at an early age, using unplugged activities as much as possible, and teach the skills necessary to do actual (block-based) coding and programming in upper primary. As a step between unplugged coding to block-based coding, we started by investing on SAM Labs app-enabled construction kits. There are many great tools out there, but SAM Labs worked well for us to connect the dots between the physical and the digital world. After that, a next step would be Arduino or Micro:bits programming at the end of Grade 5. In secondary school, the possibilities are endless from coding languages to anything our students are interested in.

As much as we think that learning to code, nowadays, is a useful skill, we do not envision all our students becoming computer programmers. We are, however, strong supporters of focusing on the computational thinking skills for all students, as this will not only help them become better at coding but – more importantly – we believe that it will help them become better learners in general.

The computational thinking pilot Grades 1 and 2: our experience

When we were asked by our leadership to start a pilot in computational thinking in the lower grades, we were of course very excited. We did not have any previous experience, so we really had to start from scratch and do a lot of research. Over the weeks that followed we tried things out, and tried to get an idea of what we think, what would be a logical way of teaching computational thinking skills in the lower grades, and used a blog to track our progress (Coorde and Dijkstra, nd).

In what follows, we describe some of our actual lessons and take the reader along on our journey so far. In the description, we cannot get around having to mention and describe in detail a few products we came across and started using. There are a lot of great tools, toys and games on the market. The products we use are simply products we liked, and which suited our specific needs.

Where to start when you want to teach computational thinking to six to eight year-olds? What are they capable of and how much learning can we pack in one lesson? Do we need a sequence of lessons to focus on a certain skill, or will one lesson suffice, and can we go on to the next skill? These were some questions we asked ourselves before starting. We did some research, thought about what skills we wanted to teach, looked at what lessons we could find online and tried to think about lessons ourselves. In the end, it was just a matter of starting somewhere and finding out through trial and error. One important decision we took quite early was to limit the amount of screen time. While we think that some screen time is important for the younger students, it should be limited. We are not alone in thinking along these lines (Deruy, 2017; Ritchie, 2017). Luckily, teaching computational thinking without the use of computer devices is not only possible but fun too!

The first lessons: giving and receiving instructions

To get the students excited, and to talk to them in terms they would be able to understand, we focused on robots. Not real robots, since we want to work unplugged, but we used the students' understanding of what a robot can or cannot do and how it functions; in other words, we focused on giving and receiving instructions.

In our first lesson, we let the students pair up. One of them was the '*computer*', giving instructions, the other student was the '*robot*', only able to do what the instructions told it to do. During the first couple of lessons, the computer was only able to give three instructions: start/stop (double tap both shoulders), turn left (tap on left shoulder) and turn right (tap on right shoulder). After getting used to these instructions and changing roles, we introduced a problem. The computers had to guide their robot through a course we set out, but there were obstacles they had to go over or under. We left it to the students to discuss which instructions (what code) they would use to have the robot deal with these obstacles.

The students loved these exercises. They loved coming up with their own instructions for evading obstacles, even though they were not practical at times. No, tapping the back of someone's knees when he/she is walking probably will not work. Of course, every now and then, some of our students would start ignoring instructions. We quickly found a solution for that. It must mean that the robot and/or computer was overheated, so it needed to cool down. We would draw a circle around them, which they could not leave until they were told to start up again.

By giving these lessons, focusing on giving and receiving instructions, our goal was to instil an intuitive way of algorithmic thinking (reformulating the problem into a series of ordered steps). The students ran into lots of problems while playing or controlling the robots. They were forced to break bigger problems into smaller ones, they were forced to do step-by-step thinking and solve the problems (troubleshooting or debugging) and they had fun while doing these activities!

The next step: the grid and writing or following code

Code does not have to look like the programming code a lot of people think of. It can be as simple as a few arrows telling you where to go, or where to move a piece on the board. Another example is the chess match descriptions in a newspaper. They give a step-by-step description of how the pieces moved on the chessboard. It is this simple depiction of code that we used in the next few lessons.

Having learnt, or at least developed, a feel for computational thinking, we started doing a series of grid-based lessons. Having worked on how to give and follow instructions, we started working on writing code. Students were given a set of worksheets where they had to guide Flurb (the character that was on the worksheets) to a piece of fruit, using arrows. After some individual exercises, each pair of students got a blank grid (a chessboard would also do) where one of them could place Flurb, the fruit and some obstacles. The other student had to write down the code (↑ ↓ ← or →) without using his or her hands to count the squares.

Over the next weeks, we elaborated these kinds of grid-based activities. We kept the students practising moving a character (Flurb) around a grid, towards its end goal. Complicating things a little bit, we also introduced obstacles on the grid, such as brick walls, dynamite or, a Grade 1 favourite, poo.

We also brought in a big grid (see Figure 9.4). Using a pre-written code, we '*ran that code*' on the grid. It was the students' job to write the code as they saw it as we were moving along the grid. After a few steps, we went back to the starting position and ran the code again, so the students could check if the code matched the steps. If not, they could debug or solve it (a term they were introduced to a week before). As it happens when thinking of and actually giving the lessons, we encountered a small problem: we

Figure 9.4 Students learning conditionals in a big grid mat

did not take perspective into account, which meant that the students on opposite sides had a different code written down.

The grid is a very useful tool when teaching computational thinking as it forces the students to think in steps, and those steps can be written down as actual, but simple code. It also creates a border and depending on the size of the grid, it will help students get an overview of how big or small the problem before them is. The bigger the grid, the likelier problems will arise, whatever the activity you use.

A different example of using a grid and code was the introduction of a *'drawing robot'*. This time the code would guide the *'marker or pencil-holding robot'* to move the pencil over the grid, telling it when to bring the marker down and start filling up the square. In a similar line of thought, we asked the students to create a drawing on one square, and figure out what code to give a robot, to copy that exact same picture.

One of the last lessons, using this *'drawing robot'*, showed us that it is not easy to follow step-by-step instructions and do exactly what the code asks you to do. We gave the students a pre-written code, and the students were challenged to be drawing robots themselves this time. The code said, for instance: *'colour in the square in black'*, *'move one square to the right'*, *'colour in the square in black'*, and so on. This resulted in a lot of different drawings. Not every *'robot'* thinks the same.

Code: some surprising results

Having worked on and experimented with coding, we have also been working on reducing the chance of running into bugs. By comparing code to a spelling test (the more words there are in a test, the likelier it is you will make a mistake), we explained the importance of limiting the number of symbols used in our code.

To do this, we introduced a new '*type of robot*' or actually a couple of robots. This time our robots (teams 1–4, consisting of our students) made one type of sound. For instance, robot 1 (or team 1) made the sound '*BOO*', robot 2 '*DZZP*', robot 3 '*TOK*' and robot 4 '*WEEE*'. To know when to make the sound, we needed a piece of code for each robot. The children came up with symbols such as squares and triangles. We then proceeded to write a piece of code and '*put*' it into our robots. When we finished a line of code, we added more and more code, until we had a long song of WEEEs, BOOs, DZZPs and TOKs.

After this, we asked the students if there was a way to shorten the code. Because, what if we had to use a code of 100 or 200 symbols, we would fill up the code grid fast! The students came up with solutions such as writing a tiny grid or using another board. But we kept asking about the code itself. After some prodding and suggesting, they did come up with a solution. We could write down one symbol, and then the number of times the sound was repeated. The students then tried to rewrite the whole code like that. They really rose up to the challenge.

As always, we tried to let students come up with a solution for a problem, and in each and every one of the Grades 1 and 2, students suggested to add the number of steps that needed to be repeated to the symbol. However, this was one of the first times we really noticed a clear difference between the students in Grade 1 and those in Grade 2. When the Grade 2 students were able to shorten more complex code (eg ↑→↑→↑→ = [↑→]3), the Grade 1 students were able to show the repetition of a single symbol (eg ♥♥♥ = ♥3). Reflecting on these lessons, we realised that the Grade 1 students might have to develop their multiplication skills and/or pattern spotting skills, before being able to solve more complex problems. We also realised that we had Grade 2 students doing Grade 7 (!) algebra, a surprising result indeed.

Intermezzo: games

Teaching computational thinking and coding should be fun for the students. We believe in play-based learning, and this should be kept in mind when approaching these lessons (see also Chapter 5). The lessons described above really felt like play to the students. Evidence of this was brought to us on more than one occasion when the Grade 1 and 2 main teachers sent us pictures of the students doing the activities we taught them during their free play.

Apart from our lessons, we also brought in some games and toys for the children to play with. There is a lot to find on the market, and we advise to look at these games and toys with a critical eye. A lot of them, we found, were very limited in educational value. Two examples of games and toys we liked and used were the Bee/Blue Bots and Robot Turtles.

Computational and digital pedagogy **147**

The Bee/Blue Bots are toys which allow you to push in the arrow keys (and GO button) on the bots to code them to move and turn. These are perfect for teaching problem-solving, sequencing, estimation and directionality and can be used in more than one way. They can be combined with language or mathematics lessons; in other words, they allow for creative use, which we find very important.

Robot Turtles is more limited in terms of creativity; however, this board game is a perfect tool for grid-based coding. Using playing cards with arrows, it is the player's job to move the turtle over the grid towards its end goal: a beautiful diamond. The game also makes use of blocking cards and shooting lasers to get rid of the blockage.

SAM Labs: STEAM and coding combined

In January 2019, we came across SAM Labs and decided to invest in their SAM Labs kits, as we felt these kits were able to service a very broad range of educational strands. The SAM Labs kits make use of wireless electronic blocks that each has a different use. There are lights, motors, sliders, buzzers, heat and light sensors and many more. All these Bluetooth-enabled blocks can connect to the others via the app to do something different (see Figure 9.5).

Figure 9.5 Students exploring SAM Labs light blocks

The educational applicability potential is big, whereas other (also great) products were too limited for our liking. With the SAM Labs kits, we can integrate STEAM, computational thinking, coding and (block-based) programming on a wide variety of projects and subjects. It also facilitates play-based learning, which we, as mentioned earlier, find very important. Another great thing is that we can use these kits in Grade 1 or 2 already all the way up to secondary. With these kits, you can go from STEAM (LEGO applicable, for instance) and CT to simple coding, to block-based coding, to actual coding as it works with Micro:bits as well.

The lessons

To prepare the students for our SAM Labs adventure, we first explored conditionals with the students. With the SAM Labs kit, the students also have to think in terms of: if < ... >, then < ... >, (or) else < ... >. All previous lessons, of logical, step-by-step thinking work up to this actual piece of coding.

An example is the following game we played: '*conditionals with playing cards*'. The rules are simple: write a conditional, like if <conditional>, then <reward>, or else <other reward>; for example: if <the card drawn is red>, then <say whoohooo>, or else <aaaaw>.

Then came the first series of lessons with SAM Labs kits. The first lesson was quite simple. We only used a button block and an RGB LED block. We explained how the blocks work and modelled how to connect and operate them. We value experiencing things first hand, so we explained what needed to be done, but we never gave away spoilers. It is so much more fun to see the looks on the faces of the students when they notice what their actions cause. It is priceless, especially once we started adding behaviour blocks (like: change colour of LED block light) and when students start trying things themselves. In the future, we will continue experimenting with these new tools, and try to find ways to integrate them within the existing curriculum. For example, Grade 2 will start a unit on city planning soon. We look forward to building a model city with them, creating working streetlights, doors that open and close automatically, windmills and who knows what else the students can come up with.

Challenges ahead

Computational thinking and coding are important skills to learn. They help to teach problem-solving skills; they help children develop new ways of thinking by breaking up big problems into smaller steps and take the fear out of making mistakes or failing. They can teach persistence in finding a way to solve problems.

Above we described the way how we, through trial and error, managed to find a way of teaching computational thinking and coding in what we think is a logical order. Reflecting on the learning process the students have been through, we can at least conclude that students love these lessons. Assessing the skills that the students acquire is our next step in the process.

To take this even further, it would also be important to look at the existing curriculum and see where computational thinking skills are already used or could be used complementary to certain other learning experiences. Examples we found already are things such as procedural writing, many mathematical activities which require a step-by-step approach, or even simpler things like getting organised. Finding a way to integrate the approach of computational thinking into regular teaching will be a challenge for us over the next few years.

Lastly, we would like to emphasise the importance of fun, play-based learning and the awareness of unplugged versus plugged teaching of computational thinking. If we are to teach our students these skills, the above is more important than ever. Play on!

GENERAL CONCLUSION

The use of ICT in schools is not new anymore. Computers have been used in most schools for over two decades now. However, their use is increasing, not only as a teaching tool, but also in the daily life of the students. Schools therefore have an important role to play in the proper way of using and learning how to work with ICT. It simply cannot be ignored. In this chapter, we talked about three strands of computer science, which we think are important areas to teach in/about: (1) digital literacy, (2) digital wellness and digital citizenship and (3) computational thinking/coding.

It is also important to teach our students how to use the vast number of tools available to them, how to utilise them for their own learning benefit and, of course, how to use them responsibly and properly in order to use the internet safely and responsibly. Students should be aware of the differences and similarities of the real and the digital world. They should learn how to create a healthy balance between the two and as a school we play an important part in this. We believe that if the students are given the right tools to have a safe and responsible digital life, they will be empowered to succeed in the twenty-first century. Learning how to use language in a digital setting requires us in education to rethink and reflect on traditional literacy.

Learning how to code, or at least learning computational thinking, is another important and relatively new skill, added to the skill set of our students, which allows them to understand and manipulate the devices they are working with every day. As we mentioned, we do not envision all of our students to become master computer programmers. However, some knowledge of the workings and use of our wide range of digital devices is necessary. Learning computational thinking will help to reach this goal, and it will also help our students become better learners.

In this chapter, we have described the challenges we faced while working on these separate topics. We have described the actual lessons we used and the results they yielded. We will continue to work on and teach these topics to our students. Much like many other schools, we are just at the beginning of this extensive process, and it will require a lot of tweaking, trying out and teaching to have a solid curriculum where the whole ISUtrecht teaching and learning community will be involved and inspired. The digital world and the interaction between the real and virtual world is constantly evolving and changing. So should we.

Reflective questions

1. Are we still focusing too much on ICT-skills instead of computational thinking in education?
2. In your opinion, should computational thinking be a vital set of skills that everyone should learn?
3. Do you think the use of new technologies benefits students' learning?
4. How does digital citizenship relate or compare to real-life citizenship?
5. What would your computational thinking lessons look like?

REFERENCES

BBC (2008) *Flying Penguin Hoax Video*. [online] Available at: www.bbc.co.uk/pressoffice/pressreleases/stories/2008/04_april/02/penguins.shtml (accessed 12 September 2020).

Blurton, C (1999) *New Directions of ICT-use in Education*. [online] Available at: www.unesco.org/education/lwf/dl/edict.pdf (accessed 12 September 2020).

Coorde, K and Dijkstra, W (nd) *Secretly Having The Most Fun in School. A Blog about Keeping Learning Fun at ISUtrecht*. [online] Available at: http://secretlyhavingthemostfun.blogspot.com (accessed 12 September 2020).

Deruy, E (2017) In Finland, Kids Learn Computer Science without Computers. *The Atlantic*. [online] Available at: www.theatlantic.com/education/archive/2017/02/teaching-computer-science-without-computers/517548/ (accessed 12 September 2020).

International Baccalaureate (2011) *The Role of ICT in the PYP*. [online] Available at: www.slideshare.net/bradycline/pyp-ict (accessed 12 September 2020).

International School Utrecht (nd) *Mission Statement*. [online] Available at: www.isutrecht.nl/organisation/mission-statement/ (accessed 12 September 2020).

Ritchie, M (2017) *Want Your Kids to Learn Coding? Start by Unplugging the Computer*. [online] Available at: www.info.thinkfun.com/stem-education/want-your-kids-to-learn-coding-start-by-unplugging-the-computer (accessed 12 September 2020).

Wikipedia (nd) *Computational Thinking*. [online] Available at: https://en.wikipedia.org/wiki/Computational_thinking (accessed 12 September 2020).

10 Rethinking literacy

Marcelle van Leenen

If it were possible to define generally the mission of education, one could say that its fundamental purpose is to ensure that all students benefit from learning in ways that allow them to participate fully in public, community, and economic life.

(The New London Group, 1996, p 60)

INTRODUCTION

Traditional notions of literacy tell us being literate means being able to read and write. The skills of reading and writing are important and irreplaceable. There is evidence to suggest that traditional handwriting, as it involves hand–eye co-ordination, is associated with academic achievement and cognitive development (James and Engelhardt, 2012). However, as we move more and more into a digital world, we need to redefine what being literate means. What does it mean to be literate in a world of constant and easily accessed information, social media, network tools, smartphones and tablets? What does it mean to be able to read and write online? A definition of twenty-first century literacy offered by the 21st Century Literacy Summit (2005, p 21) is

> the set of abilities and skills where aural, visual, and digital literacy overlap. These include the ability to understand the power of images and sounds, to recognize and use that power, to manipulate and transform digital media, to distribute them pervasively, and to easily adapt them to new forms.

More specifically, Richardson (nd) describes new literacies arising from new technologies as things like text-messaging, blogging, social networking, podcasting and video making. He also mentions that '*these digital technologies alter and extend our communication abilities, often blending text, sound, and imagery. Although connected to older, "offline" practices, these technologies change what it means to both "read" and "write" texts*' (Richardson, nd, para 4).

In today's world, most students have almost unlimited access to mobile devices. More than ever before, students are creating their own media, something not witnessed in past generations. A quick YouTube search will show an abundance of content created by young people. Another unprecedented phenomenon of this generation is that the information in students' everyday lives consists of eye witness video of current events. Current media messages are shaped through blogging, eye witness video accounts or Twitter feeds and this shapes the perceptions of viewers. This is one of the reasons why teachers have a responsibility to help educate students on these new literacies. Educators need to teach not only the traditional literacy skills students need to succeed but also the critical thinking skills that allow students to not only consume but *create* digital content. If schools do not adequately address media literacy in their curricula, students will merely be able to *respond* to stimuli created by others. Therefore, the question is not *whether* we should teach new literacies, the question is *how soon can we start*?

As becomes clear through the examples offered in this chapter, the great news is that technology offers educators a wealth of opportunities to teach not only new literacy skills, but other valuable skills, too. It allows children, as the opening quotation to this chapter mentions, to participate *fully in public, community and economic life*. As an example, students may publish their work on the web allowing not only their peers but a global audience to give feedback on their work. Through the creation and publishing of digital media students and educators share, teach and learn from each other. They learn engagement, accountability and motivation while contributing to community experience that expands their knowledge of communication in our global society. In today's networked world, participatory networked practices or '*participatory culture*' offer educators the opportunity to create authentic learning experiences for students.

This chapter highlights some practical examples of how learning about and through new media literacies can be incorporated into the enquiry classroom, and how this has been implemented in my own and other classrooms at the International School Utrecht (ISUtrecht). At the time of writing this chapter, I had just begun my new role at the school as digital literacy coach. The practices mentioned here serve as the rationale for my digital coaching plan at ISUtrecht. Two important concepts that occur throughout the chapter are described below, which are participatory culture and enquiry and technology.

What is participatory culture?

Participatory culture is an opposing concept to consumer culture — in other words a culture in which private individuals (the public) do not act as consumers only, but also as contributors or producers. Advances in technologies have enabled private persons to create and publish such media, usually through the Internet.
(Willis, 2003 as cited in Everything Explained Today, nd, para 1)

Since the technology now enables new forms of expression and engagement in public discourse, participatory culture not only supports individual creation but also informal relationships that pair novices with experts.
(Jenkins et al, 2006 as cited in Everything Explained Today, nd, para 2)

Enquiry and technology

Inquiry teachers challenge learners to come to understanding through tackling a problem, looking for connections between case studies or analyzing data they have gathered. As they engage with a learning episode through inquiry, students gradually construct and deepen those principles for themselves.
(Murdoch, 2015, p 14)

In an increasingly globalized and digital world we are inundated by huge quantities of information which is available to us almost any time and anywhere. This is vastly different from the context many teachers grew up in and demands different skills. Students need to learn how to effectively and safely locate, access, evaluate, use and contribute to this ever-evolving global information bank, and that's what inquiry is all about.

(Murdoch, 2015, p 15)

Technology and learning to be media literate can provide opportunities for authentic assessment, give access to authentic audiences, increase collaboration, diversify resources, foster enquiry and enable documentation for learning and assessment. The following sections explore these opportunities in more detail. First, the benefits of technology for the digital learning environment and assessment are discussed. The increase and advantages of online communities for learning are also explored. Then, fostering enquiry and independence through active literacy and participatory culture is described. The different ways in which technology allows for more creative research is discussed. A final word is given on the importance of the mindset of the teacher.

THE DIGITAL LEARNING ENVIRONMENT, REFLECTION AND ASSESSMENT

The concept of the environment as a participant in the educational experience, referred to sometimes as *'the third teacher'* (Reggio Emilia, nd), is one we recently discussed at ISUtrecht. During a staff meeting, we examined each other's classrooms in order to share and receive feedback about what our classroom environment communicated about our values and approaches to teaching and learning. It was then that I realised that the classroom blog can say a lot about who we are, what we do and what we value as educators. The purpose of the classroom blog is multi-faceted. Apart from home–school connections and building community, it can serve as a tool for reflection through documenting learning, a means to reach out globally and make connections with other classrooms and experts, a memory aid, a place to celebrate, share and give feedback on student learning and for students to have a voice and express creativity. It can also serve as a curation platform, or an online hub for learning, where resources are easily shared with students. It can show an intricate web of links to enquiry pedagogy. The following are a few snapshots of how I have used the blog.

We regularly visit our classroom blog as a class. Often, we start the day by reading yesterday's blog posts, which are supported by visuals of student learning and often include video. It allows us to connect with the learning that is happening, perhaps notice new things, and gives us the opportunity to generate new questions. Often, when we link back to previous learning, we get up the relevant blog post on the screen so that we can revisit what actually happened. For example, when we returned from a field trip at the end of the day, we used the blog to record our reflections. The next day, we reconnected with the event and created new questions.

The blog also allows us the opportunity to share and celebrate each other's learning and to showcase how the community is part of our learning. One of my students, who has only been learning English for a year, shared his interview with an entrepreneur on our blog as part of a unit of enquiry on the market place. He was extremely proud of this interview that his mother had helped him create and was keen to share his success. It was also an opportunity to invite and model feedback. As a result of him sharing his learning, other students started wondering about something the entrepreneur had said. It allowed us to delve into advertising and the role social media plays in developing a product or service, creating a new direction for our enquiry.

The blog allows students to publish for authentic audiences. Using the blog, students know that their work can be shared with parents, grandparents, friends on the other side of the world and anyone interested in following our class. This creates an authentic platform for feedback and builds confidence for learning.

Another valuable thing about the classroom blog is that it allows teachers to be transparent about their approaches and to create a mirror for what is valued in a classroom. For example, as a teacher, I want to model myself as a lifelong learner. At the start of the year, I spent time on creating *a community of learners*. We talked about what learning is and how it is done best. Together, we came up with many definitions and we took pictures of ourselves with quotations we developed. I did this because it connects to the concept of lifelong learning and having it up in the classroom and on the blog helps me to refer back to it throughout the year.

As an enquiry teacher, I make a point of modelling myself as a learner by being transparent and thinking out loud. '*I'm not sure, but let's see if I can find out.*' I also talk to students about being a learner in my profession and often inform my students about *why* we are doing something. '*The reason I don't want you to raise your hand, is because I want everyone to have some thinking time. I learnt that talking through our ideas is part of learning, that's why it's important that everyone gets the chance to do that.*'

For this reason, I have created a page on the class blog with the tab '*teachers learn too*' (see Figure 10.1). Parents and students can visit this page to see who I am as a learner by following me on Twitter or visiting the platform on which I curate professional articles. I might visit the page with the students to show how my decisions are informed by an article I read. The classroom and the digital environment help me model myself as a lifelong learner, something I value as an educator.

Documenting learning on a blog allows teachers to assess student understanding at deeper levels. Instead of relying on fleeting moments, videos of student interactions and images of student work can be documented to be revisited and to invite feedback from a wider community. Making decisions about student understanding is much more meaningful if they can be revisited.

Another valuable way to document and assess learning, and one that is being used by teachers at ISUtrecht, is the use of a digital learning portfolio. A tool like Seesaw is a digital platform on which students create, reflect, share and collaborate. Students show what they know using photos, videos, drawings, text, PDFs and links. This platform allows students more ownership over documentation of their learning and is a powerful tool to involve them in a meaningful assessment process. This is a closed platform and is an excellent

Rethinking literacy **155**

Teachers learn too!

Ms Marcelle is a learner too!

Who I follow and professional learning resources I curate

Figure 10.1 Screenshots from blog page

tool to build learning portfolios that show progress over time. It allows students to reflect orally or in written form. They can view and leave feedback on other students as well.

Another ubiquitous tool that through mobile devices is now at teacher fingertips is video. Video, which is also a form of meaning making, is particularly useful for student self-reflection. To understand that collaborative reading helps us better understand and appreciate literature, an activity used in Grade 4 is '*annotexting*' (Fisher and Tribuzzi, 2012). Much like annotating a text, students annotate videos of their literature discussions. After identifying the elements of a good literature discussion and recording their group discussion, students work together to annotate the video, commenting on indicators of success. This is a highly reflective and agentive way to improve metacognition.

CONNECTED LEARNING

> *Participatory cultures remind us that creativity isn't a solitary endeavor. It is nearly always to and from a community. Great ideas rarely happen in isolation. Instead, they are a part of the constant sharing back and forth of what we are learning, doing, and making. This is why it's so valuable to show our work.*
>
> (Spencer, 2019, para 14)

Connected learning, or connectivism, is a learning theory of the digital age according to which people use technology to learn and share information on the internet (Siemens, 2005). Technology reminds us that the world is an infinitely big place to share our work and connect with communities of other learners and experts. Like the enquiry classroom, new online communities allow learners to engage in deep thinking, rich conversations, writing and research. At ISUtrecht, a tool we use to build a community of readers is Flipgrid. This is a very accessible platform on which students can record themselves recommending books. It works like a board of videos that can be accessed and clicked on to hear what peers are reading.

A literacy teaching emphasis at ISUtrecht is *'to foster an enjoyment of reading'*. Thus, teaching children ways to look for new novels to read outside or just looking in the library and providing opportunities for students to read different genres is a huge part of that. Flipgrid provides an opportunity for students to connect with other students and can spark inspiration to expand their reading interest. Additionally, reading and recommending books is an authentic pursuit that adults engage in as well. Book reviews require certain structure and language features that can be explicitly taught. In this way, students are apprenticed into being digital citizens with the skills necessary to actively take part in online reading communities.

Another example of how connected learning happens at ISUtrecht is the use of Skype and Twitter to connect with experts. A Grade 3 teacher at the school wrote the following:

> *About 2–3 weeks ago I found Chris Gadbury on Instagram and Twitter and read through his blog where I found links to a number of children's books that are linked to the United Nations sustainable development goals. Since Grade 3 is focusing on those in our unit on heroes and we are writing different types of narratives in our language unit, I decided to reach out and send him an email. We had some contact through email and he was keen to set up a Skype interview with Grade 3. The students came up with a list of questions beforehand. He lives in Hong Kong and works there as an art and language teacher and writes children's books on the side.*

It is worth mentioning the extent to which social media is used by teachers to connect with other educators in order to learn from each other and to get inspiration. On Facebook, there are groups dedicated to very specific teaching areas, ranging from word study to mathematics. These online communities provide an unprecedented means to improve teaching practice. They open up classroom doors in ways previously unimaginable. They serve to support teachers and also provide a platform to celebrate and showcase examples of good practice.

Twitter is another platform used by teachers that can really accelerate learning. In a previous blog post, I have written about how Twitter helped me learn about an enquiry spelling approach – an extract of which is copied below.

> *My principal shared a Maths blog on Twitter by Graeme Anshaw that drew my attention: I loved the documentation of learning on this blogpost, but especially the blog header 'rescuing children from textbook or worksheet learning'. I saw a*

connection with my own ideas about learning, so started following Graeme on Twitter. A few weeks later, he shared a picture of student work. The image drew my attention because I could see that this showed an approach to word study that involved student enquiry. Initially I was just planning to use the activity. However, I opened the link in his tweet and that's where the learning journey really began, uncovering a network of teachers who were using the same approach. Over the next few days all I wanted to do was learn more. I spent time looking at blog posts and videos of student work from other international teachers who had used a similar approach, like Dan Allan who use Peter Bower's approach to teach spelling and word study as well as Lyn Anderson's wonderful blog.

(Houterman, 2016)

FOSTERING ENQUIRY AND INDEPENDENCE THROUGH ACTIVE LITERACY AND PARTICIPATORY CULTURE

In the introduction, I mentioned that educators need to prepare students for a future in which they know how to participate online, not only how to *respond* to stimulus created by those who know how to operate technology. An approach to teaching literacy that includes critical thinking skills to decipher media but also the *creation* of all kinds of media, particularly the kinds of media that students engage with on a daily basis, is of paramount importance to develop twenty-first century global digital citizens.

There is an ever-growing amount of web tools and applications that can be used for the creation of digital media. The use of these tools is an engaging way for students to show conceptual understanding of a unit while at the same time working on collaboration, technology, literacy, self-management, thinking, communication and research skills. The added advantage of then also publishing their creations is that it increases student motivation and awareness of audience.

During a unit of enquiry on natural disasters, a Grade 4 class collaborated on creating a news broadcast. They watched different news broadcasts and created their own success criteria of what a good broadcast looked like. Through the use of Green Screen and IMovie, students then created individual pieces such as interviews with experts, reports from the news scene and background reports which were then pieced together as one class broadcast. The children were able to use their own questions to explore the lines of enquiry in depth. For example, in learning about how the severity of a disaster depends on the location of the country, one student explored the construction of disaster-proof buildings. He then staged an interview pretending to be an expert engineer for the construction of hurricane-proof structures. With a picture of the types of structures used as the backdrop on the Green Screen and also a picture of the damage done by a hurricane in a developing country, this student explained in detail his understanding of how developing countries have limited resources to build hurricane-proof structures, hence the damage done was far greater.

In the process of piecing together the broadcast, students showed a high level of engagement and took their role and accountability in the creation of the broadcast seriously.

During an end of unit parent sharing afternoon, the broadcast was played on the big screen as a kind of premiere viewing of their hard work. Students were visibly proud of their product and the skills they developed in the process were invaluable – not easily replicated in the traditional classroom.

For home learning, students in Grade 4 are regularly encouraged to explore new webtools. Adobe Spark was recently used to create a timeline for a unit on civilisations. When a student was showing her successful product on Seesaw, other students were inspired to start using this tool as well (see Figure 10.2). As a result, a whole array of products was created using this visually appealing tool to show understanding. In this way, students are taught that they have the skills to be part of participatory culture and they can tell our technology what to do, to participate and not just be at the receiving end of it.

Figure 10.2 Student work on digital learning portfolio

One of ISUtrecht's guiding statements is:

> We use technology in an innovative and sensible way to enhance our teaching and learning. We equally appreciate the value of sensory and tactile experiences. We approach the virtual and real world as one, behaving consistently as we are moving from one to the other.
>
> (International School Utrecht, nd)

In the digital world, when we publish our work online, we are inviting feedback from a global audience. It is therefore even more important to teach students how to give feedback as responsible and active digital citizens, what that looks like and how to do it so that their peers feel empowered. This is a digital literacy skill because it is a way of actively participating in a global community, much like as the school's guiding statement says, we would hope to behave offline too. Giving feedback online is part of being internationally minded, which is the main goal of an International Baccalaureate (IB) education (International Baccalaureate Organization, 2017). When giving feedback, students can show that they appreciate the creations of others, make connections with other learners in order to learn from them, share their learning and contribute to as well as learn from the internet. In Grade 4, we therefore spend a lot of time making sure that students have the skills to give feedback. We use the ladder of feedback to comment on student work. This means that we give feedback by moving up the rungs of the ladder. The different steps on the ladder are:

1. clarify (students ask clarifying questions to ensure their understanding);
2. value (students tell what they think is good about the work);
3. concerns (students tell what they are sceptical about in the work);
4. suggest (students offer ideas on how to improve the work);
5. thanks (students share their appreciation of the work).

(terBorg, 2018)

After a while it becomes noticeable that students use this type of feedback automatically when commenting on each other's work and it becomes a routine of the classroom, as can be seen in Figures 10.3 and 10.4.

Home Learning | Unit of Inquiry

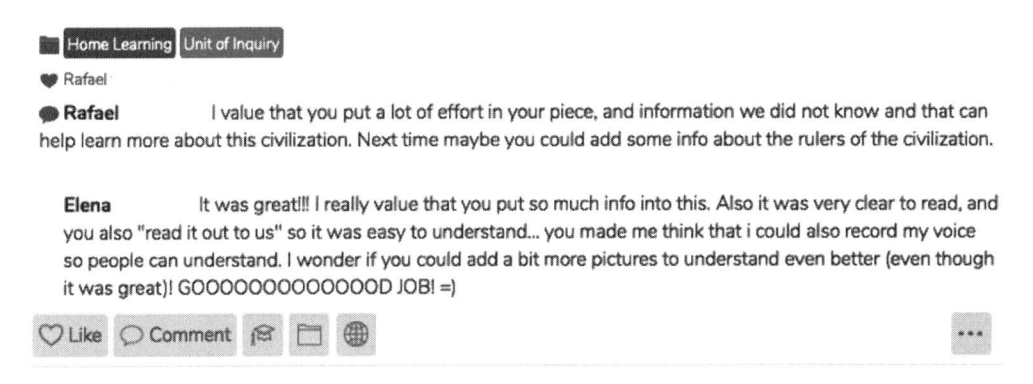

Rafael

Rafael   I value that you put a lot of effort in your piece, and information we did not know and that can help learn more about this civilization. Next time maybe you could add some info about the rulers of the civilization.

Elena   It was great!!! I really value that you put so much info into this. Also it was very clear to read, and you also "read it out to us" so it was easy to understand... you made me think that i could also record my voice so people can understand. I wonder if you could add a bit more pictures to understand even better (even though it was great)! GOOOOOOOOOOOOOD JOB! =)

♡ Like   ⌾ Comment

Figure 10.3 Students giving feedback to each other

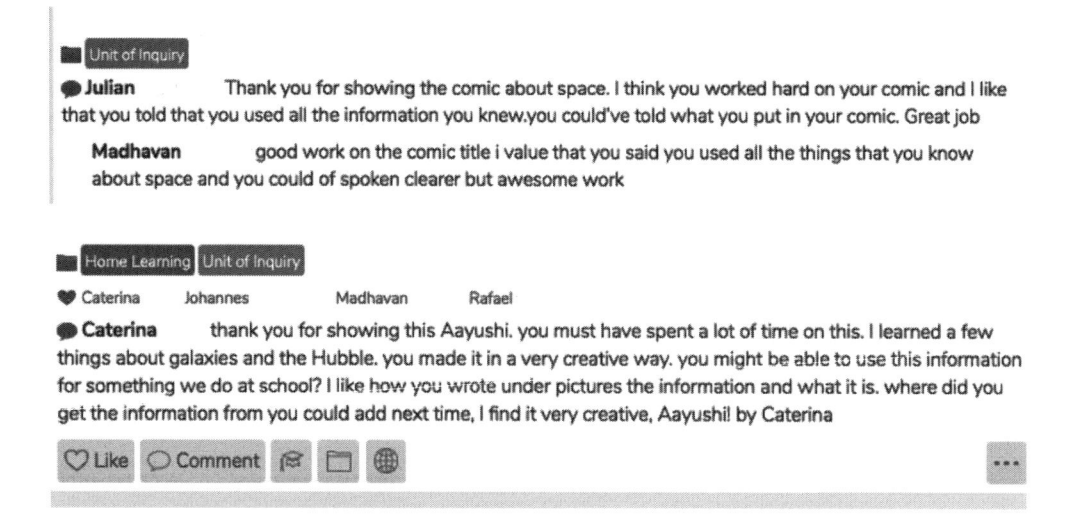

> **Unit of Inquiry**
> 💬 **Julian**   Thank you for showing the comic about space. I think you worked hard on your comic and I like that you told that you used all the information you knew.you could've told what you put in your comic. Great job
>
> **Madhavan**   good work on the comic title i value that you said you used all the things that you know about space and you could of spoken clearer but awesome work
>
> **Home Learning | Unit of Inquiry**
> ❤ Caterina   Johannes   Madhavan   Rafael
> 💬 **Caterina**   thank you for showing this Aayushi. you must have spent a lot of time on this. I learned a few things about galaxies and the Hubble. you made it in a very creative way. you might be able to use this information for something we do at school? I like how you wrote under pictures the information and what it is. where did you get the information from you could add next time, I find it very creative, Aayushi! by Caterina
>
> ♡ Like   💬 Comment

Figure 10.4 Students giving feedback to each other

RESEARCH

Enquiry teachers encourage all types of research, including interviewing experts, doing surveys and observation. However, as teachers we also know that learners rely on the internet to do research, as do their parents and most of the people they know. If a student is doing research on ancient civilisations and types Indus Valley into the search bar, Google will return 29,200,000 search results. Apart from this being overwhelming and digitally unsafe for young students, there are far more clever and efficient ways to do research. Curation platforms and online communities are the answer. During a unit, teachers collect an abundance of resources from the internet. As part of a #pyp (Primary Years Programme) hashtag search on Twitter, they may come across pictures, videos and ideas of how other classrooms have approached a unit on ancient civilisations. Teachers may have asked on the Facebook group they have joined whether anyone knows of a good video to show the decline of the Ottoman Empire. This video will not show on a Google search, because it is popular among a small number of people (teachers) and the first Google hits are based on most viewed. Teachers can then create a community themselves using a platform like Google Communities or Flipboard on which they curate all these resources to share with students. The teacher may decide to open this platform up to the whole school and parent community, so that everyone is actively collecting and curating the most relevant, up-to-date and engaging content.

Teachers can show students how to do research like this themselves. Like in the example provided earlier, a classroom Twitter account could be opened to connect with experts and search for information using specific hashtags. Once students know the power of Twitter they may be heard saying things like: '*Maybe we can see if the writer of this book is on Twitter and we can ask him questions*' or '*Can I interview this expert on Twitter about how he created the Ocean Clean-up? I want to see if I can get ideas for my product'*. Questions like these are evidence of independent learning, which is what we aim to foster in our students. We just need to show them the power of the digital tools at their disposal and how they can use them to be part of a connected world.

CONCLUSION

As this chapter has shown, teaching children to use technology as a vehicle to participate, engage with the world and make a difference in the community matches the ideals of an IB and international education. However, when we introduce technology into the classroom, we have to understand its power, and as teachers engage with it ourselves. We have to make sure our knowledge of and familiarity with the new technology is adequate enough so that the lesson material can be amplified and transformed for the better through using the technology, not just substituting paper and pen. However, technology changes at such a fast rate that as soon as we think we have mastered a new application or webtool, a new one replaces it. The disposition of the teacher is therefore very important. Showing children ways to troubleshoot, modelling a growth mindset and showing we are learning *with* the students are crucial in navigating the digital landscape.

Reflective questions

1. What changes to your current literacy programme could you make for it to include digital literacy?
2. Which authentic audiences could you connect with to support learning?
3. What opportunities do your students have to create digital content?
4. How could you use technology to document learning?
5. What tools or resources would you need to teach digital literacy skills successfully?

REFERENCES

Everything Explained Today (nd) Participatory Culture Explained. [online] Available at: http://everything.explained.today/Participatory_culture/ (accessed 12 September 2020).

Fisher, M and Tribuzzi, J (2012) Annotexting. [online] Available at: www.curriculum21.com/2012/03/annotexting/ (accessed 12 September 2020).

Houterman, M (2016) *Globally Connected: An Inquiry into Word Works*. [online] Available at: languageandliteracyforlearning.blogspot.com/2015/10/globally-connected-inquiry-into-word.html (accessed 12 September 2020).

International Baccalaureate Organization (2017) *What Is an IB Education?* Cardiff: International Baccalaureate.

International School Utrecht (nd) *Mission Statement*. [online] Available at: www.isutrecht.nl/organisation/mission-statement/ (accessed 12 September 2020).

James, K H and Engelhardt, L (2012) The Effects of Handwriting Experience on Functional Brain Development in Pre-literate Children. *Trends in Neuroscience and Education*, 1(1): 32–42.

Murdoch, K (2015) *The Power of Inquiry: Teaching and Learning with Curiosity, Creativity and Purpose in the Contemporary Classroom*. Northcote Vic: Seastar Education.

Reggio Emilia (nd) The Environment as the Third Teacher. [online] Available at: https://reggioemilia2015.weebly.com/environment-as-a-third-teacher.html (accessed 12 September 2020).

Richardson, W (nd) New Literacies in the Classroom. [online] Available at: https://modernlearners.com/new-literacies-in-the-classroom/ (accessed 12 September 2020).

Siemens, G (2005) Connectivism: A Learning Theory for the Digital Age. *International Journal of Instructional Technology and Distance Learning*, 2(1): 3–10.

Spencer, J (2019) Students Should Share Their Process, Not Just Their Product. [online] Available at: www.spencerauthor.com/seven-reasons-to-show-your-work/?fbclid=IwAR3PuNIC-Pjpo5EQRRggcAcmYzlHd1nFBAbNkqY6y0x_c5ABOz93J-2i188 (accessed 12 September 2020).

terBorg, S (2018) Ladder of Feedback. [online] Available at: https://sonyaterborg.com/2018/10/21/ladder-of-feedback/ (accessed 12 September 2020).

The New London Group (1996) A Pedagogy of Multiliteracies: Designing Social Futures. *Harvard Educational Review*, 66(1): 60–92.

21st Century Literacy Summit (2005) *A Global Imperative: The Report of the 21st Century Literacy Summit*. Austin, Texas: The New Media Consortium.

11 Towards new mathematical thinking

Idalet de Haan

INTRODUCTION

'Grade 3s, take out your maths books. Write the date on the right-hand side. The date is 13-03-1997. Write the title "multiplication" on the left-hand side in you book. Put your pencils down and eyes on the board when you're done'. Miss Sonja writes the date and heading on the board and turns around. *'Everyone done? Put your pencils down, no fiddling'*. All the children sitting at their decks arranged in rows place their pencils on their desks. *'Right... today I'm going to show you how to multiply 2-digit numbers with a 1-digit number. First you write the 2-digit number at the top. Then you write the 1-digit number under the 2-digit number. Make sure the units line up with each other. Like this:'* She writes the following equation with chalk on the black board:

$$\begin{array}{r} 24 \\ \times\ 3 \\ \hline \end{array}$$

'First you will multiply the 4 with the 3. So, 4 × 3, who can tell me what 4 × 3 is? Put up your hand if you know the answer. Alice, what is 4 × 3?'

'12'

Most of us know the end to this lesson. This was a traditional mathematics lesson of my childhood, in which the teacher stood in front of the class and the children had to watch him/her solve a mathematical problem on the board. After that they received the instructions to either solve similar problems in their textbook or copy problems from the board. Assessment was done by the teacher or students and the final mark was based on the correct answers by the student.

This is a perfect way to teach children to become workers in the industrial age, in which they are taught in uniformity; the learning is outcome- or product-oriented and the personal worth is dependent on performance. However, we live in a world where we need to prepare students for jobs that most probably do not exist yet, jobs they might even need to create for themselves. We teach students who live in a world which is ever-changing, information overloaded. We need to make a mind shift from teaching children to follow orders and steps provided by the teacher to taking initiatives, from being dependent to taking personal responsibility, from product-oriented to process-oriented (Bluestein, 2012).

Teaching during the COVID-19 lockdown in South Africa as a substitute teacher made me realise once again how important it is to step away from the product-oriented approach, to the process-oriented approach. Suddenly, all around me teachers used to the traditional approach were confused about how to deal with the change of going online. It was a big step for me as well, and it was hard work. But now suddenly, the question arose: '*How do we assess the students when they cannot write tests?*' We cannot give them marks. Because of this product-oriented approach they were used to, the teachers were unable to focus on life skills that are way more important than a final mark. This was such a rich opportunity to teach time-management, open-ended questioning, critical thinking, technology skills, the importance of good communication, digital wellness, digital etiquette, ownership and personal responsibility. In this time, the focus could have shifted from testing knowledge to fostering and improving skills. This situation further reinforced my perception that we need a shift in the way we approach teaching and learning.

Throughout this chapter, I explain how we teach mathematics lessons with an enquiry- and concept-based approach by provoking learners to get engaged and actively participate during lessons to build upon their own understanding. I touch upon pre-assessment that guides the planning of the lessons to create differentiated opportunities for children to progress on their own level, as well as summative assessment and student reflection. Furthermore, I discuss the importance of social learning in which students are encouraged to have conversations with and seek advice from each other. Lastly, I stress the importance of building mathematical knowledge from concrete to abstract and using real-life examples to help students to create an understanding of mathematical concepts.

CREATING CONCEPTUAL UNDERSTANDINGS TO GUIDE OUR LEARNING

At the International School Utrecht (ISUtrecht) where I taught for three years, we adhered to a concept-based approach to teaching mathematics (see also Chapter 6). Concept-based mathematics moves away from the traditional approach to teaching and learning, where the focus is on drill and kill rote memorisation (Wathall, 2018). A concept-based approach aims for learners to explore and investigate mathematical concepts, rather than the traditional approach in which the teacher models mathematical skills and content, and learners show their understanding by repeating those skills. Our aim was to actively engage students to enjoy, enquire and discover mathematical concepts by taking on an inductive teaching approach. We presented students with problems and examples that led them to seek patterns (see also Wathall, 2018). According to David Sousa (2011), researcher on how the brain learns, human beings have an innate quality to pattern seek.

To create meaningful experiences and lessons, we tried to connect the mathematics (and other disciplines) with the current theme/unit of enquiry as much as possible. For example, during a marketing unit, we focused on money or during an explorers unit we did map work. However, integrating mathematics to the unit topics is not always possible, and thus we did teach stand-alone mathematics units as well. When planning a lesson, we decided on the outcomes and created conceptual understandings that we wanted the children to reach through learning experiences. These conceptual understandings drove the planning of our lessons not only to develop knowledge, which is lower-level cognitive work, but also to stimulate complex thinking (Erickson et al, 2017).

Our brainstorming often took place in the form of sticky notes and a big sheet of white paper. We brainstormed all the content and vocabulary we would like to cover as well as the mathematical processes we would focus on. Two or more concepts were combined to create a sentence of understanding, or generalisation that was timeless, universal and abstract. Therefore, instead of having verb-driven objectives, we created generalisations (Erickson et al, 2017). Table 11.1 below shows a list of concepts that were turned into generalisations.

Table 11.1 Concept and generalisations

Concepts	Generalisations or conceptual understandings
Measurement Area Perimeter Relationships Formulas Models	• Linear measurement is used to determine the perimeter and area. • There is no direct relationship between area and perimeter. • Through manipulating models, we can prove our formulas work. • With the correct vocabulary, we can explain our thoughts and opinions.

Table 11.2 illustrates more examples of generalisations created for different mathematical topics.

Table 11.2 Generalisations

Shape and space	Time	Multiplication
• Transforming shapes using tessellation and reflection does not change the properties of the shape. • Symmetrical objects have parts which can be matched by rotating, reflecting and translating. • Nets contain the same 2D shapes in the right relationship to each other. • Shapes are grouped and named according to their properties.	• Natural time cycles (including your internal clock) are dependent on latitude. • Time zones are dependent on longitude. • Digital and analogue are two different ways of visualising and expressing time. • Re-reading a word problem and key words help us identify what is being asked.	• Properties of number help us understand multiplication. • Different strategies can lead to the same answer. • Rounding, imagining number lines or diagrams and using properties of number help us to estimate calculations. • Mathematicians recreate different representations to show patterns in multiplications.

We created these conceptual understandings to not only focus on content and skills, but also help students to use the facts and skills to recognise patterns, links and transferable ideas (Erickson et al, 2017). When creating generalisations, we also took into account the seven mathematical processes, which help students to understand, learn and do mathematics. These seven mathematical processes are:

1. students apply their knowledge through *problem-solving*;
2. through *reasoning and proving*, students solve mathematical problems;
3. student *reflect* on their abilities and strategies used to solve problems;
4. students select different *tools and computational strategies* to solve problems;
5. students *connect* mathematical ideas and concepts, also to other disciplines;
6. students create visual *representations* of mathematical problems;
7. students *communicate* their understanding to express what they have learnt.

The mathematical processes help students to develop conceptual understandings and connect conceptual understandings to knowledge and skills (Ontario Ministry of Education, 2005).

With these conceptual understandings, we created three columns; the first column contains the conceptual understandings we have developed. In the second column, we wrote down the evidence we needed from students in order to demonstrate their understanding. Lastly, we brainstormed the learning experiences that best help students to show their understanding. When thinking about experiences, we tried to incorporate both lower (ie facts and skills) and higher (ie conceptual) levels of thinking (Erickson et al, 2017). Table 11.3 is an example of the three-column sheet we created in order to guide our lessons.

With this basic outline, we first decided on the pre-assessment (ie diagnostic assessment) where we assessed the children in order to find out what they already know. After that we also created the summative assessment, since that was the moment where students were asked to show their learning. The pre-assessment can be an activity starting out with a problem, or a discussion in which the children share their pre-knowledge of the topic. The pre-assessment determines the students' abilities and needs, which helped us to plan good differentiated lessons, in order to accommodate the abilities and meet those needs. The summative assessment is the final assessment activity or test at the end of the unit. We planned this prior to the lessons. We determined what we wanted the students to understand and be able to do at the end of the mathematics unit. Assessment is discussed more at the end of this chapter (see the section *Assessment of mathematics*). Next, I move on to talk about the enquiry approach and how to use that in mathematics.

ENQUIRY-BASED APPROACH IN MATHEMATICS

After the pre-assessment, we started planning the lessons. We planned our lessons with an enquiry-based approach which is an inductive approach to teaching (see also Chapter 7). More specifically, enquiry-based learning builds on the idea that people

Table 11.3 Generalisations, evidence and experiences

Generalisations	The evidence we need	Experiences should include
Symbols help us visualise items and their locations on maps.	• Explain the purpose of a key. • Read a map by using a key. • Designate appropriate symbols to the key. • Draw symbols that are representative of their features.	Using an atlas and using the symbols to identify the scale, locations and objects through questioning. On a trip to the park, the children must make a map with a key to represent the area.
Locations on earth are described by longitude and latitude.	• Show/draw the longitude and latitude lines. • Find locations on a map by looking at the longitude and latitude.	Using an atlas, the children will identify, through questioning, the longitude and latitude. Making a grid (representing longitude and latitude) on a carpet where the children will plot/find different co-ordinates.
Co-ordinates and grids help us organise maps.	• Draw the grid and the co-ordinate mapping styles. • Differentiate between grid and co-ordinate location.	Create/read maps of different locations.

are born with an inherent curiosity to understand the world around them. Students' questions and wonders drive the learning in an enquiry-based classroom and the teachers facilitate students to answer their questions with multiple tools and resources (Chiarotto, 2011). Students are encouraged to explore by using multiple senses and get the opportunity to interact with the concrete world to develop abstract thoughts (Pataray-Ching and Roberson, 2002). It is not a rigid methodology and focuses on the process of learning rather than on covering the outcomes of the curriculum (Chiarotto, 2011). The teacher assists learners by setting up and planning engaging situations and by listening to the learners, asking open-ended questions, encouraging student thought and recording observations. Enquiry-based learning promotes investigation, exploration, research and study, rather than just merely answering questions (Kuhlthau et al, 2007).

Enquiry can be presented by a cycle with phases – this is called the *enquiry cycle*. Pataray-Ching and Roberson (2002, p 498) state that *'the inquiry cycle provides a curricular framework that puts the learner at the centre of the curriculum'*. There are multiple ways to present the enquiry cycle. Pedaste et al (2015) identified and summarised the core features of enquiry-based learning by identifying the following five phases:

1. *orientation*;
2. *conceptualisation*;
3. *investigation*;

4. *conclusion*;

5. *discussion*.

The enquiry cycle is not a linear process from one phase to the other, but rather moves back and forth between these phases. Figure 11.1 below displays a visual representation of the phases.

Orientation

Introducing and tuning into the topic and stimulating curiosity

Conceptualisation

Creating questions and hypothesis to investigate

Investigation

Doing investigation, experiments and research by collecting, organising and analysing data

Conclusion

Noticing patterns and relationships, drawing conclusions, making inferences and judgements

Discussion

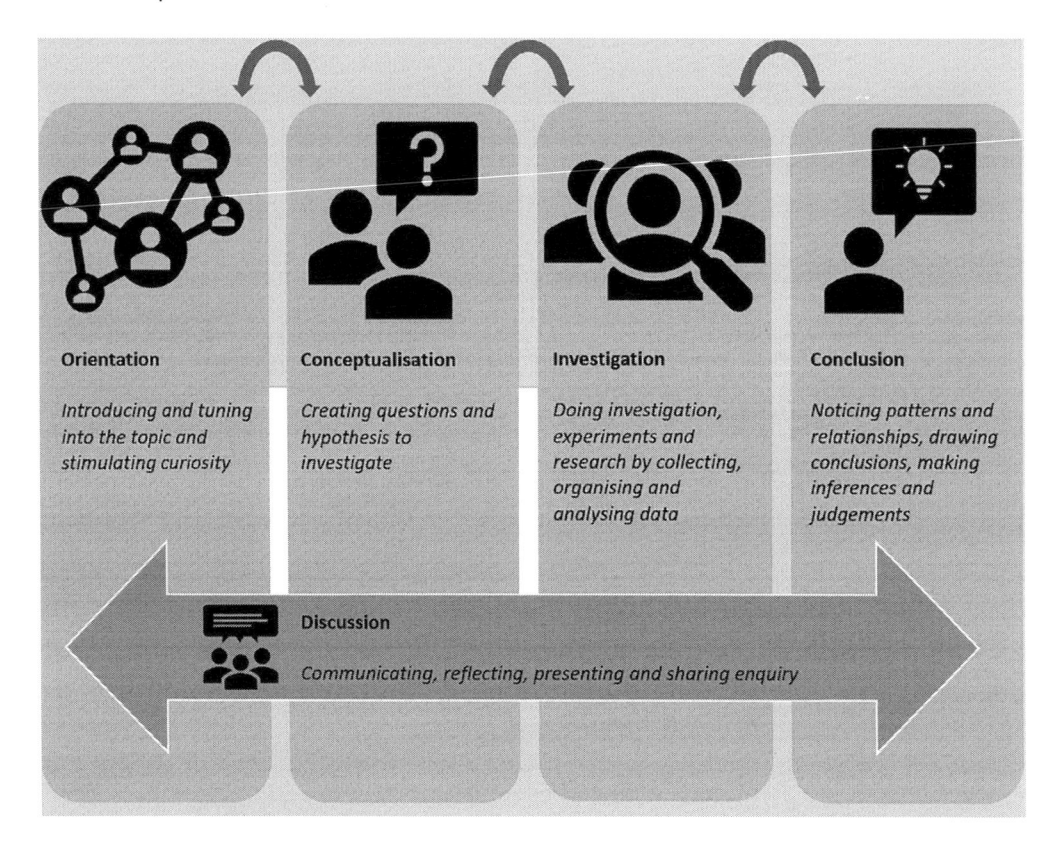

Communicating, reflecting, presenting and sharing enquiry

Figure 11.1 Enquiry cycle
(Adapted from Pedaste et al, 2015, p 56)

An enquiry begins with the orientation phase in which the topic is introduced with the purpose to stimulate curiosity. It is very important here to introduce the topic in a provoking manner in order to move on towards the next phase, that is, the conceptualisation phase. During the orientation, we want to introduce the topic, make the children curious and stimulate them to go investigate. The provocation can be something as simple as an interesting problem or question, a peculiar object like a protractor or ruler, a funny story or books, information presented in a different way or various resources. Table 11.4 contains some examples of provocations used to introduce different topics and possible questions that can rise for the conceptual phase. The conceptual phase is the phase in which questions and hypotheses are created to explore during the next phase, that is, the investigation phase. Students are encouraged to ask questions which are used by teachers to plan lessons during the investigation phase.

Table 11.4 Provocations and questions

Topic	Provocation	Possible questions
Volume and shape	Give the students a challenge to create a popcorn container for a movie theatre. The container should hold 100 pieces of popcorn. After creating the container, they can test their containers by filling it up with 100 pieces of popcorn. (Do not show the amount of popcorn at the start of the activity.) Have a discussion afterwards about what their initial thoughts and strategies were when creating the container, by asking questions.	What does 100 pieces of popcorn look like? Will the container change in size if we fill it with marbles/blocks? How do we express the size of a container? How do we measure volume? How will you know how to create a container for more/less popcorn? Is popcorn a reliable measuring tool? Why/Why not? How do we measure the volume of a rectangle/round container?
Number	Make different representations of numbers with blocks. For example, make a pile with 20 blocks, put 20 blocks in a long line, make two rows of ten, four rows of five, stack the blocks in ten columns of two each, make a row with three, seven, four and six blocks. (Instead of only representing the number 20, you can also represent different numbers simultaneously.) Guide the children by asking questions about the different representations, such as: which pile do you think has the most blocks? How do you know how much is in each representation? Which representation do you need to count/or not? Which representation shows the amount the best?	What makes some representations clearer than the rest? Why are they clearer? Can we come up with other ways to represent the number 20 with blocks? How do we express our representations by using the correct vocabulary? How can we present numbers by using other items in the class/or on paper? Where would we use the representations in real life?
Data-handling	Give the children a provoking problem, like 'The average temperature in the Netherlands was 17 °C this week. Give the possible temperatures it could have been throughout the week to reach that average'. You can add a table partly filled out.	Are there more possibilities for this problem? What does average mean? What do we need to take into account when we calculate the average? What could have been the highest/lowest possible temperature that week? Would it be possible? What time of year would you get this average? Why?

Mon	Tues	Wed	Thus	Fri	Sat	Sun
24 °C				20 °C		

The teacher can guide the children in creating potential questions to investigate, and record the questions as drivers for the investigation phase. The aim is to create open-ended questions that can be investigated, as opposed to closed questions with a yes or no answer. For instance, at ISUtrecht, we created wonder walls with the questions we came up with.

During the investigation or exploration phase, students make discoveries related to their questions and collect evidence to support their findings (Pedaste et al, 2015). The teacher provides opportunities to do hands-on activities that lead to the discoveries. This can be done by giving different supplies to solve problems, providing the students with resources to investigate and record findings, or giving them materials to manipulate and create with. Table 11.5 below demonstrates a few activities in which students get the opportunity to explore, solve problems and answer questions. We usually tried to create open-ended problems with more than one correct answer. These types of problems foster high-level thinking and motivate children to dig deeper into a problem. Subsequently, correct answers can be given at different levels, therefore adhering to the different abilities (Sullivan and Lilburn, 2017).

Table 11.5 Investigation

Question	Activity
What strategies can we use to measure elapsed time?	Give the children a (differentiated) problem to solve elapsed time, such as how much time do you spend sleeping/at school/doing homework?
	Challenge them to find different strategies to solve the problem. Give them timelines, clocks, blocks, white boards, etc, to solve the problems.
	Have them share their solutions and compare their strategies at the end and discuss which strategies work best. During this discussion, the teacher can provide correct terminology, such as elapsed time, starting time, end time, duration, etc.
Where do we use fractions in our daily lives?	Give the children magazines from which they can cut out different pictures where they can possibly use fractions. They can create posters and show how they will cut the different objects into fractions and name the possible fractions they will cut them into. Have them present their findings to the class and have a conversation about their findings.
	Give the children different types of fruit and have them cut the fruit in fractions for a fruit salad. Have them express how they cut the fruit, how many pieces there are and what each piece represents. Have them cut the same fruits differently in the same amount of piece and compare the fraction pieces.
Can we measure the area of an object that is not a square?	Give the children the challenge to find the area of the triangle. Take a paper that is a square metre and cut it in half, so it creates two right-angled triangles. Ask them what the area of the triangle would be. Let them write down their thoughts.

Question	Activity
	Pose the next question – can the area of a triangle be measured with squares and expressed in square metres? Or how will you express the area of a triangle? Have the children come up with theories which they then have to reason out and prove.
	If the formula to measure a square is length × width, what will the formula be to measure a triangle?
	Present them with other shapes to create formulas for those shapes, such as a trapezoid, octagon, equilateral triangle or circle.
How do I know how many objects there are?	Tell the students that you counted six of something in the classroom. They need to find the possible answer and discuss how do they know it is six.

During the conclusions phase, students share, defend and present their findings from the investigation phase to the teacher and their peers by using mathematical language. This can be done in multiple ways, for example, in small group meetings, classroom discussions, PowerPoint presentations and making videos. At ISUtrecht, we recorded the discoveries by creating posters and wall charts to refer back to when needed. For instance, we created a wall chart when we compared fractions. The wall chart with our understandings and correct vocabulary helped students communicate their understandings. Since they were part of the process of creating the poster, they knew where to look and find the information when needed in the following activities. Another way to consolidating the students' learning at the end of a mathematics lesson or unit is to have the children create a concept map on what they have learnt. They can create this either collaboratively or individually. The consolidation can also be a video clip which they can create with tablets, in which they explain their findings or strategies in a few minutes. The advantage of this is that you can share it with parents or/and use it for formative (and even summative) assessment. In the past, we have used an online platform where students can share their work with each other and their parents. However, it is important to make sure that you have the parents' consent to post photos and the students' work.

Take note that in the *enquiry cycle* displayed in Figure 11.1, the discussion phase permeates the whole enquiry process, rather than being a phase on its own. The discussion phase provides opportunities for students to communicate their findings and to help the teacher clarify any misconceptions. Discussion can be encouraged by asking questions to help the students communicate their understandings so far and to help them to go deeper in their learning. Here are some example questions that can be asked.

- How do you know that is the correct answer? Why do you think that?
- What strategy did you use? How did you come up with this strategy?
- Will this strategy work on a different problem? Have you tried it with another problem?
- Can you think of a different strategy that might also work?
- What materials in the classroom (or elsewhere) can you use to prove your answer?
- Why is your strategy not working? Have you tried something else?

- Have you tried someone else's strategy? Can you explain their strategy in your own words?
- Why is your answer not the same as Sarah's? Does that mean one of you are incorrect? Why/why not?
- How will this apply to...?
- What do you think of Ben's strategy? Do you agree with his strategy? Why/why not?
- Can you explain your strategy step by step in order for others to follow?

Reflection can be defined as the process of critically thinking about our behaviours, attitudes, beliefs and values. It is a vital part of any learning process. Reflection is shown to be a very effective way to guide students to become more motivated and take charge of their own learning (Roberts, 2008). Reflection can be completed informally and during lessons, for example, by asking students to indicate with their thumbs up, down or in the middle on how they are progressing through an assignment, dealing with their teamwork or understanding the content. In what follows are some examples on how reflection can be implemented in a more formal manner and at the end of a lesson to guide students to think about how and what they have learnt.

- Two stars and a wish

Two stars and a wish (also known as two roses and a thorn) is a reflection strategy in which students write down or say two things they are proud of or did well. Then they have to fill in a wish, something they would like to get better at, learn more about and need help with. The students can also give two stars and a wish when providing feedback to peers. This type of reflection teaches students that there is always room to grow and improve. Another alternative to two stars and a wish could be two hopes and a wonder.

- Helps and hinders

Students reflect on their learning behaviour by filling in what helps and what hinders their learning. This is very useful as it helps students make better choices when taking on a learning activity in the future. Moreover, it gives feedback to the teacher where he/she can guide the student best.

- Traffic light

Students can use the colours of a traffic light to reflect on their learning. The lights can present different issues. For example, the red can represent *'Something that really challenged me was ...', 'I really don't understand ...', 'I should stop doing ...',* or *'A mistake I made today was ...'.* Orange can represent *'I'm still wondering about ...', 'I still need to improve ...', 'I'm going to think about...'* or *'... was really interesting today'.* Green, in turn, can stand for *'I'm going to keep on ...', 'I was really successful with ...',* or *'I'm really proud of ...'.*

- Exit slip

Have the students fill out an exit slip at the end of the lesson. The question on the slip can be different every time. For example, have the students fill out three things they have learnt, two skills they have developed and one issue they still need to improve on. The students can also just write down a question they still have about the topic or rate themselves on a continuum.

These are just a few examples of how students can reflect upon their learning. There are many more creative ways, such as creating a drawing, making a video or writing down their feelings. Reflection helps us to keep on developing our skills and to know how effective we are. Next, I discuss how to differentiate when teaching enquiry lessons.

DIFFERENTIATION

Differentiation is an approach to learning and teaching in which students' differences are acknowledged and addressed (Tomlinson, 2014). Differentiation takes place when learning is planned and structured to meet the different needs and abilities of students (see also Chapter 2). It is important to make students feel valued as individuals with their own strengths and weaknesses. In order to do that, one must create an environment where students are protected, respected, included, challenged and supported (Whitworth et al, 2013). One way to create a safe environment is by having conversations with the children about how people are different, how they learn and think differently and like different things. In my lessons, I provide personal details about myself, to show the learners my strengths and weaknesses. I let them (respectfully) point out what they think my weaknesses are. Then they are asked to reflect on their own skills, what they are good at and what they should be working on. These reflections can help the students to understand that we are all at different levels, and have our own strengths and weaknesses that we have to work on. This is also applicable in mathematics. Some students can solve problems and get a correct answer, but they are unable to explain how their strategy works or clearly communicate how they solved the problems; others can come up with very creative ways of solving problems but are unable to work in a group and allow others to come up with ideas. Skills such as group work, communication and organisation can also be developed and worked on in the mathematics lesson, alongside the content. Table 11.6 gives some examples on how differentiation can be applied to mathematics lessons.

Enquiry-based learning can provide multiple ways to differentiate learning to match the diverse learning styles of learners (Guido, 2017). Differentiation can take place by differentiating access to content, adjusting the process, or lastly the product through which students show their understanding (Whitworth et al, 2013). At ISUtrecht, we planned the enquiry activities to meet students' needs by providing a range of content and ways to process it. Enquiry activities allow you to meet your students' learning needs and preferences (Guido, 2017). Good mathematics enquiry lessons are tiered lessons, which is a differentiation strategy that addresses the same generalisation for all levels, but students arrive at this understanding by following different pathways (Adams and Pierce, 2004). Table 11.7 explains a lesson on multiplication, in which students solve problems using different strategies, addressing the same generalisation (ie *multiplication problems can be solved in a variety of ways*), but at different levels.

Table 11.6 Differentiation examples

Differentiation	Example
Access of format: The material being presented	Provide different ways for students to access information on linear measurement by addressing different senses. Here are some examples. • For your pre-assessment, you can gather that some students already have good knowledge about linear measurement. Create small groups where these students explain the content using white boards or other materials. • Have an expert (eg an architect) come to school and share how he/she uses linear measurement in his/her field. • PowerPoint presentation by the teacher. • Watch a video about linear measurement.
Process: The activities students do to make sense of the material	There are multiple ways to present activities for students to develop and practise their skills; here are some examples when drawing and recognising number. • Drawing numbers in sand. • Looking at flash cards and tracing them. • Playing a game with a friend. • Creating numbers with playdough. • Practising on a computer.
Product: The outcome or assessment of the material	There are multiple ways to produce a product. For example, when covering a topic like shape and space, students can be asked to create different 3D shapes by choosing one or more of the following materials. • Paper, scissors and sticky tape. • Playdough. • Toothpicks and Blu Tack. • Drawing 3D shapes. Students can be challenged to create more interesting shapes, like octahedron or hexagonal prism.

Table 11.7 Differentiated lesson plan

Differentiated lesson on 'multiplication'

Enquiry question: *What strategies can I use to multiply one-digit numbers with two-digit numbers?*

The teacher lays out different materials, such as base-ten blocks, chains, graph paper, white boards, number lines and even calculators. Then she/he presents the following problem: A farmer packs 34 apples into four boxes. Altogether he packs 136 apples. Is that correct? By using the different materials, how many *ways* (or strategies) can you think of to prove whether it is correct or not?

Students can work in pairs or groups, using the different materials set out to prove whether the statement is correct. They will come up with different strategies and share their finding at the end.

The figures illustrate some examples of possible solutions students could come up with when using the manipulatives:

In Figure 11.2, the number of apples is presented by the chains. The chains are grouped in tens and units. Putting the tens and units chains together and then adding up the total gives the final answer.

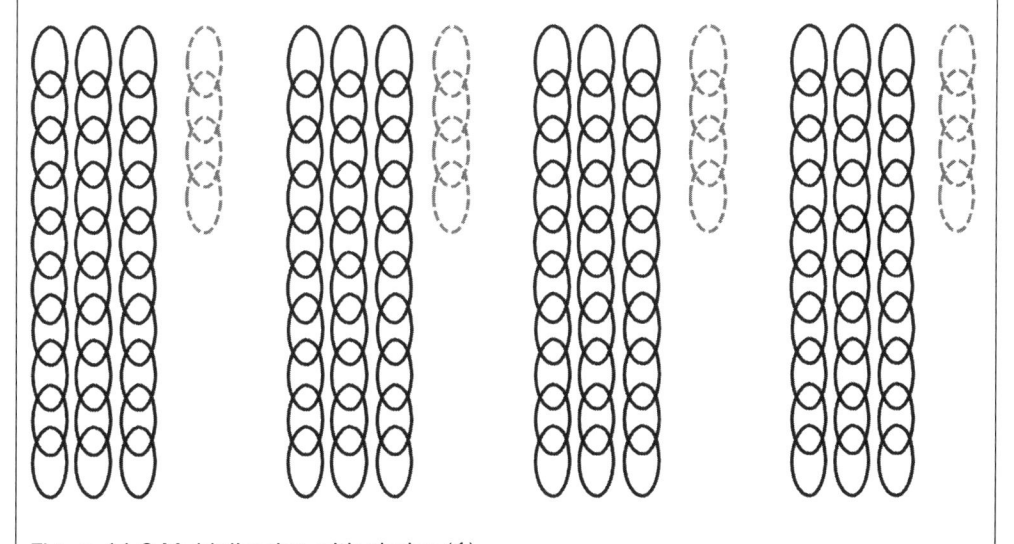

Figure 11.2 Multiplication with chains (1)

176 TEACHING AND LEARNING IN INTERNATIONAL SCHOOLS

Figure 11.3 shows a different presentation with chains, where the solid chains symbolise tens and the dashed chains units.

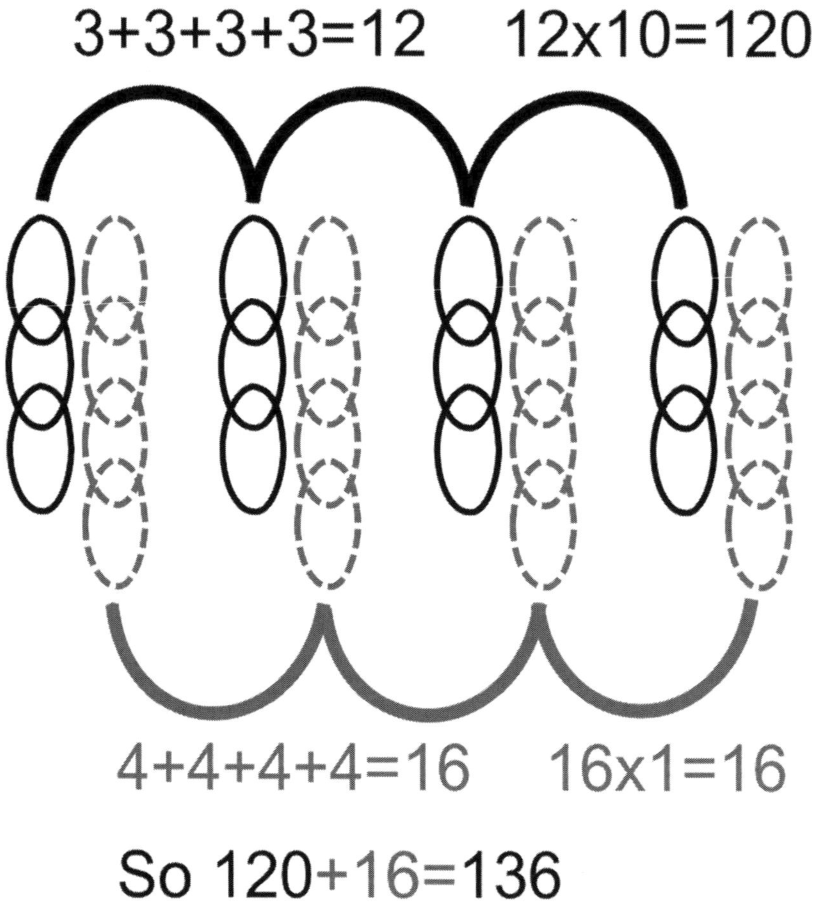

$$3+3+3+3=12 \quad 12 \times 10 = 120$$

$$4+4+4+4=16 \quad 16 \times 1 = 16$$

So $120 + 16 = 136$

Figure 11.3 Multiplication with chains (2)

Very similar to the chains, Figure 11.4 shows how base-ten blocks can be added together. These blocks really help students understand how numbers are made up of units, tens, hundreds, etc.

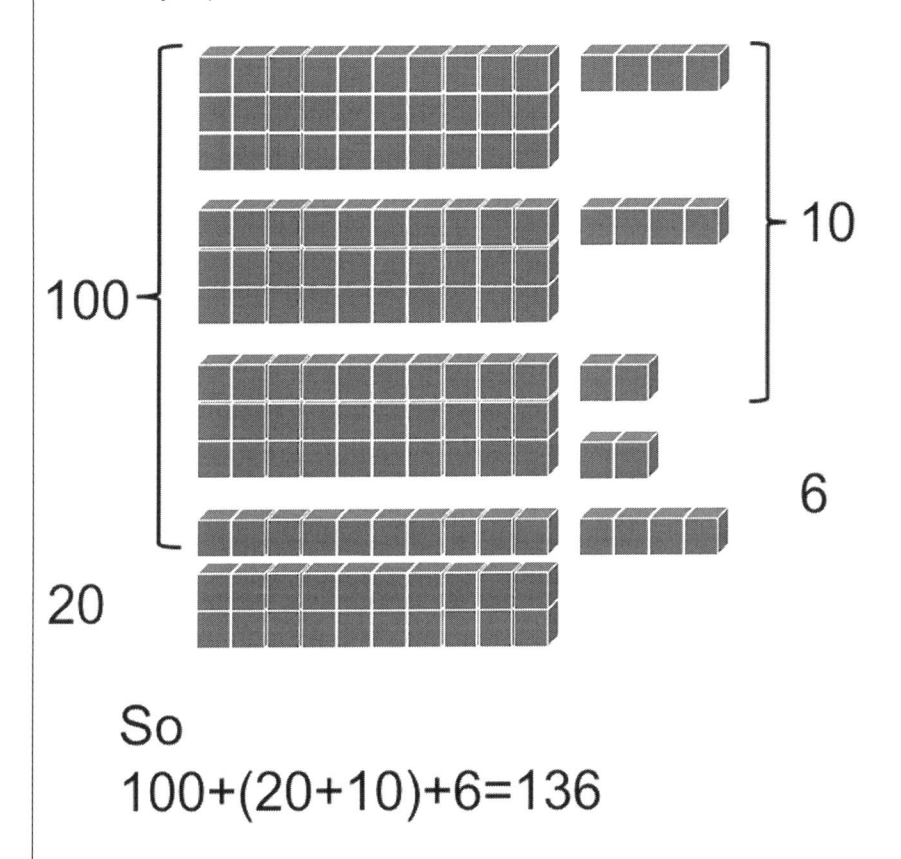

So
100+(20+10)+6=136

Figure 11.4 Multiplication with base-ten blocks

Figure 11.5 below shows an example where the number 34 (first four times 30 and then four times four) is repeatedly added on a number line. By decomposing the numbers into tens and units, it becomes easier to add them together.

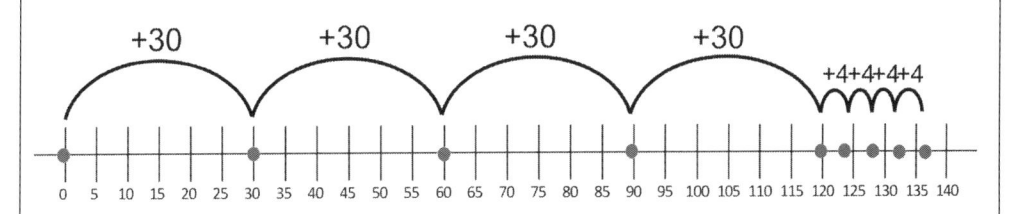

Figure 11.5 Multiplication with a number line

Figure 11.6 beneath demonstrates more abstract strategies and methods, such as doubling, repetitive addition, the traditional method and breaking numbers apart.

```
   34              1           34 × 4          30+30+30+30=120
 + 34             34         (30+4) × 4        4+4+4+4=16
 = 68           ×  4          30 × 4 = 120
 + 68          = 136           4 × 4 = 16      120+16=136
 = 136                        120+16=136
```

Doubling   Traditional method   Breaking numbers apart   Breaking numbers apart and repetitive addition

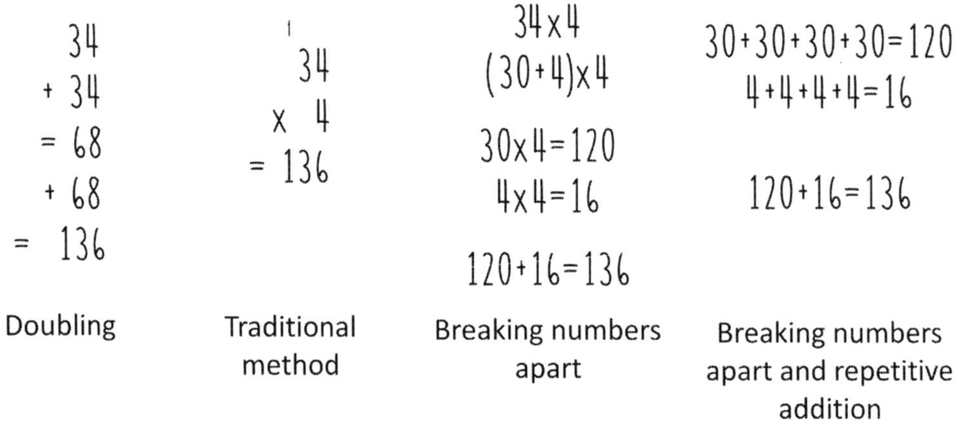

Figure 11.6 Abstract strategies

After coming up with as many strategies as possible, the students get the opportunity to share their findings. Different photos, charts or posters can be created to display the possible strategies on the wall. Through discussion, students can reflect on the various strategies and decide which strategies work best, take less time or make the most sense to them.

By providing more problems, the students can get the opportunity to try out their peers' strategies. They can be asked to explain the strategy to each other. Below are three possible tiers at which the students can work (the teacher can alternate between these groups).

Tier I: Students are expected to know at least their own and one/two other strategy. They can work in small groups to solve problems together and explain different strategies to each other.

Tier II: Students are expected to solve problems using at least three different strategies and try out a fourth strategy that challenges them. They have to be able to explain how the strategy works at the end, using appropriate vocabulary.

Tier III: Students investigate alternative methods. Figure 11.7 illustrates some alternative ways to do multiplication. These strategies provide the students with the opportunity to investigate how they work and why. My personal favourite is the *Russian peasant method*', which really challenged my students in the past. The students can be given the task to create videos for an online platform where they need to explain how the strategy works and the logistics behind this strategy.

→

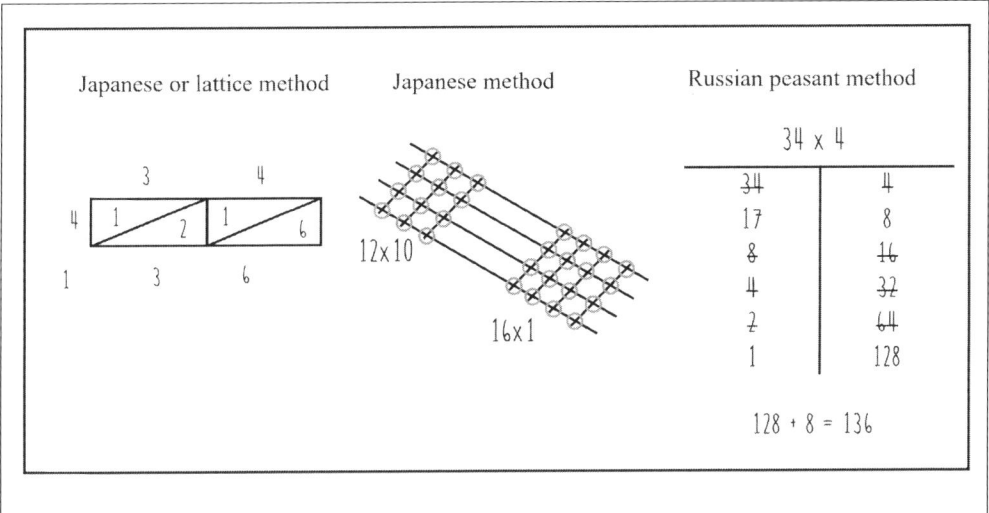

Figure 11.7 Alternative methods

When creating differentiated groups, I generally do not tell students which level, what content or activity I think would suit them best, but I rather explain the levels and then give them the opportunity to make a choice. Even though I create groups in advance according to the students' abilities, I allow them to choose the level or activity they want to work on. When I notice that students might choose beyond or below their level, I will observe them first and then have a conversation with them based on how there are doing on that specific activity. For example, if Sarah were to choose an activity that is too easy for her, I would approach her and ask her questions like *'Why did you choose this level?'* *'Do you think this is the right activity based on how well you did in your pre-assessment?'* *'How can you challenge yourself more?'* *'Do you think you learn anything if you choose activities that you can get the answer to so quickly?'* When the teacher asks these questions, the students start to think about their own learning and reflect on whether learning is actually taking placing, rather than just the outcome or high grade at the end. This way the students are part of their own learning journey, being guided by the teacher to understand and develop their abilities.

ASSESSMENT OF MATHEMATICS

Assessment is an ongoing process during enquiry. As already mentioned earlier in the chapter, we planned our assessments at the beginning of the mathematics unit to begin with a clear and understandable vision of what we wanted the students to achieve throughout the unit (Zumach, 2016). The assessment guides the rest of the lessons, since it determines the students' pre-knowledge, what they need to learn throughout the mathematics unit and what should be taught to them. We as a school provided structured feedback rather than grades, because we wanted learners who focus on the learning process that takes place rather than the achievement. We assessed what the students did well, their strengths, as well as where they need to improve on, their weakness. Pre-assessment (also known as diagnostic assessment), formative assessment and summative assessment should be part of the enquiry. Both the content and mathematical processes should be monitored and assessed (Fry, 2014). It is important that students are aware of what is being assessed, especially during summative assessments. Assessment should be done by both the teachers and students and it is vital to reflect on the assessment afterwards in order to set future goals and improve skills. Furthermore, self-assessment helps students to monitor their own learning and to develop into independent, self-directed, lifelong learners. Students can be guided to reflect on their learning by using '*I statements*' that they need to place on a continuum from never to always. For example, '*I was on-task*', '*I understand different strategies*', '*I work well with my group members*'. By providing 'I statements' students become increasingly more familiar with the process of self-evaluation (Zumach, 2016).

Pre-assessment (or diagnostic assessment) is used to determine students' knowledge and skills, and therefore the foundation to build on new knowledge and develop skills further. It is done at the beginning of the unit, topic or lesson, and helps to determine how best to differentiate in class and where students might need extra attention (Swearingen, 2002). A pre-assessment can be a short activity where students show what they already know, and teachers identify what to teach and whether there are any misconceptions. Most traditionally in a mathematics classroom, a pre-assessment will take the form of a test, but there are other ways to pre-assess students as well. Listed below are some ideas I have picked up along my teaching journey that move away from tests.

- Students create a concept map on what they already know about the topic. You can even provide a list of concepts/words that will be explored throughout the unit which they can use to create the concept map. For example, for data handling you can use concepts, such as data, graphs, patterns, comparison, attributes and classification. This exact same activity can be done at the end, and then the students can compare their two concept maps to see their development and improvement, and no matter the ability there will be progress.
- The teacher presents cards with statements, to which students give their opinions, for instance, '*agree*', '*disagree*' or '*do not know*'. This can also be done by moving around in the class, where each area represents an opinion. There can be statements such as, '*There is a strong connection between area and perimeter*', '*There are other ways to present the number three*', or '*Multiplication is a different way to calculate addition problems*'.
- Students fill out a KWL (ie know, wonder, learnt) chart shown. First, they fill in what they already know about the subject, then what they are wondering about. At the end, they fill in what they have learnt.
- Give the children different concepts that will be explored throughout the unit and have them rank the concepts from easy to hard.

Formative assessments are done throughout the unit to inform the teacher of students' progress, understanding and needs, in order to plan for the next lessons, improve own instruction and guide students to deeper understanding and develop their skills (Swearingen, 2002). Formative assessment can be the discussions you have with the children and observations during and after their enquiries. Listed below are some alternative ways to do formative assessments.

- Create carousel charts in which students are presented with a statement, word or open-ended problems and students need to write down what they think and then pass it on to the next student or group.
- Have the students fill out a self-evaluation questionnaire in which they share what they have learnt so far and their struggles.
- Have the students write in their reflection journals. The teacher can provide prompts to help them write reflections. Some examples of such are challenges they encountered and new knowledge they gained or questions they still have. This will give the teacher feedback on how the students received the lesson material and what to teach them next.

Summative assessments are the final assessment conducted at the end of the mathematics unit that assesses skills, conceptual understandings and knowledge of the students. It provides information on the progress and the achievements, first to the students, but also to the parents and the teachers (Swearingen, 2002). Traditionally, a mathematic summative assessment would take the form of a test; however, these tests are usually aimed at the average students, making others feel incompetent. A test usually only focuses on getting the answers right, rather than assessing deeper thinking skills and understanding. The emphasis at the end is on the level of achievement, rather than the process of learning. Listed below are some alternative ways to assess the students' learning as a process.

- Open-ended problems. The students can be asked to solve an open-ended problem, which allows them to answer the question according to their ability. Table 11.8 illustrates some examples of open-ended problems.

Table 11.8 Open-ended problems

Open-ended mathematics problems
I bought a candy bar at the shop. I got €1.67 change. What coins might have made up the change?
A soft drink costs five units of a country's money. What country could this be? Have the students study money from different countries and the exchange rate.
Ben's bicycle shop sells bicycles and tricycles. Ben counted a total of 30 wheels. How many bicycles and tricycles might there be? Show two different answers for this question.
There are ten squares that are 1 cm² each. If packed together, what will the perimeter be? Come up with different solutions.

- Creating a concept map with the generalisations. Students expand on the generalisations, by creating a concept map showing their understanding of the different concepts. They can give real-life examples to explain the concepts and elaborate on them by using correct vocabulary. Table 11.9 shows an example rubric which the teacher can use to assess the concept map.

Table 11.9 Rubric

	Emerging	Developing	Consolidating	Exceeding
Student was able to connect their learning experiences to the generalisations.				
Student showed understanding by giving real-life examples and using the correct vocabulary.				
Student actively participated during different activities.				

- Creating a video. Ask the children to create a video to explain the lesson material. By teaching others, students show deep understanding, since they need to know the material before they will be able to explain it to someone else. As a class, you can discuss the criteria and create a rubric for making a video.

In addition, parent involvement helps children to achieve better and reflect and build on their experiences. One way to engage parents is with digital portfolios; at our school, we use an online platform to communicate with parents (there are many digital sources out there to create digital portfolios). We share our daily activities and students can post videos and documents on this site to show their work. The parents can watch the posts from home and comment on these or have conversations with their children at home.

CONCLUSION

In conclusion, teaching with a concept-based approach helps children to understand the 'big ideas' and how these apply to the real world. They learn how to make meaning of the content and skills they are learning and transfer their understanding across different disciplines. Along with teaching with an enquiry-based approach, which is an open-ended approach to learning, encouraging students to be curious by asking questions makes the learning go deeper. Students are encouraged to be actively involved in the learning process, which motivates them to take ownership of their learning. These approaches help students to develop skills which are needed to be lifelong learners and prepare them for the working life. When teachers use a concept- and enquiry-based approach, students can reach the same understanding, but be guided to that understanding at different levels. An enquiry classroom welcomes students at different levels, without making them feel frustrated or left-out. Furthermore, the process of learning is celebrated, rather than the level of achievement. As a teacher who taught in a very traditional setting during the first years of my career and then moved on to an international school, one of the biggest differences I saw was in the students' motivation. All the students enjoy coming to school and take part in the learning activities with curiosity. They have a voice and they shape the lessons as we go along. As a teacher, it excites me to see how they develop, how their understanding of their own abilities increases and how they are constantly willing to improve and learn more.

Reflective questions

1. How do you go about planning for a mathematics lesson to ensure students are actively engaged and participating?
2. Do you have an inductive or deductive approach to your teaching? Which do you think is more important? Why?
3. How do you encourage both students and parents to focus on the process of learning rather than the product?
4. How do you differentiate your mathematics lessons to ensure everyone is learning?
5. Can you think of alternative ways to assess students' learning during a mathematics unit rather than a standardised test?

REFERENCES

Adams, C and Pierce, R (2004) Tiered Lessons: One Way to Differentiate Mathematics Instruction. *Gifted Child Today*, 27(2): 50–65.

Bluestein, J (2012) *Industrial Age vs. Information Age*. [online] Available at: https://janebluestein.com/2012/industrial-age-vs-information-age/ (accessed 12 September 2020).

Chiarotto, L (2011) *Natural Curiosity: Building Children's Understanding of the World through Environmental Inquiry: A Resource for Teachers*. Oshawa: Maracle Press Ltd.

Erickson, H L, Lanning, L A and French, R (2017) *Concept-based Curriculum and Instruction for the Thinking Classroom*. Thousand Oaks, CA: Corwin Press.

Fry, K (2014) *Assessing Inquiry Learning: How Much Is a Cubic Metre?* [online] Available at: https://files.eric.ed.gov/fulltext/EJ1093367.pdf (accessed 12 September 2020).

Guido, M (2017) *All about Inquiry-based Learning: Definition, Benefits and Strategies*. [online] Available at: www.prodigygame.com/blog/inquiry-based-learning-definition-benefits-strategies/ (accessed 12 September 2020).

Kuhlthau, C C, Maniotes, L K and Caspari, A K (2007) *Guided Inquiry: Learning in the 21st Century*. London: Libraries.

Ontario Ministry of Education (2005) *The Ontario Curriculum, Grades 1–8: Mathematics*. [online] Available at: www.edu.gov.on.ca/eng/curriculum/elementary/math18curr.pdf (accessed 12 September 2020).

Pataray-Ching, J and Roberson, M (2002) Misconceptions about a Curriculum-as-inquiry Framework. *Language Arts*, 79(6): 498–505.

Pedaste, M, Mäeots, M, Siiman, L A, de Jong, T, van Riesen, S A N, Kamp, E T, Manoli, C C, Zacharia, Z C and Tsourlidaki, E (2015) Phases of Inquiry-based Learning: Definitions and the Inquiry Cycle. *Educational Research Review*, 14: 47–61.

Roberts, C (2008) Developing Future Leaders: The Role of Reflection in the Classroom. *Journal of Leadership Education*, 7(1): 116–30.

Sousa, D A (2011) *How the Brain Learns*. 4th ed. Thousand Oaks, CA: Corwin Press.

Sullivan, P and Lilburn, P (2017) *Open-ended Math Activities: Using 'Good' Questions to Enhance Learning in Mathematics*. Sausalito: Oxford University Press.

Swearingen, R (2002) *A Primer: Diagnostic, Formative, & Summative Assessment*. [online] Available at: https://lincs.ed.gov/professional-development/resource-collections/profile-476 (accessed 12 September 2020).

Tomlinson, C (2014) *The Differentiated Classroom: Responding to the Needs of All Learners*. 2nd ed. Alexandria, VA: ASCD.

Wathall, J C (2018) *Concept-Based Mathematics with Jennifer Chang Wathall*. Interviewed by A McBride, 18 May. [online] Available at: www.aplusedtech.com/2018/05/18/concept-based-mathematics-with-jennifer-chang-wathall/ (accessed 12 September 2020).

Whitworth, B A, Maeng, J and Bell, R (2013) Differentiating Inquiry. *Science Scope*, 37: 10–17.

Zumach, K (2016) *Assessment in Inquiry-based Learning: The Rationale and Design of a Handbook for Teaching and Assessing Key Learning Facets* (Unpublished master's thesis). Vancouver Island University: Nanaimo. [online] Available at: https://viurrspace.ca/bitstream/handle/10613/2924/Zumach.pdf?sequence=1&isAllowed=y (accessed 12 September 2020).

12 Fostering multilingualism

Melanie Post Uiterweer, Anssi Roiha and Helen Absalom

INTRODUCTION

We live in an extremely multilingual reality as there are currently more than 7000 languages spoken in the world (Ethnologue, 2018), making multilingualism an important factor in many domains of life. In the global work market, the mastery of more than one language has moved from an asset to a prerequisite. The importance of language skills is nothing new particularly as the European Union released a recommendation in 1995 that all European citizens should have the ability to communicate in at least two community languages, in addition to their mother tongue (European Commission, 1995). This aim, though ambitious, highlights the importance of multilingualism and shows how essential it is on a policy level as well as a social one.

While multilingualism is not a new phenomenon, according to Aronin and Singleton (2008), it has evolved throughout the years rendering multilingualism no longer limited to certain geographical areas but rather ubiquitous. Previously multilingualism had often been perceived as the privilege of certain social classes and disciplines but nowadays concerns a wide range of people across different professions and social strata. Multilingual communicative situations had also previously been characterised by their slowness, as they occurred mostly in written form or face-to-face situations, whereas now they are increasingly instantaneous and can occur over distances (Aronin and Singleton, 2008).

In this chapter, we focus on how to foster multilingualism in schools. We draw on examples from the International School Utrecht (ISUtrecht) where a broad range of languages are spoken by both children and staff. There are more than 50 different nationalities in our school and due to the school's unique demographic, students at ISUtrecht learn content and skills in a multilingual environment surrounded by several languages. As the language of instruction in the school is English, a very high percentage of our students are constantly operating in a language (English) other than their home language. As the school is in the Netherlands, Dutch, which is the official language of the country, is also explicitly taught to all students. Many students live in a multilingual home environment as their parents use a language or languages other than English or Dutch. Thus, the majority of the students at ISUtrecht have a broad linguistic repertoire upon which they can draw.

As well as a multilingual student body, the staff at ISUtrecht comprises 27 different nationalities. The English spoken by the teachers at ISUtrecht varies in terms of vocabulary, syntax and grammar and the students receive both non-native and native-speaker models for language-learning. For the students, this illustrates that languages can be spoken in a variety of ways. It also endorses the notion that different ways of speaking the same language do not equate to deviance. Acknowledging the diverse linguistic backgrounds fosters the mindset that multilingualism entails adapting one's own language use according to the context and interlocutors. This corresponds well with the current world in which non-native speakers of English exceed the native speakers (Trudgill and Hannah, 2017).

To start this chapter, we briefly define multilingualism and give an overview of multilingual education and its research. In the subsequent sections, we introduce practices that schools can use to sustain the linguistic diversity of the whole school community. We have divided the section into two main parts: Dutch language acquisition and micro- and macro-level multilingualism practices.

DEFINING MULTILINGUALISM

Multilingualism is sometimes used interchangeably with bilingualism and plurilingualism as all three can be defined in a variety of ways. Bilingualism and multilingualism are sometimes differentiated so that the former refers to the use of two or more languages, whereas the latter purports to the use of three or more languages. However, both bilingualism and multilingualism can also be synonymously defined as the use of two or more languages. Bilingualism is also often regarded as being subsumed under multilingualism. Plurilingualism, in turn, is sometimes used when talking about individual-level multilingualism (Cenoz, 2013).

Multilingualism is currently the most frequently used term in the field and it is prevalently defined as '*the acquisition and use of two or more languages*' (Aronin and Singleton, 2008, p 2). Similarly, the European Commission (2007, p 6) defines multilingualism as '*the ability of societies, institutions, groups and individuals to engage, on a regular basis, with more than one language in their day-to-day lives*'. Multilingualism can further be divided into additive and subtractive multilingualism. Additive multilingualism refers to a situation in which a new language that is added to the individual's linguistic repertoire does not displace the prior languages. Subtractive multilingualism relates to situations in which the new language replaces the existing ones. Additional distinctions can be made between receptive and productive multilingualism or balanced and unbalanced multilingualism. The former refer to the levels of understanding or using a language, whereas the latter relate to the levels of proficiency in different languages and the relationship between them (Cenoz, 2013).

In this chapter, we use multilingualism as a generic term to refer to two or more languages and view it both as an individual and a societal phenomenon. Thus, all students at ISUtrecht can be considered multilingual as they all have had some exposure to English as the language of the curriculum, and are all studying Dutch and living in the Netherlands surrounded by social Dutch. In addition, students come to ISUtrecht with a developed home language other than English and sometimes a host-country language from a previous country of residence due to their parents' transient lifestyle.

Another term that relates to multilingualism is translanguaging. This refers to a unitary linguistic repertoire consisting of several languages (Vogel and García, 2017). In essence, translanguaging means using all one's linguistic resources to communicate and express oneself. According to García (2009, p 140), translanguaging is *'the act performed by bilinguals of accessing different linguistic features or various modes of what are described as autonomous languages, in order to maximise communicative potential'*. The term is also used to talk about an educational approach that fosters students' multilingualism in teaching and learning. Therefore, the practices described in this chapter reflect and embody translanguaging.

MULTILINGUAL EDUCATION AND RESEARCH FINDINGS

Considering the concept of multilingualism presented above, multilingual education can be defined as *'the use of two or more languages in education provided that schools aim at multilingualism and multiliteracy'* (Cenoz, 2009, p 4).

We take our first example from a national context: Canada has a long tradition of multilingual education due to the French immersion programmes which were developed in Quebec in the 1960s when English-speaking parents deemed it desirable for their children to be fluent in French thus being better placed to integrate into society. Since the inception of such programmes, one of the main concerns for policymakers and parents has been whether students in immersion education reach the same learning outcomes as those in a monolingual teaching programme. This model of immersion has been widely studied and the corresponding research shows that immersion students achieve at least the same outcomes as students studying in their first language (Cummins and Swain, 1986; Swain and Lapkin, 1982). Lazaruk's (2007) review suggests that immersion education can also benefit creative thinking skills and enhance metalinguistic awareness.

Geographically closer to our own ISUtrecht context, in Europe, multilingual education has been implemented following the approach called *Content and Language Integrated Learning* (CLIL). Perceived as an umbrella term that encompasses several models of implementation (Coyle et al, 2010), CLIL can be seen to stem from immersion education and is considered by some as having more commonalities with immersion education than differences (Mehisto et al, 2008; Somers and Surmont, 2012). Others, in turn, differentiate CLIL from immersion, for instance, in terms of the language objectives, starting age or teaching materials (eg Lasagabaster and Sierra, 2010). From a vast amount of research on CLIL, despite some variation, studies in general indicate that, similarly to immersion, CLIL is not detrimental to students' content learning (eg Dalton-Puffer, 2011; Graham et al, 2018; Pérez-Cañado, 2012).

From the above examples, we perceive that multilingual education carries many benefits as it has been shown to develop significantly higher competences in the *'target'* language than that which is achieved by merely formal language teaching (Lazaruk, 2007). In addition to such language gains, children being introduced to different languages may also gain advantages on an attitudinal level (Björklund and Mård-Miettinen, 2011).

In the sections that follow, we explore multilingualism at ISUtrecht. The first part is concerned with Dutch language acquisition and aims to illustrate how multilingualism can be acknowledged, nurtured and developed in formal language teaching. The second part focuses on multilingualism at ISUtrecht more holistically and endeavours to showcase how multilingualism can be integrated into the school programme on both

THE ISUTRECHT COMMUNITY

> *We are a close-knit and welcoming community of students, staff and parents. We all approach life from a different culture and background and with the languages we know. We find each other in our common goal: to create a stimulating learning environment in which everyone feels at home. We strive to be culturally competent; we are grounded in our own cultures, yet curious about others.*
>
> (International School Utrecht, nd)

'*Community*' is one of the four pillars of the ISUtrecht mission statement and we see this reflected in the statement above which clearly describes the emphasis on the school being a community. As a multilingual community, ISUtrecht embraces its linguistic and cultural diversity and the school strives for its students to develop their language skills to their fullest potential. English is the main instructional language and the students' academic language. But even more importantly, the students are strongly encouraged to maintain and further develop their home languages. ISUtrecht runs a robust after-school Home Language programme where students can choose to study their home language at an age-appropriate academic level. As the host country of ISUtrecht is the Netherlands, the school aims to help the students also develop the necessary cultural and communicative competence to function and participate within the Dutch community.

DUTCH LANGUAGE ACQUISITION

> *Learning to speak another's language means taking one's place in the human community. It means reaching out to others across cultural and linguistic boundaries. Language is far more than a system to be explained. It is our most important link to the world around us. Language is culture in motion. It is people interacting with people.*
>
> (Savignon, 1983 as cited in Clementi and Terrill, 2013, p 59)

During the Dutch language acquisition lessons, students learn the Dutch language and about Dutch culture through songs, games, word cards, speaking, reading and writing exercises. The lessons are designed to benefit the students' cultural awareness, international mindedness and language-learning needs. Students do not only experience full language immersion during the Dutch language acquisition lessons, but also begin to understand the language and the processes of language-learning itself which are also deemed essential skills. Considering this, in the Dutch lessons, students also learn to express what they are doing and why they are doing it. They find connections across languages while developing techniques, skills, attitudes and understandings. Translinguistic connections make and create a deeper and better understanding of the (Dutch) language. In this learning, students experience the Dutch language in a safe environment, willing to try and daring to make mistakes. The Dutch department emphasises how making mistakes can help us learn and further develop. The entire language-learning process aids, supports and encourages students to become lifelong language learners.

Fostering multilingualism

At ISUtrecht, primary students have Dutch twice a week for 45 minutes. In the early years, emphasis is on play-based learning where students experience and develop their language in their stations and during other playful activities (see also Chapter 5). In upper primary, we connect to the language focus they are working on within their regular class setting. If, for example, their language focus is poetry, Dutch teachers plan and teach accordingly making transdisciplinary connections to strengthen concepts.

Even though the aim of these lessons is primarily to improve the students' proficiency in Dutch, we also acknowledge and employ all their linguistic resources. One way to nurture multilingualism organically is to look for connections across the languages represented in any one class. With younger learners, this can be done in a relatively simple manner; for instance, students can write the same sentence in their own language, or languages they are competent in, on the board. An example of this is an activity where we made a connection between the Dutch language, the academic language and the home language. Looking at sentence structures, we discussed similarities and differences, trying to discover patterns. We used a sentence from a text we were reading and we discussed how it changes in English – this is also a good way to show that Google translate often cannot be used to translate entire sentences. Students proceeded to write the sentence in their own language (see Figure 12.1). Every single student was involved in comparing the various languages and their conventions; for instance, lexical items, syntax or use of capital letters.

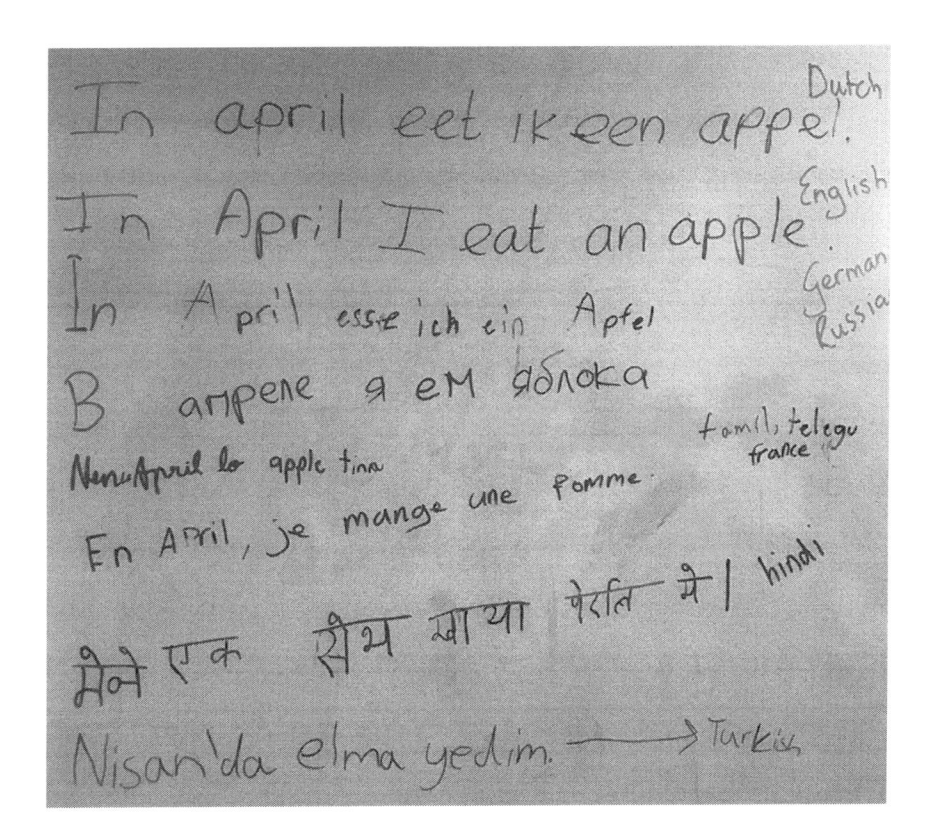

Figure 12.1 Finding similarities and differences between languages

The students showed a lot of interest in the other languages and enjoyed trying to speak them. They gave instructions on how to pronounce the words and provided feedback, both positive and constructive. Moments like these only take a few minutes and can easily be incorporated in various lessons and daily activities. With older students, the different languages can be compared and discussed in a more analytical way. These types of activities can have manifold purposes: they make multilingual visible and normalise it, they demonstrate to students how competence in one language can work as a useful resource in learning other languages and they increase the students' metalinguistic awareness. Language-learning should be an ongoing and engaging process, based not only on the level of the language students are practising but also on the students' intellectual development. The next part explains more about how we try to create more depth and challenge students' academic skills when learning a new language.

Another example of an activity we did regarding sentence structures is having the students practise new language in an interview setting. Our unit was about '*animals and their habitats*' and for this interview, we asked one student to be the interviewer and another student to pretend to be an animal who could speak and answer questions. We started by modelling the activity and then the students were divided into pairs to practise independently of the teacher. The students were enthusiastic and truly engaged, as they had the opportunity to act, were able to demonstrate student autonomy and decision-making and were very eager to find out more about an animal they were interested in. After this activity, we brainstormed about the questions asked and we chose a few questions to put on our wall. The children quickly recognised the structures of the sentences and we decided together to colour-code our sentences accordingly (green for a verb/action word, yellow for who and grey for the 5 Ws+H (who, what, where, when, why and how)). During the process, we compared the sentences to the students' home languages and once again identified both similarities and differences.

Very important in this short exercise, much like in all learning, is student agency (see Chapter 1). Even though the activity was structured and planned, the students still had a choice, a voice and ownership. They decided who was the interviewer, which animal they were interviewing, the sentences they wanted to put up, where they wanted them and in which colours. Their input dictated the process of the activity, and therefore the result made sense and they were proud of the work they did.

Summative assessment

In our Dutch lessons, we make connections to different languages, to the unit, to the language focus, to everyday events and activities and to various cultures and experiences. During the six to eight weeks that we work on one of our units, we begin by exploring where we want our students to go through the key concepts of the Primary Years Programme. What is it we want to achieve? What do we want them to understand? What do we want them to remember? And how can we get there? Often, we try to include the students in this too. We let them set an intention for a lesson or even a unit, a goal they want to reach and how they think they can achieve their goal. We also make sure that we connect to different languages and that we incorporate the use of their home languages in all our lessons.

Imagine you are a student, ten years old and just moved to a new country. At your new school, you need to learn Dutch, a language you do not speak. Being shown videos and singing songs aimed at students half your age is not very engaging, or enjoyable. Even though you do need to learn the basics, this does not mean that the intellectual level of the lesson has to be at the same level as your knowledge of that language. In our enquiry-based teaching, we endeavour to investigate content which is significant, challenging, relevant and engaging. How do we do this during our Dutch language acquisition lessons? In what follows is an example of some of our summative assessments for one of our lower primary units.

At ISUtrecht our units in the Dutch lessons spiral, which means we teach the same topic in every classroom, while increasingly broadening and deepening the explanations, activities, complexity, practices and sophistication. The following unit is about art (ie light, colour and shape), and each class has their own language focus. For example, Grade 2 focused on descriptive writing, while Grade 3 focused on persuasive writing.

Also of significance is that during this unit, King's Day was celebrated in the Netherlands. King's Day is a national celebration and a culturally important event. Incorporating King's Day into our unit planning helped make our lessons more relevant and engaging for the students. We tried to think about a way to incorporate these different aspects in our unit. After brainstorming, deciding on the key and related concepts, the central idea, the conceptual understandings and the standards, we came up with this summative assessment (see Table 12.1).

Table 12.1 The summative assessment of a Dutch unit

Grade	Summative assessment
Grade 2	Make a drawing that consists of two elements. One part shows the celebration of King's Day in the Netherlands and the other one a comparable festive event from your own culture. What connections can you make? What is different?
Grade 3	Persuading the King to make a change in the Netherlands. What is it that you'd like to see differently and how can you persuade the King to make this change? Use a drawing or poster to represent your ideas.

A new unit of enquiry is introduced through exploring the knowledge and language tools related to this topic that the students already have. The students are motivated to share their interests and enquire into our topic. This is a great moment to also incorporate their home language, for example, when brainstorming (see Figure 12.2).

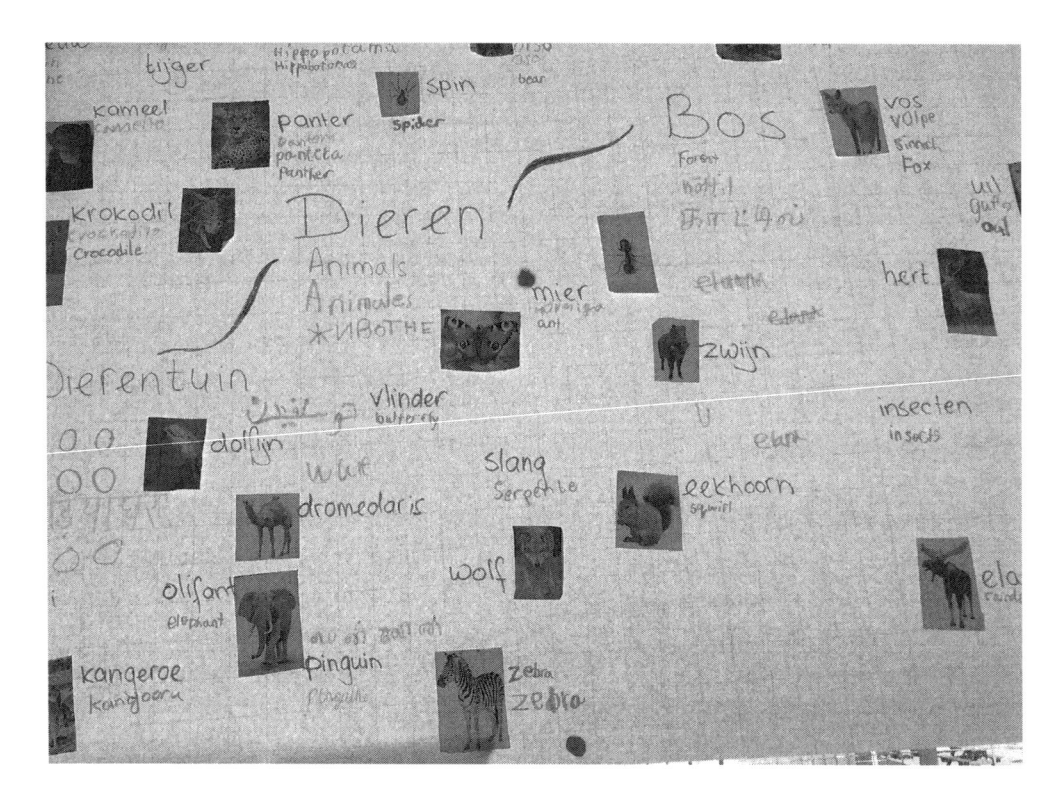

Figure 12.2 Animal vocabulary in different languages

With teacher guidance, students set goals for a lesson and their unit and are subsequently supported in reaching or adjusting the goals they set. In our lessons, we provide them with the necessary language tools, and we work on understanding, memorising and using the new vocabulary. The students look at sentence structures and verbs and compare all of these with the academic language and their home language.

For the unit, Grade 3 drawings and letters were sent to the King. We even received a written response to thank the students for taking an interest in the environment and to let us know that their suggestions and ideas would be forwarded to the according ministers. The students were incredibly proud of the work and the King's response to their work provided an authentic and culturally significant language experience.

This section of the chapter has been written from the point-of-view of a Dutch language teacher. It is important, however, to keep in mind that *all* teachers, whether art teachers, PE teachers or classroom teachers, are language teachers and an important responsibility lies with all these teachers to ensure inclusion of multilingualism in the class. In the next part of the chapter, we look at how we can support multilingualism in the classroom at a more general level. The most important points raised in this part are summarised in Table 12.2.

Table 12.2 Multilingualism in Dutch language acquisition

> ✓ The aim is to introduce students to the Dutch language and culture, while creating awareness of language relationships. The students benefit from learning the language of their host country, but also from the experience and process of learning, or further developing, a new language.
>
> ✓ Parental involvement and support are very important when learning a new language.
>
> ✓ Maintaining the academic level and challenging the students' intellectually is key, even if they do not speak this new language yet. Using students' home languages helps in this.
>
> ✓ Our goal is to create lifetime language learners.

TEACHING PRACTICES THAT PROMOTE MULTILINGUALISM

Promoting multilingualism should be a whole-school approach that involves all stakeholders. This can be done through a combination of various micro- and macro-level practices. In schools with linguistically diverse students, multilingualism should transcend all learning. The aim is to bring different languages to the forefront and make them visible not only within the language policy but also within the school. Code-switching (ie the alternation between languages) should also be normalised both for the students and for the staff. In educational contexts such as ISUtrecht, where there is only one official instructional language (ie English), other languages can be acknowledged in various activities throughout the school day. Next, we introduce several practices that facilitate and promote this objective.

Practice which may well have been derived largely from the communicative method in which the target language was emphasised and the home language given lower or no status often led teachers and parents alike to discourage the use of the home language or mother tongue. This approach has since been understood to prove detrimental to students' learning let alone their attitude towards multilingualism. ISUtrecht implements a policy which takes the students' home languages into account. This is essential, as many times new students have had no previous exposure to English. At the start of an academic year, teachers find out about their students' home languages and linguistic repertoires. This is done through the '*language profile*' which is introduced by the English Language Acquisition (ELA) department and which appears as a prerequisite to understanding a student's prior knowledge in the revised International Baccalaureate (IB) standards and practices (International Baccalaureate, 2018).

Language profile

Informed by IB guidelines and the '*Translanguaging Stance*' advocated by García et al (2017), ISUtrecht has introduced the language profile to help create a strong picture of each child's individual linguistic repertoire. Previously, teachers had employed forms filled in by parents to guide their planning for and implementation of effective translanguaging strategies. However, on closer inspection of our children's language backgrounds, we observed that although we were able to glean language-background information from parental forms and informal chats to the students, we lacked a deeper understanding of the complex nature of the relationships between the languages used by each child. The ELA department devised and introduced the language profile to the staff and students in the first weeks of term. Through the creation of their language profiles, students were encouraged to think profoundly about their functional as well as emotional relationships with their languages: how and where and why they used certain languages in certain contexts. We move now to the process of that in the following section.

> Children drew an outline of their bodies and then added facial features and a heart. They then depicted all the languages they used through a colour-coded key which corresponded to colours used on various parts of themselves. Students showed how they used their ears, voice, mind, and mouth to describe how they employed their receptive and productive language skills in and for different languages. Children coloured their heart to show their emotional connection to those languages. We take an example from younger children in Grades 1 and 2:
>
> *I coloured my hands yellow for Dutch. Because I go to football club after school and the coach speaks Dutch during the training. So I coloured my hands to show Dutch.*
>
> The teacher suggested that perhaps the student meant feet, instead of hands, to which the student answered:
>
> *I'm the goal-keeper.*
>
> In this way, we as teachers cannot only get a more robust understanding of the child's perspective on their languages usage but also with which languages they feel emotionally more connected.
>
> Children thought deeply about the visual connection between their languages. Many of the children coloured not separate parts but rather two colours over one another. One Grade 1 girl described this as using the languages 'at the same time and together'. She went on to say: 'So here, I coloured orange… it's not really orange, well it is really orange because it's Hindi and English at the same time… and they are yellow and red, so together they make orange. Ha! It's like an art lesson.'

The language profile is a living document to which is added as new language experiences happen or are remembered. Many children who have come from a country other than their home country have used the language profile as a springboard to the rekindling of language memories of a previous school language.

As the children publish their work on a digital platform, we have also noticed that they are keen to present in their home language as they know that their grandparents in their home country will access their footage. This they have done with ease as they look at the visuals and key and describe what they see bilingually or trilingually in some cases. Knowing their audience informs the form of the text and sharing with grandparents gives them a real audience and an authentic task.

At the beginning of the following academic year, children revisit their language profiles and discuss their growth as language users, preparing a new profile and using the language of comparison to express and explore the concept. The information gleaned from the language profiles is used to inform further teaching and planning. It also guides teachers in the later placement of students as they move up the school.

Other teaching arrangements and practices that foster multilingualism

In the case of new students enrolling in the school, we attempt to place them in a class where other student(s) speak their mother tongue. The school has very positive experiences of this as it allows the new students to have a peer who can facilitate their learning and start in the new school using the communication set with which they are most familiar. Within the classes, students for whom English is an additional language are buddied with same or (if that is not possible) similar-language children. Students for whom English is an addition language are explicitly encouraged to share and talk about their learning with their peers who speak the same language to ensure their understanding and to create a sense of security. These types of practices also reflect the current understanding of viewing multilingualism as the norm, and making use of a child's complete linguistic repertoire.

Continuous parental support is essential for the students' additional language skills as well as the maintenance of the home language. Not only is it helpful to have parents motivate their children, the ongoing development of their home language also helps children make translinguistic connections and provides the schemata for any subsequent new languages learnt. It is essential that all stakeholders are aware of the current thinking in the field of second-language acquisition and multilingual learning and teaching and the crucial role that the home language has to play in that. At ISUtrecht, the ELA department organises workshops for parents and teachers on multilingualism and its importance.

Working with parental support towards the maintenance of the home languages is of paramount importance. Parents are custodians of the home languages and by discussing school topics in their home languages, they can ensure that students understand the concepts and teachings as well as develop their home language skills. A useful practice is to inform the parents at the beginning of each unit about the topic and the key concepts that will be covered during that unit. For instance, prior to a water unit, the Dutch department advises the parents to discuss complex concepts (eg precipitation, condensation, matter, filtration, irrigation, transformation, etc) in their home languages.

Different languages should explicitly be included in classroom practices, so that all languages represented in the class and school are shown to have equal status. One relevant dimension with regard to this is the physical learning environment. The linguistic repertoire of the students in any class is evident in the environmental print of that class. Multilingualism can be reflected in the classroom displays and labels. For example, posters that contain words or sentences in various languages can be pinned on the wall. As the school follows concept-based teaching (see Chapter 6), the teachers at ISUtrecht often ask the students to define the key concepts in their home languages. The different definitions can be illustrated on the wall. The classroom should also have a wide range of multilingual literature where students can familiarise themselves with different languages.

At the beginning of the school year, the parents can be asked to donate or loan books in their own language to the school. In the case of a school library, it is useful to have a section of books in several languages and the students should be urged to read and loan those as well. Having a range of books in various languages stimulates students to read in their own language and encourages them to learn more about other languages too. An option is also to create multilingual books together. The class can choose a famous story and each student can translate a part of it into their own language. This multilingual book can then be printed for everyone. Alternatively, the students can make a multilingual movie and add subtitles to it.

At ISUtrecht, teachers pay attention to the students' linguistic background in various teaching activities. When enquiring into a new topic, students are encouraged to research and seek information in their own languages. In the early stages of a child's English and Dutch language acquisition, teachers ask students to do their writing assignments in their own language which another student, teacher or a parent can translate. Students can also start their stories or texts in their own language and finish them in English or vice versa. Harnessing technology to support language research and publishing, students are encouraged to use online translation programs to better understand the topics discussed. Digital technology also enables teachers or other students to speak into a translate recorder and the students can then listen to that in their own language to scaffold their learning.

In addition, teachers at ISUtrecht use a lot of visual support in their teaching which guides the learning of the students who have challenges in comprehending the teacher's input. Some students have small notebooks in which they collect useful vocabulary. The notebooks can be divided into three columns so that students can write the words in English and their definition in their own language as well as draw an illustration as a visual cue. Particularly with new students who have had little or no exposure to English, having a *remember book* can be very helpful and they can add new and important words to the book throughout the school day. Additionally, parents going over these words at home, adding the translations in their own language, is beneficial for the student's understanding and the memorisation process.

Multilingualism can also be incorporated into the school day in more informal ways. One feasible practice is to carry out certain classroom routines always in different languages. One student can be in charge each week and teach the other students certain greetings or phrases in her/his mother tongue. The class can practise them and use this language in everyday interactions in familiar situations. At ISUtrecht, many teachers incorporate multilingualism in their morning assemblies and greet each other in their home languages. In many classes, the birthday celebrations are sung in various languages and songs in different languages are frequently listened to. Having the student (or a parent or guardian while the student helps his/her classmates understand what is being said) read a book out loud in his/her home language is both a linguistically and cognitively engaging activity.

In addition to these micro practices that can be implemented on a daily basis, schools can foster multilingualism on a more macro-level. Schools or individual teachers can organise different events and theme days/weeks of which the function is to celebrate multilingualism. Parents can be asked to assist in organising these types of events and they can hold workshops in which they teach students a few phrases in their own language. Parents can also be in charge of home language reading clubs for students. If there are no parents available, speakers of different languages can also be invited to video-call in.

At ISUtrecht, we annually celebrate International Mother Language Day. During the week leading up to the day, the teachers have carried out several language awareness activities in their classrooms. Students have written poems in their own languages or taught some sentences in their language to their peers. In addition, the classes listened to songs and watched videos in different languages or teachers and students explored the etymology of relevant words and indicated where in the world their word/language is from on a map.

Students also wrote letters to each other in their home languages and posted them in a central postbox. The postbox was emptied and the letters delivered on International Mother Language Day to the relevant students. Additionally, on the day the school organised an assembly where students were given the opportunity to perform skits, songs, poems and readings in the home languages. Footage was compiled and played in the communal area for guests to enjoy over the following weeks.

The practices described above are only a few examples and each school can come up with several others to foster and acknowledge the linguistic diversity of the school community. It is important that the staff's multilingualism is also made visible so that it is not restricted to the students. The staff can take part in the multilingual activities and when comparing different languages in class, teachers can also include their own language and other languages they know. These actions reflect the notion that multilingualism is something that concerns adults as well and can be seen as a resource in one's work. Table 12.3 summarises some of the ideas covered in this section.

Table 12.3 Good practices to foster multilingualism in class

✓ Promote multilingualism in class continuously and in different ways (eg language displays, encourage students to share their home languages).
✓ Bring various languages systematically forth (eg classroom routines every week in different languages → students can instruct).
✓ Compare and analyse languages, observe similarities.
✓ Allow the students to use their home languages in classrooms to ensure understanding.
✓ Organise events that promote and normalise multilingualism (eg language day).
✓ Inform the guardians on the benefits of multilingualism and make use of their support.

CONCLUSION

The language of instruction at ISUtrecht is English but this does not mean that English is used to the detriment of other languages nor does it mean that English obtains a hegemonic status dismissing the students' home languages. In order for us to ensure equal access to the curriculum and to celebrate our distinct identities, we encourage children to draw upon prior knowledge which is their richest linguistic resource – their home language. Through carefully planned multilingual design, students can use their stronger resource and develop English at the same time. So many students come to school already literate in a language other than English. If you know a concept in one language, you know that concept, and you do not need to relearn that you just need the language to express it in a way which can be reached by all. In this chapter, we have argued that multilingualism should be acknowledged in second-language acquisition contexts and that schools should implement several micro- and macro-level practices that support the coexistence of various languages. In essence, we have endeavoured to showcase several such practices. However, the chapter is by no means exhaustive and teachers can come up with their own practices that better suit their context. The aim of this chapter has rather been to demonstrate that, as opposed to explicitly and formally teaching various languages, different languages and their variants can be promoted by small actions during the students' school days. This makes the students aware of the multilingual realities surrounding them and consequently creates mutual respect, which has a direct bearing on the students' attitudes towards diversity and identity and is reflected in the school's ethos.

Reflective questions

1. Are you aware of all the languages present in your students' lives?
2. How do you promote multilingualism in your class and in various subjects?
3. Do you allow the students to use their mother tongue in the classroom?
4. Are there any schoolwide practices that support multilingualism in your school (eg theme days, mother-tongue classes)? Can you think of some additional ones?
5. When you teach a (foreign) language, do you look at similarities and differences between languages? Do you try to let the students find patterns?
6. Do all the parents acknowledge the importance of maintaining one's first language? How could you raise more awareness of this among the parent community?

REFERENCES

Aronin, L and Singleton, D (2008) Multilingualism as a New Linguistic Dispensation. *International Journal of Multilingualism*, 5: 1–16.

Björklund, S and Mård-Miettinen, K (2011) Integrating Multiple Languages in Immersion: Swedish Immersion in Finland. In Tedick, D J, Christian, D and Fortune, T W (eds) *Immersion Education: Practices, Policies, Possibilities*. Bristol: Multilingual Matters.

Cenoz, J (2009) *Towards Multilingual Education: Basque Educational Research in International Perspective*. Bristol: Multilingual Matters.

Cenoz, J (2013) Defining Multilingualism. *Annual Review of Applied Linguistics*, 33: 3–18.

Clementi, D and Terrill, L (2013) *The Keys to Planning for Learning: Effective Curriculum, Unit, and Lesson Design*. Alexandria: American Council on the Teaching of Foreign Languages.

Coyle, D, Hood, P and Marsh, D (2010) *CLIL. Content and Language Integrated Learning*. Cambridge: Cambridge University Press.

Cummins, J and Swain, M (1986) *Bilingualism in Education. Aspects of Theory, Research and Practice*. London: Longman.

Dalton-Puffer, C (2011) Content-and-language Integrated Learning: From Practice to Principles? *Annual Review of Applied Linguistics*, 30: 182–204.

Ethnologue (2018) *Summary by World Area*. [online] Available at: www.ethnologue.com/statistics (accessed 12 September 2020).

European Commission (1995) *Teaching and Learning: Towards the Learning Society*. Brussels: European Commission. [online] Available at: https://europa.eu/documents/comm/white_papers/pdf/com95_590_en.pdf (accessed 12 September 2020).

European Commission (2007) *Final Report: High Level Group on Multilingualism*. Luxembourg: European Communities.

García, O (2009) Education, Multilingualism and Translanguaging in the 21st Century. In Mohanty, A, Panda, M, Phillipson, R and Skutnabb-Kangas, T (eds) *Multilingual Education for Social Justice: Globalising the Local*. New Delhi: Orient Blackswan.

García, O, Johnson, S I and Seltzer, K (2017) *The Translanguaging Classroom: Leveraging Student Bilingualism for Learning*. Philadelphia, PA: Caslon.

Graham, K M, Choi, Y, Davoodi, A, Razmeh, S and Dixon, L Q (2018) Language and Content Outcomes of CLIL and EMI: A Systematic Review. *Latin American Journal of Content and Language Integrated Learning*, 11(1): 19–37.

International Baccalaureate (2018) *Programme Standards and Practices*. Cardiff: International Baccalaureate.

International School Utrecht (nd) *Mission Statement*. [online] Available at: www.isutrecht.nl/organisation/mission-statement/ (accessed 12 September 2020).

Lasagabaster, D and Sierra, J M (2010) Immersion and CLIL in English: More Differences than Similarities. *ELT Journal*, 64(4): 367–75.

Lazaruk, W A (2007) Linguistic, Academic, and Cognitive Benefits of French Immersion. *Canadian Modern Language Review / La revue canadienne des langues vivantes*, 63(5): 605–27.

Mehisto, P, Marsh, D and Frigols, M (2008) *Uncovering CLIL. Content and Language Integrated Learning in Bilingual and Multilingual Education*. Oxford: Macmillan Education.

Pérez-Cañado, M L (2012) CLIL Research in Europe: Past, Present, and Future. *International Journal of Bilingual Education and Bilingualism*, 15(3): 315–41.

Somers, T and Surmont, J (2012) CLIL and Immersion: How Clear-Cut Are They? *ELT Journal*, 66(1): 113–16.

Swain, M and Lapkin, S (1982) *Evaluating Bilingual Education: A Canadian Case Study*. Clevedon: Multilingual Matters.

Trudgill, P and Hannah, J (2017) *International English: A Guide to Varieties of English Around the World*. London: Routledge.

Vogel, S and García, O (2017) Translanguaging. In Noblit, G and Moll, L (eds) *Oxford Research Encyclopedia of Education*. Oxford: Oxford University Press.

13 Intercultural competence

Carren Ward, Megan Tregoning and Rynette de Villiers

*A school flourishes or withers
depending on the quality of communication
within the community*

Rynette de Villiers

INTRODUCTION

A large part of the way we communicate with each other is determined by our cultural baggage and our curiosity to get to know more about the people around us. In our work, we meet people with such a wealth of knowledge and such a deep understanding of other cultures, people who make us want to do better, fighting against bias and prejudice, trying to avoid forcing individuals into cultural boxes. Yet, time and again we find ourselves making assumptions about how people think and act, solely based on what we perceive to be their culture. For us, intercultural competence is not about tolerating or allowing everything from everyone. It is about developing an understanding of our own cultural baggage, while being curious about other people's cultural baggage, celebrating the things we have in common. And if we are lucky, we get to '*borrow*' some of the great things of another's culture and combine it with our own. This journey has also meant coming to terms with the fact that in order to learn intercultural competence, we had to learn that we can never be completely accepting of everything in other cultures; and that this is not per se necessary in order to work together.

We live in an era in which information and people are more accessible than ever. The internet and travel have allowed us to broaden our horizons now more than ever before. Developments in communication technology mean that we are no longer limited by geographic boundaries. We live, physically and virtually, side by side with people from vastly different backgrounds, with a wealth of ideas, knowledge and experience that differs from our own. While this has provided us with a chance to evolve, it also challenges us to step outside our comfort zones.

There are several parts of the world that remain largely culturally homogenous. Many cities across the globe have undergone a significant evolution due to immigration and accessibility. This means the educational, business and almost all areas of society have become culturally diverse. With increasing global diversity, intercultural competence is a topic of immediate relevance. Our culture is what motivates most of our interactions, values and norms. When we encounter someone from a different culture, it can be challenging for us to relate and communicate effectively with them.

In this chapter, we define what intercultural competence is, focus on its importance in both an educational and global setting as well as address the challenges faced at an international school. We try to do this using a combination of research and stories from our own community which includes more than 50 different nationalities.

WHAT IS INTERCULTURAL COMPETENCE?

Intercultural competence is a complex concept. To narrow it down, it *'typically describes one's effective and appropriate engagement with cultural differences'* (Arasaratnam, 2016, para 1) or is defined as the ability *'to co-create shared spaces, teams, and organisations that are inclusive, effective, innovative, and satisfying'* (Cultural Detective, nd, para 3). Situations we find ourselves in are neither *'intercultural'* nor *'not intercultural'*, but they simply possess a certain degree of interculturality. This is because intercultural competence does not only apply to people of different national cultures meeting, but can also apply to a person coming from a different context, with different experiences and a different understanding of the world. We see the collision and interaction of various backgrounds and views daily and intercultural competence is how we deal with these situations.

Most people feel confident and comfortable in their own cultural and social situations and when taken out of this, they may feel uncomfortable. This emotion stems from the fact that it feels as if we are not communicating naturally. Intercultural competence means taking learnt competencies of how to deal with these situations and applying them to the unknown contexts. This then allows us to communicate and interact effectively even in the most diverse and unfamiliar situations. Intercultural competence is not a complete learnt ability or skill, but one that is constantly evolving. It really is a lifelong journey.

There are three widely accepted main areas within intercultural competence, namely: *knowledge*, *skills* and *attitudes*. The following three are adapted from Deardorff (2006, 2009).

Knowledge

Our intercultural knowledge starts with our own cultural awareness. We are unable to understand and communicate with other cultures until we have an understanding of that of our own. This also means reflecting on our own learnt prejudices and biases. Often, we are unaware of these ideas and require critical introspection to discover them. The following example from our school illustrates this.

> An Argentinian teacher came into the head of school's office, rather upset, wanting the head to have a talk to a Dutch student. The student, standing close behind her, equally upset, was determined to have his say. It was summer and uncommonly hot at the time. It turned out that the student, who was wearing flip-flops, had slipped off his shoes under his desk and stretched out his legs in front of him. The teacher was extremely upset with his rudeness and disrespect, while the student was confused and irritated with the unnecessary 'over-reaction' from the teacher's part. After a short discussion, they understood that in some countries, it is incredibly rude to show the soles of your feet, while in other countries, it is

> completely acceptable and even expected to take off one's shoes when entering someone's home. This conflict resulted in a unit in individuals and societies which was shared with the whole school in our quest to gain more knowledge about other cultures.
>
> This is one of many examples, but the point is that it is essential on our journey to intercultural competence, to be curious about other cultures and consider responses and actions from other people in a cultural light, always trying to develop a better understanding and knowledge of another's individual cultural baggage.

Culture-specific knowledge is the deep understanding of ideas, customs and social behaviours of other cultural groups. This is something that requires time and commitment to master and understand. Socio-linguistic awareness is a vital part of this knowledge because knowing when certain ways of interacting are appropriate or not is extremely important for effective and non-offensive communication. This also refers to body language, tone of voice and manner in which issues can be addressed.

Skills

The most important skill that underpins intercultural competence is the ability to create an open and comfortable dialogue. These dialogues allow for the chance to share, listen and question, which leads to a deeper understanding of an individual and their culture. The skills that we need to create such dialogues do not differ greatly from those needed in any other relationship. These involve:

- listening;
- observing;
- evaluating;
- the ability to see the world from another's perspective;
- the ability to 'let go' of own perspective.

At the International School Utrecht (hereafter ISUtrecht), we implicitly practise these skills daily, but essentially, it is of importance that a school offers explicit opportunities and professional development for its staff to develop skills with regard to intercultural competence. It should become part of the DNA of the community, modelled by the staff and shared by the whole community.

Attitudes

The attitudes we have towards others reinforce any competencies from the other two areas. The four most important attitudes to foster intercultural competence are as follows.

204 TEACHING AND LEARNING IN INTERNATIONAL SCHOOLS

- *Respect*. This is the ability to value each other's cultures.
- *Open-mindedness*. This means allowing others to express ideas and opinions that may form part of their cultural identity without judgement.
- *Curiosity*. In order to become more interculturally competent, we need to view difference as a learning opportunity. This means that we are actively interested in other cultures and experiences with them.
- *Discovery*. This means to tolerate ambiguity and view it as a new discovery and not an uncertainty.

Although Deardorff (2006) mentions knowledge of our own culture, which does include our own set of values, we see that in some instances, values can be added as its own separate area. Byram et al (2002, p 13) state: *'It is not the purpose of teaching to try to change learners [sic] values values, but to make them explicit and conscious in any evaluative response to others'*. This quote not only applies to the educational realm, but to all people interacting with one another. The possibility of acceptance of a different set of values is vital to intercultural competence. Acquiring these competencies and skills is a process, which can be described as moving from a *mono-cultural mindset* to an *intercultural mindset*. Most people live with a mono-cultural mindset without realising it. Once again, this means that this process begins with critical introspection.

MONO-CULTURAL TO MULTICULTURAL MINDSET

Organisations such as the Intercultural Development Inventory offer services to 'test' and measure the level of intercultural competence within an organisation. Figure 13.1 is adapted from the Intercultural Development Continuum as presented by the Intercultural Development Inventory (nd). This continuum begins with the denial phase. Most people

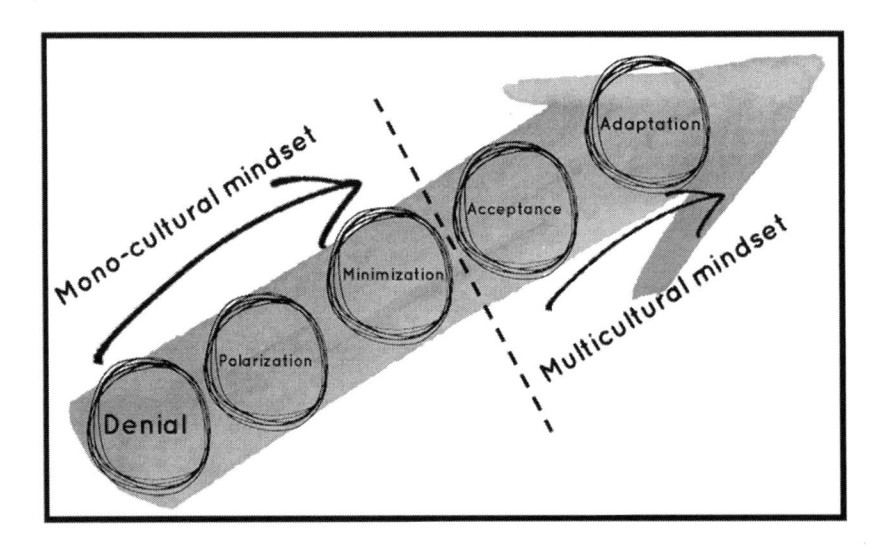

Figure 13.1 Mono-cultural versus multicultural mindset
(Adapted from Hammer, 2019, as cited in Intercultural Development Inventory, nd)

who have begun the journey towards intercultural competence have moved past this stage and realised the need to change. However, there are many people who are living within this stage and it is worth exploring each step in the continuum in order to gain a better insight into people we interact with who may not share the same phase as ourselves. The explanation of these phases has been adapted from the Intercultural Development Inventory (nd).

Denial

This stage mostly consists of the belief that our differences cannot be defined as simply 'cultural'. Most people within this stage will avoid others they perceive as different as they have a very limited capability to understand and respond in an appropriate way. It is also common that people within this stage have had very little contact or experience with other cultures and thus tend to operate on the knowledge gained from broad stereotypes and generalisations. This mindset lends itself more commonly to the dominant culture in a certain environment. As non-dominant cultures tend to have to engage with other cultures in a more open way, they tend to be less likely to maintain a denialist phase. Due to this, cultural diversity and the need for intercultural competence can often be overlooked.

Polarisation

Polarisation equates to a cultural mindset that has a strong sense of 'us versus them'. Polarisation takes on two forms, namely: *defence* and *reversal*. Defence means that an individual will view cultural differences as threatening to their own way of life. People may feel scared that they will have to lose their own cultural identity in order to understand that of another. Reversal refers to individuals who see another culture as 'ideal'. This may occur when people take up a 'cause' of a certain oppressed cultural group. However, this is mostly done without accurate knowledge of what the said cause means to the actual group of individuals it is affecting.

Minimisation

Minimisation can be seen as an evolutionary period between the very mono-cultural mindsets within the denial and polarisation phases, to a more intercultural or global mindset that we see within acceptance and adaptation. This stage is when people become aware of factors that allow for a commonality between groups of people. There are two groups of these commonalities: *similarities* and *universalism*. Similarities refers to the things that most humans share, such as basic needs. Universalism refers to values and principles that are shared globally. Minimisation can be observed in two forms. The first is an underscoring of commonalities due to a mostly dominant culture having a very limited self and other cultural knowledge. The second is an awareness of commonalities as a strategy for navigating the values and practices which are largely determined by the dominant culture group. This mainly affects the non-dominant cultures within a diverse environment. This is commonly a coping mechanism and promotes a 'go with the flow' attitude. This form of minimisation can lead to people feeling like they are not heard or valued within a diverse group.

> ## What does this mean for international schools?
>
> It is so easy to get stuck in a mono-cultural mindset in an environment such as an international school. We actually have developed a kind of monoculture within our school. Let us look at the general profile of our families.
>
> - All have some form of international background, generally with an open-minded approach to other cultures.
> - Most are of middle-high economic income.
> - We are lovers of good food, travel and the arts.
> - Our parent community is highly educated, understanding the value of education and exposure for their children.
> - We are all together in one host country that actually determines quite a lot of the choices we make while living here.
>
> Yes, we come from different cultural backgrounds, but in our 'bubble', we have created our own, comfortable monoculture. So, we have to do better, try harder to work our way to that next level of intercultural competence.

Acceptance

When an individual enters the acceptance phase, they begin to recognise and appreciate cultural difference and commonality in both their own and other cultures. This is also when curiosity really starts to bloom. People will start to explore situations, for example, how certain cultures' values or behaviours could work in different environments. This also involves self-reflection and then comparison between one's own culturally learnt perceptions and behaviours and then the perceptions and practices of different cultural groups. Even though individuals within this phase are curious to the differences within cultures, they may not yet be able to adapt to these differences. This is also a stage that forces individuals to confront behaviour or values that are in direct contradiction to their own. During the acceptance phase, people tend to gain a deeper cultural understanding, but are mostly unable to reconcile all the disparities with their own culture. Every now and then, we get authentic glimpses of this phase at our school.

> A heart-warming moment was a couple of years ago when we decided to change the service provider for our after school care centre. Changing the provider meant that our students would be collected by the company and walk a block or two down the road. At the time, there were Israeli families who made use of the after school care facility. These families were concerned about the safety of their children during this vulnerable moment in the day. Taking into account the host country

> and the safe freedom of movement people enjoy here, there initially was very little understanding for what was seen as an 'over-protective over-reaction'.
>
> During a rather heated meeting with the school and the after school care company, our parents asked for a moment alone to deliberate as a group. To this day, we do not quite know what happened in that meeting, but when they came out, they had one voice, which included requests for basic, but reasonable safety measures. The parents never explained who required what. Somehow, they not only gained a cultural understanding of each other's situation during that hour, but were able to implement this new knowledge in a constructive solution for the whole community.
>
> It was a moving moment, one we will not easily forget.

Adaptation

The biggest transformation that we can observe within the adaptation mindset is that of the individual's actual behaviour. They are working towards being able to act in authentic and culturally appropriate ways, depending on the given situation. We also can observe a shift in a person's cultural perspective, to that of someone who is able to experience situations from a culture other than their own. This process is one that can take place over a long period of time. Once an individual reaches the adaptation phase, they will continue to grow within it. As discussed before, reaching intercultural competence is not a definite skill that can be acquired. As cultures evolve and change, so must an individual's way of interacting with them.

INTERCULTURAL COMPETENCE IN PRACTICE

Intercultural competence is clearly a competence that is of the utmost importance in the modern world. It is also something that can be seen at any age and in all spheres of society. This means that as a teacher, there is a certain responsibility to both model such competence and persevere to instil it in students. It has become one of the most vital life skills in order to flourish in society. In the following section, we outline the practices that support intercultural competence within ISUtrecht.

Creating intercultural competence at ISUtrecht

Intercultural competence should be infused in all areas of a school. But how does a school go about creating this? ISUtrecht has taken a lot of care when developing the school and its vision. The ethos of the school is its foundation and every choice that is made is a conscious one in order to preserve the aim of the school. Therefore, much thought has been taken when creating the mission statement, hiring the staff, choosing the teaching methodology and in any other decision made. All of these choices have been made with the heart of intercultural competence in mind and can be felt in every aspect of the school.

The moment one enters the ISUtrecht building, they are surrounded by a warm feeling of acceptance. They see children, parents and teachers of all cultures and nationalities interacting together with respect and good will. The atmosphere is safe and welcoming. As an expat, who is still finding one's way in this new country, it is comforting to have a place to go to where one feels at ease and welcomed. This atmosphere is created by a multitude of things, one being the mission statement of the school.

> *A community learning for world citizenship*
>
> *We are a close-knit and welcoming community of students, staff and parents. We all approach life from a different culture and background and with the languages we know. We find each other in our common goal: to create a stimulating learning environment in which everyone feels at home. We strive to be culturally competent; we are grounded in our own cultures, yet curious about others.*
>
> *We communicate across cultures, using music to form strong bonds. That is why we offer an exciting music programme accessible to all students and connected to the rich music tradition of the city of Utrecht.*
>
> *We give special attention to the physical and social environment we learn and work in. We value and care for the natural world and model responsible behaviour. Our learning environment is one in which every person can express themselves safely and freely.*
>
> *We use technology in an innovative and sensible way to enhance our teaching and learning. We equally appreciate the value of sensory and tactile experiences. We approach the virtual and real world as one, behaving consistently as we are moving from one to the other.*
>
> *We are a community of life-long learners.*
>
> (International School Utrecht, nda)

This mission statement is the heart of school. It provides the foundation that allows our students to flourish in their learning and be valued for who they are, as individuals having various cultural backgrounds that provide different perspectives to deepen learning for all. Being an international school, ISUtrecht recognises that a person's culture is one of the things that influences everything he or she does. Our families are proud of where they come from, who they are, the languages that they speak and the traditions that they celebrate. A person's culture provides the roots that are needed for growth. ISUtrecht honours the importance of each individual's culture and aims to tap into the various ideas and perspectives of each person in order to create a completely diverse learning experience, which can be viewed from various angles. As our mission statement states: '*We strive to be culturally competent; we are grounded in our own cultures, yet curious about others*' (International School Utrecht, nda, para 3). ISUtrecht values the many cultures that we have in school. This is apparent not only in the mission statement, but also in the staff that works at the school.

ISUtrecht staff

Our staff is one of the most important contributing factors in making ISUtrecht the success that it is. Their understanding and openness to intercultural competence with their students, our parent community, colleagues and themselves have enriched the school, have made it feel like an extension of home for many families and provided a safe haven for our students to excel in their education. A lot of care is taken when hiring new staff members. The senior leadership team looks for people who have the knowledge, skills, attitudes and values that match the essence of the mission statement. Our staff is composed of 27 different nationalities, many of whom speak several languages and have lived abroad in more than one country. Each person comes from a different walk of life, but the one thing that unites us is our strive for intercultural competence (see Figure 13.2).

Where are you from?

We find it more and more complicated to answer this question. Does this mean the country we are born in? The one we have spent most of our lives in? The one that had the biggest impact on our education? The one our parents are from? It is a minefield of social missteps waiting to happen.

We have a lot of fun on our staff app group. Sharing things we are proud of. There are a lot of apps related to food, and sometimes, we are simply fooling around. One afternoon, a staff member posted this picture (see Figure 13.2) and asked the question. Where are we from?

It turned out to be the United Kingdom, the United States and Brazil. We are so quick to link a person's cultural look to a culture when clearly this is not a realistic option anymore.

Figure 13.2 Teachers of ISUtrecht

Our curiosity requires a different question. Perhaps, we should be asking: *'Which cultures have formed your values and beliefs?'*

Our staff is open-minded and curious about learning new things. We are not scared of differences or new challenges. Instead, we welcome and try to learn from them. This attitude along with the knowledge, skills and values of the teacher is important because it determines the entire tone and learning environment of the classroom. The level of learning at ISUtrecht is high and carries an energy that radiates from every classroom. The children are willing to take risks, voice their opinions and honour and understand each other's perspectives. The children feel safe and recognised. This is accomplished not only through the attitude of the teacher, but also by the classroom environment.

Creating safe learning environments through the International Baccalaureate (IB) learner profile

At the start of every school year, it is essential to create a safe learning environment. Children will only dare to 'spread their wings' if they feel accepted, valued and heard. At ISUtrecht, teachers and students often use the IB learner profile as one of the main ways to encourage children to better themselves and create a nurturing classroom environment.

The learner profile is often used to make classroom agreements where the desired attitudes and behaviours are decided on together by the students and teacher. These agreements set the foundation for the rest of the school year and provide an atmosphere that welcomes everyone to be reflective, risk-taking and enquiring but also accepting of new ideas and ways of doing things. '*The development of these attributes is the foundation of developing internationally minded students who can help to build a better world*' (International Baccalaureate, 2017, p 3). These positive attributes make it safe for students to be themselves, share who they are without having the fear of being rejected and as a result the children are open to learning about different perspectives. These classroom agreements help in laying the groundwork for students to become interculturally competent.

The learner profile is not only addressed at the beginning of the school year, but it is also focused on while teaching each new unit of enquiry. At this time, the teachers consistently model and label these profiles, bring attention to situations and students who display these positive behaviours and repetitively draw connections to good actions and the goal profile(s) being taught. The early years has the '*habit of the week*' in which, through role play, the children see what a good and bad example of a learner profile attribute is. They also have the '*sunshine of the week*' in which one student gets special attention and nice comments from their friends are written onto a picture of a sun. Many times the learner profile attributes are used to describe the sunshine of the week. This is a nice reflection of the students' understandings since the attributes are used at free will.

Grade 4 encourages the students to 'catch' moments when their friends are displaying a learner profile attribute. The action is then written on a sticky note and stuck up next to the attribute that was reflected. They also have used the learner profile in many activities, such as during international mother language day (see Chapter 12). The children connected the learner profile to themselves when speaking their mother tongue. For instance, one child said, '*I am a risk-taker when I try to speak someone's language*' or '*I am a communicator when I speak my own language*'. These activities and daily reminders to strive towards a learner profile attribute keep the notion of goodwill for themselves and for others at the forefront of their minds.

Students who learn to interact in a principled, respectful, enquiring and open-minded manner welcome change and new things that are different than what they are used to. It has been recognised time and time again that as our students practise using the IB learner profile in their daily lives, they mature into young adults who become '*active, compassionate lifelong learners*' (International Baccalaureate, 2010, p 1). This is exactly the goal of the IB learner profile.

Developing a safe learning classroom environment requires not only teachers who are modelling the learner profile themselves, but also teachers who understand the learning process of their students and are willing to take risks in their own learning. Thus, they should practise being lifelong learners, like their students, by questioning opinions, researching topics and enquiring.

> *Taking part in international projects, professional associations, governmental initiatives, exchanges will promote all the aspects of intercultural dimension in language teaching. Such experience involves teachers in being intercultural learners themselves, in taking risks, analyzing and reflecting on their own experience and learning – and drawing consequences from this for their work as teachers.*
> (Byram et al, 2002, p 28)

ISUtrecht encourages their teachers to continually keep on learning. It provides professional development at school, online and abroad. ISUtrecht wants their teachers to learn new things, apply them in their classes, reflect on their discoveries and share their findings with the rest of the staff. In doing this, the teachers' wealth of knowledge increases and stimulates others around them. In addition, our teachers also understand the learning process that their students experience and can better facilitate and relate to them.

Approach to learning

The approach to learning in a school is very important. It can either foster intercultural competence or smother it. A collaborative learning approach where there is a '*sharing of knowledge and a discussion of values and opinions*' (Byram et al, 2002, p 20) among the students and teachers promotes intercultural competence. This discussion allows students to exchange opinions and learn about different perspectives on various topics. At ISUtrecht, we follow an enquiry-based approach to learning (see also Chapter 7). Direct instruction is kept to a minimum as the emphasis is on discovery, questioning, making connections, reflecting and transferring of knowledge. '*The PYP [Primary Years Programme] strongly promotes constructivist, conceptual and enquiry-based learning. This allows learners to explore their own questions, construct new knowledge and transfer these ideas to a conceptual level of understanding*' (International School Utrecht, ndb, para 4). This type of learning is extremely collaborative. The students learn from each other as much as they learn from their teacher. The teacher is not an authoritative figure who feeds information from only one point of view, while the students remain passive learners. Instead, as Byram et al (2002) state: '*the teacher's task is to help learners ask questions, and to interpret answers*' (p 11) and the teachers '*do not need to be the sole or major source of information*' (p 8).

The students at ISUtrecht are often doing their own research via conducting interviews, sending out surveys and looking up information and coming to their own conclusions based on what they have enquired into (see Figure 13.3). This enquiry-based approach

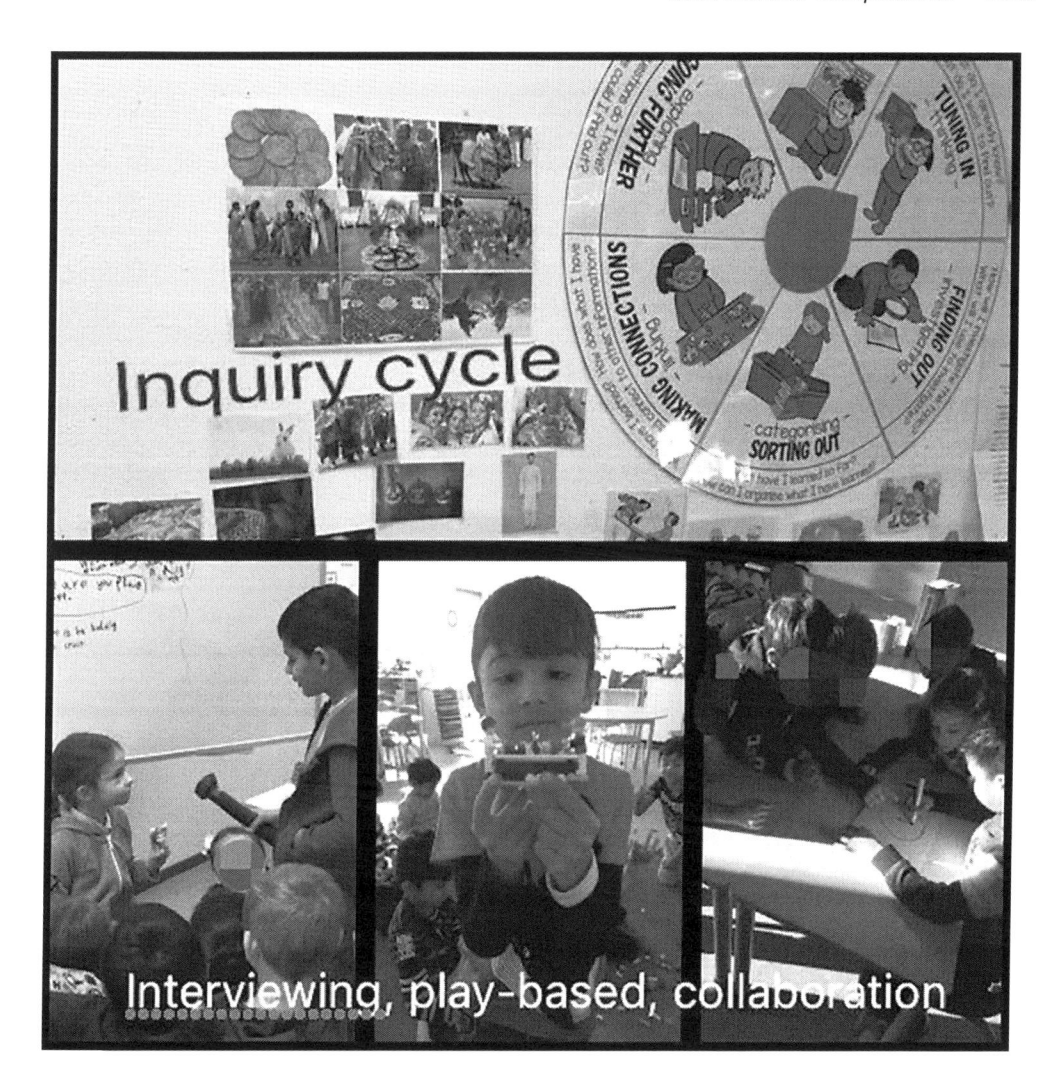

Figure 13.3 Enquiry-based learning in the early years

to learning requires students to work co-operatively with each other, to be able to understand different perspectives and ask questions about the things they do not know about. Therefore, our teachers need to have the knowledge and skills to understand that people from various cultures might work differently, have points of view that are opposing and other cultural nuances that one might bring to the group when working together. The guidance of the teacher and the safe classroom environment are fundamental elements for success in these situations. When that is intact, along with great enquiry, then the different perspectives that are shared in the classroom help the students understand their learnings through multiple points of view. A result of this is an understanding of differences that is celebrated because the knowledge of the students is growing. The more and more the students are able to see things through another's eyes and be open to trying out new ways of doing things, the more interculturally competent individuals are being developed.

Examples of developing intercultural competence in the classroom

Here are a few specific examples of how some classrooms at ISUtrecht are developing intercultural competence in their students. In Grade 1's communities and perspective unit, they focused on their school community and the classroom daily routines. In order to gain a broader perspective, each class reached out to other schools around the world, such as schools in California, Dubai and Thailand, to ask what their school routines were. Videos were shared between the schools and the students were able to ask interview questions to the students from these schools about their curiosities. Many similarities and differences were recognised, questioned, compared and finally understood on both sides as to why schools in different parts of the world had different routines from what they were used to. After researching various school communities, the Grade 1 students decided to now look at how their own personal customs differed from the other children in the class and from people from other countries. They looked at foods, traditional celebratory attire, ways of greeting and ways of showing respect. The students researched this information, interviewed their families and friends, as well as guest speakers, and created surveys to gather as much information as possible. They showed their knowledge through role play, making different foods from various countries, practising the many ways of showing respect and so much more (see Figure 13.4).

Figure 13.4 Grade 1 students being open-minded to sampling different foods and learning about various traditions from around the world

Intercultural competence 215

This unit opened the students' minds to other cultures and taught them that there are multiple ways of doing the same thing and that one way is not better than another. A new-found respect was discovered.

The Grade 3 students just finished learning about how experiencing different cultures promotes international mindedness. The students spent some time learning about their nationality and what clothing, sports, religion, food, language and celebrations are typical for their home country. A huge chart was created by the students displaying this information.

The students had a lot of pride for their own country, but through this process, began to recognise the similarities and differences between the countries. They filled out Venn diagrams comparing three completely different countries and saw that even though they come from different parts of the world, their customs, foods and sport interests were not so contrasting after all. They learnt about each other's cultures by sharing with each other and honouring the differences.

The students also learnt that a person cannot be defined by their nationality and easily stereotyped. Questions were posed asking if two or more children who came from the same country actually had the same personality or shared the same values or dressed the same or ate the same traditional foods. When discovering that the answers were 'no' for almost every comparison, the students' learning was extended. They learnt that stereotyping a person by looking at just where they come from can lead to problems. Instead, they realised that it is helpful to be aware of the cultural customs of a country when interacting with others, but one should always get to know the individual first and not generalise him or her based on where they come from. This was a valuable lesson learnt in intercultural competence.

In order for intercultural competence to be effective, it is essential for the students to collaboratively talk and share their ideas. The teachers at ISUtrecht facilitate this through many means such as gallery walks, wonder walls, think/pair/share time and having a variety of mixed groupings throughout the day. Using any of these strategies allows students to see their classmates work, hear other people's opinions, share their own opinions and reflect on what was learnt. Many classes also make an effort to include the students' languages and customs in their daily routines, such as in the morning greeting or goodbye song, by singing happy birthday in various languages, doing cultural dances and simply learning words to communicate with their English language acquisition (ELA) students (see also Chapter 12). In the early years, some teachers make home visits in order to learn more about their students. They gain valuable insight into the child when seeing him or her in their home environment such as the family's customs and routines, the relationship that is shared between the parent and child and the things that interest the child. The teacher is able to see the child as a whole, become more interculturally competent about that child and as a result become a better teacher who can connect with that student on a more personal level.

In order to stimulate the awareness of multiple perspectives, it is important for a school to use resources from different countries, which naturally have different points of view. *'Materials from different origins with different perspectives should be used together to enable learners to compare and to analyse the materials critically'* (Byram et al, 2002, p 19). At ISUtrecht, we have books, magazines, newspapers, art and music from all around the world and in several languages. We have materials that are told from the perspectives of different characters in various books. We invite guest speakers in to share their personal history and knowledge and use the expertise of our international staff and student body for their insight. In addition, our students and teachers use the internet as a source of information to gain more than one perspective of what is being learnt. Many students, especially the ELA students, get so excited when seeing a video or having a book read to them that comes from their own country. A sense of pride can be felt as they can relate to the material. Thereafter, students are more open to learning via other materials from other countries and can easily see that there are different points of view on the same topic.

The manner in which the learning outcomes are differentiated is also an important factor with intercultural competence. Most schools use a standard scope and sequence which lists all the skills and concepts the students in a particular grade need to achieve by the end of the year. A scope and sequence does not look at the individual child and consider his or her needs or cultural background. ISUtrecht does not work with a scope and sequence, but instead, we use the First Steps Program (2013) for stand-alone mathematics and language in addition to enquiry-based learning. First Steps (2013) is a continuum that tracks each student individually based on their ability and puts them in a certain phase of learning. The phases list what concepts and skills the child has learnt and what he or she should be working towards to reach the following phase.

This approach is different from a scope and sequence because the phases of First Steps (2013) are not grade-dependent. The needs and abilities of the child come first, independent of the grade that he or she is in. Intercultural competence is recognised in the First Steps (2013) curriculum:

> *Reading, writing, speaking, listening and viewing, on the other hand, are practices that often rely on social and cultural expectations.... Introducing students to the ways in which language is used to get things done is a subtle and changing art that varies according to a student's social and cultural understandings. Teachers confronted with these understandings recognise the similarities and differences between the literacy being taught in schools and the literacies that students use at home and in the community.... They wake up each morning to different family arrangements and speak different languages, dialects and forms of English. They view the day's events through a unique personal lens and have different social and cultural ways of doing things. Dale nods his head to his brother to indicate that it is time to head off to school. Khaleda engages in a long and practised routine of kisses, 'high-fives' and personalised farewells. Alejandra sends off a brief email with digital photos to her dad before racing out the door. Yet for all their differences, Dale, Khaleda and Alejandra share a basic human desire to communicate by making meaning.*
>
> (First Steps, 2013, p 32)

First Steps (2013) combined with enquiry-based learning truly recognises that there are many ways people learn and that this may be demonstrated differently in all parts of the world. The First Steps Program (2013) and enquiry-based learning are wonderful philosophies of learning that focus on the individual child and the intercultural competence that each person brings to the classroom.

CONCLUSION

> **How can we work towards intercultural competence and clear communication within our staff?**
>
> With a rapidly growing school, we realised that we needed to make clear agreements within our staff community to keep our communication as clear as possible. A professional development day was planned to align our approach to communication.
>
> We first had to acknowledge that the way we communicate is hugely influenced by our cultural background. After workshops during which we developed an understanding for how this impacts the way we interpret what we hear from our students, parents, colleagues and leadership, we made firm agreements as we moved forward.
>
> - First, we agreed to accept, as a starting point, that everyone in our school community has *good intentions*. We all want the same things, the best possible learning and working environment for our students and for ourselves.
> - Second, we agreed to continue *open communication* when a colleague exhibits behaviour that does not correspond with our school mission statement.

Many factors need to be considered when introducing intercultural competence into a school. ISUtrecht is making steps towards this goal through:

- setting a foundation in our mission statement;
- hiring an open-minded staff;
- creating a safe environment using the learner profiles;
- offering professional development to our teachers;
- collaborative student learning;
- recognising and celebrating our cultural differences in the units of enquiry and in our daily routines;
- using a variety of materials from various countries which have different perspectives;
- using an enquiry-based approach to learning with the First Steps Program (2013) for the stand-alone units.

People come from all walks of life. We have our own beliefs, morals and traditions. Yet, as Byram et al (2002, p 5) have said people should acknowledge the '*respect for individuals and equality of human rights as the democratic basis for social interaction*'. This is a tall order to reach, but one that brings peace and harmony among people. We still have a way to go, but ISUtrecht is making huge steps in this direction and we are proud of the nurturing, interculturally competent atmosphere of the school.

> *Reflective questions*
>
> 1. What approach(es) to learning guides your school? Does it align with your philosophy?
> 2. What are the benefits of being a facilitator of learning instead of always giving direct instruction?
> 3. What does intercultural competence look like to you? What evidence that this is happening would you see in your classroom?
> 4. What are the main baseline agreements every school should have to develop intercultural competence?
> 5. Do you plan your lessons with intercultural competence in mind?

REFERENCES

Arasaratnam, L A (2016) Intercultural Competence. In Nussbaum, J F (ed) *Oxford Research Encyclopedia of Communication*. Oxford: Oxford University Press. [online] Available at: https://oxfordre.com/communication/view/10.1093/acrefore/9780190228613.001.0001/acrefore-9780190228613-e-68 (accessed 12 September 2020).

Byram, M, Gribkova, B and Starkey, H (2002) *Developing the Intercultural Dimension in Language Teaching: A Practical Introduction for Teachers*. Strasbourg: Council of Europe.

Cultural Detective (nd) *Why Intercultural Competence?* [online] Available at: www.culturaldetective.com/why/intercultural-competence.html (accessed 12 September 2020).

Deardorff, D K (2006) Identification and Assessment of Intercultural Competence as a Student Outcome of Internationalization. *Journal of Studies in International Education*, 10(3): 241–66.

Deardorff, D K (2009) Implementing Intercultural Competence Assessment. In Deardorff, D K (ed) *The SAGE Handbook of Intercultural Competence*. Thousand Oaks: SAGE.

First Steps (2013) *Linking Assessment, Teaching and Learning*. 2nd ed. Perth: Department of Education WA.

Intercultural Development Inventory (nd) *IDI General Information: The Intercultural Development Continuum (IDC™)*. [online] Available at: https://idiinventory.com/generalinformation/the-intercultural-development-continuum-idc/ (accessed 12 September 2020).

International Baccalaureate (2010) *The IB Learner Profile*. [online] Available at: www.ibo.org/globalassets/publications/recognition/learnerprofile-en.pdf (accessed 12 September 2020).

International Baccalaureate (2017) *What Is an IB Education*? Cardiff: International Baccalaureate.

International School Utrecht (nda) *Mission Statement*. [online] Available at: www.isutrecht.nl/organisation/mission-statement/ (accessed 12 September 2020).

International School Utrecht (ndb) *Primary Years Programme.* [online] Available at: www.isutrecht.nl/pyp/primary-years-programme/ (accessed 12 September 2020).

Index

acceptance phase, in intercultural competence, 206–7
acting out scenarios, 76, 79
adaptation phase, in intercultural competence, 207
Adobe Spark (digital platform), 158
agree/disagree, assessment strategy, 112
approaches to learning (ATL) skills, 37
Arduino software, 142
Armstrong, T, 26
Aronin, L, 185
assessment
    determination, 92–4
    diagnostic assessment, 38
    and differentiation, 30–1
    and enquiry-based learning, 108–14
    and feedback, 109–10
    and feedback determination, 92–4
    formative assessment, 38, 109, 110, 180–1
    and learning environment, 38–9
    levels, 108
    peer assessment, 114
    pre-assessment, 108, 180
    self-assessment, 114, 180
    strategies
        agree/disagree, 112
        compass points, 113
        CSI (colour, symbol, image), 112
        I used to think, now I think, 111
        Kahoot!, 112
        make a connection, 113
        question me the answer, 112
        see think wonder, 111
        think-pair-share, 110–11
        3, 2, 1 thinking routine, 113
        thumb actions, 112
        what makes you say that?, 113
    summative assessment, 38, 109, 181–2
    in teaching mathematics, 179–82
        formative assessments, 180–1
        pre-assessment, 180
        self-assessment, 180
        summative assessments, 181–2
attitudes, in intercultural competence, 203–4

Bee/Blue Bots, 147
bilingualism, 186
Bloom, B, 86
Blurton, C, 133
brainstorming, in teaching mathematics, 165
broadcasts, in literacy, 157–8
buddy strategy, 45
Byram, M, 204, 212

call stations, 57
Canada, multilingual education in, 187
Care, E, 32
carpets, 27, 57
choice theory, 37
classroom. *See also* learning environment
    blog, 153–4
    routines, and multilingualism, 196
    transdisciplinary approach, 127–8
    Twitter account, 160
classroom management. 36, 47–9
    early years
        buddy strategy, 45
        exit tickets, 45–6
        'Get your wiggles out' strategy, 47
        glitter strategy, 46
        overlapping or multi-tasking strategy, 46
        relaxation strategies, 46–7
        restaurant strategy, 44
        rules and routines, 45
        shout it out vs whispering strategy, 46
        singing strategy, 44
        teaching social stories, 44
        technology. 44–5
    learning environment
        and assessment, 38–9
        student-focused, 37–8
    theories, 36–7
    upper classes
        counting backwards, 41
        fairy lights strategy, 43
        greeting the children at the door, 39
        home languages strategy, 43
        labelling strategy, 42
        light on strategy, 41
        positive reinforcement, 40
        rules and routines, 39–40
        secret garden, 41–2
        shout out box and wall, 41
code-switching, 193
collaboration, 51, 54, 64, 115
    benefits of, 52
    definition of, 52
    between leadership and teachers, 60
    between parents and school, 63–4
    participants, 52–3
    between school teachers, 55
        different grade level, 57–8

Index **221**

        same grade level, 55–7
        subject areas teachers, 58–9
    between students, 62–3
    between teachers and leadership, 60–2
    and transdisciplinary learning
        and teaching, 124
compass points, assessment strategy, 113
computational thinking/coding, 134, 140–3, 149
    challenges to, 148–9
    pilot Grades 1 and 2, 143
        code, 146
        games, 146–7
        giving and receiving
            instructions, 143–4
        grid and writing/following
            code, 144–5
        lessons, 148
        SAM Labs, 147–8
concept crunch, 96
concept-based teaching and learning, 86–7, 88, 95, 102
    challenges to, 100–1
    planning for, 91
        assessments and feedback
            determination, 92–4
        engagements
            development, 95–100
        goal identification, 91
    teachers' experiences, 102
    in teaching mathematics, 164, 182
    value of, 101–2
    whole school alignment, 88–91
    Wiseman's learning journey, 87–8
concepts
    characteristics of, 86
    definition of, 86
conceptual understandings, in mathematical
    processes, 166
connection, 53
connectivism, 155–7
constructivist learning theory, and
    differentiation, 20
Content and Language Integrated
    Learning (CLIL), 187
continuous assessment, in support system, 23
controlled enquiry, 106
co-operative and collaborative play, 70
counting backwards, 41
critical thinking
    importance of, 139
    in literacy, 157
CSI (colour, symbol, image), assessment
    strategy, 112
culture specific knowledge, 203
curation platforms, in literacy, 160–1
curiosity, in intercultural competence, 204, 206, 210, 214
curriculum, 17
curriculum documents, 90

Davies, A, 110
Deardorff, D K, 202, 204
decisions, 86
defence, in intercultural competence, 205
denialist phase, in intercultural competence, 205
Dewey, J, 36
diagnostic assessment, 38
dialogues, skills in intercultural competence, 203
differentiation, 19, 31–2, 33
    and assessment, 30–1
    and constructivist learning theory, 20
    definition of, 20–1
    genius hour, 24–5
    and learning environment, 26–8
    and multiple intelligences, 20–1
    providing challenges to students, 25
    research on, 21
    and support materials, 29–30
    and teaching arrangements, 24–6
    in teaching mathematics, 173–9
    and teaching methods, 28–9
    theoretical underpinnings, 20–1
    and Zone of Proximal Development, 20
digital citizenship education, 134, 136–7, 140, 149
    and fake news, 139
    safe online talk, 140
    and self-reflection, 137–8
digital learning environment, 153–5
    and digital portfolio platforms, 154
    classroom blog, 153
    video, 155
digital learning portfolio, in literacy, 154–5
digital literacy, 135, 139, 149, 159
digital media creation, in literacy, 157
digital pedagogy, 133
digital technology, in multilingualism, 196
digital tools, in literacy, 161
digital wellness, 134, 135–6, 149
Diploma Programme (DP), 121, 136
direct instruction, 97, 212
discovery learning, 97
discovery, in intercultural competence, 204
Division Council (DC), 63
drama, 59, 79
Dutch language acquisition, in
    multilingualism, 188–93

education, types of, 119–20
egalitarianism, 53
English Language Acquisition (ELA) department, 193
English language acquisition (ELA) students, 215
English language acquisition (ELA) teacher, 59
enquiry
    and technology, in literacy, 152
    controlled enquiry, 106
    free enquiry, 106
    guided enquiry, 106
    structured enquiry, 106

222 INDEX

enquiry cycle phases, 167–73
    conceptual, 168
    conclusions, 171
    discussion, 171
    investigation or exploration, 170
    orientation, 168
enquiry-based teaching and learning, 96, 117, 173, 191, 212, 216
    and assessment, 108–9
        clarity of learning intentions, 109–10
        self- and peer assessment, 114
        student involvement in designing assessment criteria, 110
        thinking activation and analysis, 110–14
    benefits, 105
    definition of, 104–5
    in early years, 114–15
    importance of, 106–8
    in intercultural competence, 217
    in teaching mathematics, 166–73, 182
    in upper primary, 115–17
Erickson, L, 86, 101
Estrada, I, 19
European Commission, 186
exit tickets, 45–6

Facebook, 156, 160
fairy lights strategy, 43
fake news, 107, 139
feedback, 45
    and assessment, 109–10
    determination, 92–4
    positive feedback, 61
feedback ladder, in literacy, 159
First Steps Curriculum, 58, 216–17
flexible grouping, 24
Flipboard, 160
Flipgrid, 156
Ford, E, 36
formal assessment, 30
formative assessment, 30, 38, 109, 110, 180
Franklin, B, 7
free enquiry, 106
free play, 12
French, R, 86, 96

gaming, 81
Garcia, O, 193
Gardner, H, 20–1, 27
generalisations, 91, 94, 165, 173
genius hour, 12, 24–5
'Get your wiggles out' strategy, 47
Ginott, H G, 36
Glasser, W, 37
glitter strategy, 46

golden time, 29
good intentions, in intercultural competence, 217
Google Communities, 160
Gordon, T, 36
Green Screen, 157
greeting the children at the door, 39
Gribkova, B, 204, 212
Griffen, P, 32
Groot Koerkamp, T, 69
grouping, 24
guided enquiry, 97, 106
guiding play, 73

Herbst, S, 110
holistic learning, 123
home languages
    as classroom management strategy, 43
    multilingualism, 193, 195
home learning, process of, 11
home visits, in intercultural competence, 215
Hughes, B, 71
Hutchins, N, 106

I used to think, now I think, assessment strategy, 111
ICT, 29, 38, 133, 149
ICT-skills/digital literacy, 134, 135
idea wall, 114
immersion education, 187
IMovie, 157
inclusive education, 52
independent learning, 161
individualisation, 20
inductive teaching approach, in teaching mathematics, 164
information and communication technology (ICT). See ICT
interconnected learning, 58–9
intercultural competence, 201–2, 207–9
    acceptance phase in, 206
    adaptation phase in, 207
    approach to learning, 212–13
    attitudes, 203
    creation of, 208–9
    definition of, 202
    denialist phase in, 205
    examples of, 214–17
    knowledge, 202
    and learning outcomes, 216
    minimisation phase in, 205
    mission statement, 208–9
    mono-cultural and multicultural mindset, 204
    polarisation phase in, 205
    safe learning environment through IB learner profile, 211–12
    skills, 203
    staff, 209
Intercultural Development Continuum, 204

Intercultural Development Inventory, 204
interdisciplinary learning, 121
International Baccalaureate (IB), 1, 121
    education, 159
    guidelines, 193
    learner profile, 37, 211–12
    model of concepts, 86–7
    model of enquiry, 107
    programmes. 121
    standards and practices, 193
international mindedness, 215
International Mother Language Day, 197
International School Utrecht (ISUtrecht), 203
    after-school Home Language programme, 188
    assessment system, 30–1, 108, *See also* assessment
    collaboration at, 53, 124, *See also* collaboration
    community approach, 53, 64
    community learning for world citizenship, 208
    conceptual growth in, 88
    connected learning at, 156
    differentiation at, 21–3
    English as language of instruction, 198
    enquiry-based approach in teaching mathematics, 173
    First Steps Curriculum, 216–17
    flexible grouping at, 24
    ICT in, 133
    intercultural competence at, 208
    and language profile, 193–7
    learning environment. *See* classroom management; learning environment
    mission and vision statement, 14, 136
    and multilingualism, 185, 188
    and new literacies, 152
    non-native and native-speaker models for language-learning, 185
    open-door policy, 60
    people's skills 'dictionary', 62
    planning at, 125–7
    play-based teaching and learning. *See* play-based teaching and learning
    providing challenges to students, 25
    PYP curriculum, 17, 119
    reflection routines, 29
    skills determination, 128
    staff, 209
    steps towards intercultural competence, 217–18
    student agency. *See* student agency
    and students' home languages, 193
    teaching methods, 28
    unit planner, 126
    units in Dutch lessons spiral, 191
    vertical approach to curriculum, 57
    See also individual entries

Kahoot!, as assessment strategy, 112
King's Day, in Dutch language acquisition, 191
knowledge, in intercultural competence, 202–3
Kohn, A, 9
Koomen, H M Y, 60

labelling strategy, 42
language learning support, 22
language profile, in multilingualism, 193–7
language tools, in Dutch language acquisition, 192
language focus, in Dutch language acquisition, 189
learning approaches, 128
learning environment, 26–8, *See also* classroom
    and assessment, 38–9
    and play, 72
    student-focused, 37–8
    transdisciplinary approach, 127–8
learning intentions, clarity of, 109–10
learning outcomes, 216
lifelong learning, 53, 62
light on strategy, 41
lines of enquiry, 11, 55, 59, 91, 96
linguistic repertoire, in multilingualism, 195
literacy, 151–2, 161
    and connected learning, 156
    creation of digital media, 157
    and digital learning environment, 153
    enquiry and technology, 152
    new literacies, 151–2
    and participatory culture, 152, 157–60
    research, 160
'lucky dip' strategy, 37

MacKenzie, T, 105
macro concepts, 86
macro-level practices, in multilingualism, 197, 198
make a connection, assessment strategy, 113
Marschall, C, 86, 96
mathematical processes, 166
mathematics teaching and learning, 163–4
    and assessments, 179
    concept-based approach, 164–6
    differentiation approach, 173
    enquiry-based approach, 166
    mathematical processes, 166
    play-based approach, 78
    pre-assessment, 166
    and reflection, 172
    summative assessment, 166
mathematics, integrating to unit topics, 164
McTighe, J, 86, 91
media consumption, 136–7
media literacy, 152
micro concepts, 86
Micro:bits programming, 142

micro-level practices, in multilingualism, 197, 198
Middle Years Programme (MYP), 69, 79–82, 121, 136
minimisation phase, in intercultural competence, 205–6
Mitchell, P H, 121
mixed aged classrooms, 62–3
mono-cultural mindset, 204–7
Montessori, M, 86
morning stations, 12
Morrison, K, 8
multicultural mindset, 204–7
multidisciplinary learning, 121
multilingual education, 187–8
multilingual literature, in multilingualism, 196
multilingualism, 185–6
    additive multilingualism, 186
    balanced and unbalanced multilingualism, 186
    definition of, 186–7
    Dutch language acquisition, 188
    and ISUtrecht community, 188
    and language profile, 193
    multilingual education, 187
    nurturing of, 189–90
    receptive and productive multilingualism, 186
    and staff in multilingual activities, 197
    subtractive multilingualism, 186
    and teaching practices, 193–7
    translanguaging, 186
multiple intelligences, 20–1, 27
multi-tasking strategy, 46
Murdoch, K, 52, 62, 104, 106, 109, 114
music lesson, 79

natural objects, 29
Nevin, A I, 20, 52
new literacies. See literacy
New Parent Connectors (NPC), 64

online communities, in literacy, 156, 160–1
online resources, unreliable and fraudulent, 107
open communication, in intercultural competence, 217
open enquiry, 97
open-ended materials, 14
open-ended play materials, 12
open-mindedness, in intercultural competence, 204, 210
outside play, 12
overlapping strategy, 46

parent involvement, in teaching mathematics, 182
parental support, in multilingualism, 195
parents and school, collaboration between, 63–4
Parents Support Group (PSG), 63
Park, J, 120
participatory culture, in literacy, 152, 158–60

Pataray-Ching, J, 167
pedagogy, 17
Pedaste, M, 167
peer support, 24
peer assessment, 114
peer-to-peer feedback systems, 11
performance assessment, 30
personalisation, 20, See also differentiation
physical learning environment, and multilingualism, 195
Piaget, J, 86
planning sessions, collaborative approach, 55–7
play
    and development, 69
    guiding play, 73
    learning computational thinking skills through, 141
    and learning environment, 72
    observation roles, 73
    phases and forms of, 70–1
play-based learning and teaching, 69, 82
    in Dutch language acquisition, 189
    in early years, 73–5
    mathematics learning, 78
    in Middle Years Programme, 79–80
    future of, 81–2
    science classes, 80, 81
    physical education lesson, 79
    in primary years, 76–9
    specialist teachers, 78–9
    and technology, 78
    theories, 69–73
plurilingualism, 186
polarisation phase, in intercultural competence, 205
positive feedback, 61
positive reinforcement, 40
pre-assessment, 30, 108, 166, 180
Primary Years Programme (PYP), 12, 17, 28, 37, 48, 119, 121, 122, 136, 190
process-oriented teaching, 164
product-oriented teaching, 164
Project Zero, 92
provocations, in enquiry cycle phases, 168
#pyp, 160

question me the answer, assessment strategy, 112

reciprocality, 53
reflection, 29, 45, 53
    and digital wellness, 137–8
    formal implementation of, 172
    informal implementation of, 172
    in teaching mathematics, 172–3
Reggio Emilia, 26, 41
related concepts, 86
relaxation strategies, 46–7
remember book, in multilingualism, 196
research, in literacy, 160–1

respect, 53, 204, 215
responsible thinking process, 36
restaurant strategy, 44
reversal, in intercultural competence, 205
Richardson, W, 151
Richart, R, 86
Roberson, M, 167
Robot Turtles, 147
role play, 76–7, 79
rules and routines, 39–40, 45

safe environment, in teaching mathematics, 173
safe online talk, 140
SAM Labs, 142, 147–8
SAM Labs kits, 147–8
school agency, support factors, 15–17
screen time, 136–7
seating arrangements, 27
second language acquisition, 198
secret garden, 41–2
see think wonder, assessment strategy, 111
Seesaw (digital platform), 154, 158
self-assessment, 114
self-reflection, and digital wellness, 137–8
shared values, 53
shout it out strategy, 46
shout out box and wall, 41
similarities, in intercultural competence, 205
singing strategy, 44
Singleton, D, 185
skills, in intercultural competence, 203
Skinner, B F, 36
Skype, 156
socio-linguistic awareness, in intercultural competence, 203, 216
solitary play, 70
Son, J, 120
Sousa, D, 164
specialist teachers, role in play-based learning, 78–9
Spencer, J, 155
Spilt, J L, 60
stand-alone mathematics units, 164
Starkey, H, 204, 212
stereotyping, in intercultural competence, 215
structured enquiry, 97, 106
student agency, 7, 69
    choice to read, 9
    and connection, 15, 16
    definition of, 7–8
    differentiation of
        early years, 14
        primary, 14
    dispositional dimension, 8
    in Dutch language acquisition, 190
    in formal planning, 10
        early years, 10–11
        primary, 11
    implementation process, 15
    in informal planning, 11
        early years, 11–12
        primary, 12
    motivational dimension, 8
    and play, 72
    positional dimension, 8
    research findings on, 8–9
    social benefits of, 9
    supported and modelled during lesson, 13
        early years, 13
        primary, 13–14
student support teachers, 59
student voice, 8, See also student agency
student-focused learning environment, 37–8
students' motivation, in learning activities, 183
students who need extra challenges, support for, 23, 25–6
students' stations, 41
Sullo, B, 37
summative assessment, 30, 31, 38, 109, 166, 181–2
support materials, and differentiation, 29–30

teacher effectiveness training, 36
teachers' stress, 60
teaching arrangements, 24–6
teaching assistants, 56
teaching methods, 28–9
teaching social stories, 44
technology, 38
    in classroom management, 44–5
    in literacy, 158, 161
    and play-based learning, 78
Thijs, J T, 60
think-pair-share, 110–11
Thousand, J S, 20, 52
3, 2, 1 thinking routine, assessment strategy, 113
thumb actions, assessment strategy, 112
Tomlinson, C A, 20
traditional mathematics lesson, 163
traditional teaching approach. See product-oriented teaching
transdisciplinary teaching and learning, 119–20, 121, 122, 129–30
    background, 120
    classroom, 127–8
    collaboration, 124
    in Dutch learning acquisition, 189
    learning approaches, 128–9
    planning, 125–7
    themes, 122–4
translanguaging, 186
Translanguaging Stance, 193
translinguistic connections
    in Dutch language acquisition, 188, 189–90
    in multilingualism, 195
trust, 53

twenty-first century literacy, definition of, 151
Twitter, 156, 160

UK National Union of Teachers, 60
universalism, in intercultural competence, 205
unplugged activities, 141, 142

van Kuyk, J J, 69
Vaughn, M, 8
video, in digital learning environment, 155
Villa, R A, 20, 52
virtual reality, 81
Visible Thinking routines, 92
visual arts, 59
visual support, in multilingualism, 196
Vogel, S, 193
Vygotsky, L S, 20

wall charts, 171
Wall of Fame, 61
well-being, and student agency, 9
what makes you say that?, assessment strategy, 113
whispering strategy, 46
whole school alignment, 88–91
Wiesmann, 120
Wiggins, G, 86, 91
Williams, D, 110
Williams, P, 9
wonder walls, 115, 170
work centres, 27
worksheets, 30

Zone of Proximal Development, 20